THE RESURRECTED GOD

THE RESURRECTED GOD

KARL BARTH'S TRINITARIAN THEOLOGY OF EASTER

JOHN L. DRURY

Fortress Press
Minneapolis

THE RESURRECTED GOD

Karl Barth's Trinitarian Theology of Easter

Copyright © 2014 Fortress Press. All rights reserved. Except for brief quotations in critical articles or reviews, no part of this book may be reproduced in any manner without prior written permission from the publisher. Visit http://www.augsburgfortress.org/copyrights/ or write to Permissions, Augsburg Fortress, Box 1209, Minneapolis, MN 55440.

Scripture quotations are from the New Revised Standard Version Bible, copyright © 1989 by the Division of Christian Education of the National Council of the Churches of Christ in the USA. Used by permission. All rights reserved.

Cover design: Alisha Lofgren

Library of Congress Cataloging-in-Publication Data

Print ISBN: 978-1-4514-8280-5

eBook ISBN: 978-1-4514-8437-3

The paper used in this publication meets the minimum requirements of American National Standard for Information Sciences — Permanence of Paper for Printed Library Materials, ANSI Z329.48-1984.

Manufactured in the U.S.A.

This book was produced using PressBooks.com, and PDF rendering was done by PrinceXML.

CONTENTS

Acknowledgments		vii
Abbreviations		ix
1.	Introduction	1
2.	The Verdict of the Father and the Generation of the Son	13
3.	The Direction of the Son and the Procession of the Spirit	71
4.	The Promise of the Spirit and the Periochoresis of God	125
5.	The Resurrected God	175
Bibliography		185
Index		193

Acknowledgments

Against the grain of typically atomistic academic culture, I have been blessed to work within a number of collaborative theological communities. The students, faculty, and staff at Princeton Theological Seminary have carried me along as I carried this work through to its completion. The fellowship I experienced among the doctoral students in theology is unparalleled. There is no better incubator for scholarship than lively, rigorous debate within the context of loving, respectful friendship. Being advised by Professor Daniel Migliore was an unspeakable honor. I am especially grateful for his timely and substantive feedback, which consistently improved the concision, clarity and coherence of my argument. Professors Bruce McCormack and George Hunsinger have been my theological mentors for a decade. Their fingerprints can be readily detected on every page of this work. I am also thankful to Professors Ellen Charry and Darrell Guder for contributing to my formation as a teacher. And the always-helpful staff of Speer library, Ph.D. studies office, and mailroom each played their essential roles. They can claim more credit for our theological work than they perhaps ever realize and surely more than we ever acknowledge.

My formal theological training began at Indiana Wesleyan University, where I recently returned to serve as professor of systematic theology. I am especially thankful for the collegiality among the faculty, both then and now. It is pure joy to teach alongside Bud Bence, Steve Lennox, Ken Schenck, and the many others who shaped me, sent me off, and welcomed me back. I hope they will find this work a worthwhile first return on their investment.

My first theological community, however, was and always will be my family. My father, mother, and brother not only supported me as any healthy family would, but also stimulated my work through lively conversations on topics religious and otherwise. The same goes for my wife Amanda, who is a theologian in her own right, though of the decidedly more practical variety. Our ongoing dialogue has provided continual inspiration, though I am more grateful for the fun and humor she brings to my life. I am thankful also for how she loves and cares for our children, especially as the final stages of the project coincided with the arrival of our daughter, Clara. This project was born around the same time as my son. Since they both turned three this year, I dedicate this Trinitarian reflection on the firstborn from among the dead to my own firstborn: Sam.

Abbreviations

CD   Barth, Karl. *The Church Dogmatics*. 4 vols. in 13 parts. Edinburgh: T&T Clark, 1956–69, 1975.

KD   Barth, Karl. *Die kirchliche Dogmatik*. 4 vols. in 13 parts. Munich: Chr. Kaiser, 1932, and Zürich: Theologischer Verlag, 1938–65.

1

Introduction

"He is God not of the dead, but of the living."[1] With these words, Holy Scripture testifies to the God of the living, the God who raises the dead.[2] This project inquires into this God. I argue that it befits God to be the God of the living because God is the living God, that is, Father, Son, and Holy Spirit. The God of the living is the triune God.

Where may this living God be sought? The central locus of the living God's self-disclosure is *the resurrection of the crucified Jesus Christ*. In the Easter event, God is once for all revealed as the living God and the God of the living. In this event, God is revealed as the Father who raised Jesus Christ from the dead; as the Son who was raised, who arises, and who will be present even to the end of the age; and as the Holy Spirit by whom the Father raised Jesus Christ, in whose power Jesus Christ arises, and in whose promise Jesus Christ is present. The God who acts in the Easter event is the living God—Father, Son, and Holy Spirit.

This is the Trinitarian grammar of Christ's resurrection as it comes to expression in Karl Barth's mature theology. Barth stands with the tradition in identifying the triune God as the *subject* of Christ's resurrection. However, he differs from the tradition in two important ways. First, he exposits the Trinitarian grammar of the Easter event in a dialectical fashion, so that the distinctive participation of each triune person comes more sharply into focus in accordance with the shifting christological motifs of *Church Dogmatics* IV/1–3. This dialectical strategy highlights the differentiated unity with which the triune God acts in the Easter event. Barth thereby avoids both the tendency of traditional theology to render moot the Trinitarian differentiation in God's

---

1. Mark 12:27a; Matt. 22:32b.

2. For a recent survey of the relevant biblical texts from both testaments, see Kevin J. Madigan and Jon D. Levenson, *Resurrection: The Power of God for Christians and Jews* (New Haven: Yale University Press, 2008).

external works and the tendency of much contemporary theology to regard the triune persons as autonomous agents among whom the works of God are divided.³ This dialectical approach is Barth's first major contribution toward a Trinitarian theology of Christ's resurrection.⁴

Second, and at a deeper level, Barth asks after the Trinitarian ground of Christ's resurrection. The triune God is not only the subject, but also the *basis*, of Christ's resurrection. In view of his thoroughgoing commitment to divine self-correspondence, Barth treats Easter's Trinitarian grammar as a point of entry for inquiring into the ground of the Easter event in God's own life. In doing so, Barth shows that he does not merely apply the doctrine of the Trinity as a set of grammatical rules to the case of Christ's resurrection; rather, he re-conceptualizes the doctrine of the Trinity in light of the Easter event. So, over the course of his reflections, a striking picture of the living God emerges, one in which Barth speaks of the generation of the Son as a movement of grace, of the procession of the Spirit as a history-in-partnership, and of divine perichoresis as a purposive communication. By means of these various re-conceptualizations, Barth testifies to the triune God's readiness for resurrection. This readiness

---

3. For examples of the former, see the discussion of Jesus Christ as God raising himself as man in Athanasius, *On the Incarnation*, §20, §26, and §32, and the more sophisticated account of the same in Thomas Aquinas, *Summa Theologica* III, q. 53, a. 4. For examples of the latter, see Jürgen Moltmann, *The Trinity and the Kingdom* (Minneapolis: Fortress Press, 1993), esp. chs. 3–5, as well as the far more subtle account in Robert W. Jenson, *Systematic Theology*, Vol. 1 (Oxford: Oxford University Press, 1997), esp. Part II. Karl Rahner is an important critic of the tradition on this question, who, like Barth, avoids the tri-theistic tendency of much contemporary theology; see "Remarks on the Dogmatic Treatise 'De Trinitate,'" in *Theological Investigations*, Vol. IV (Baltimore: Helicon, 1966), 77–104, and *The Trinity* (New York: Crossroad, 1997). Although I will have occasion to cite Rahner positively, he does not develop his Trinitarian reflections in direct connection with Christ's resurrection, as does Barth in *CD* IV/1–3.

4. Perhaps this is good a time as any to identify both my indebtedness to as well as my difference from Moltmann's classic *The Crucified God* (New York: Harper & Row, 1974). The title of this book (*The Resurrected God*) is a riff on Moltmann, and the recurring phrase "Trinitarian theology of Christ's resurrection" also alludes to the title of a central section of *The Crucified God* (ch. 6, sect. 5, "Trinitarian Theology of the Cross," 235–49). Beyond these titular allusions, the substantive decision to treat Christ's resurrection and the doctrine of the Trinity as mutually interpreting is a twist on Moltmann's thesis: "The material principle of the doctrine of the Trinity is the cross of Christ. The formal principle of knowledge of the cross is the doctrine of the Trinity" (ibid., 241). However, inspiration is not endorsement. For one, the shift from the cross to the resurrection itself entails a critique of the one-sidedness of *The Crucified God*. Furthermore, I defend Barth's model of the Trinity (as one subject in three modes of being), which Moltmann explicitly rejects in both *The Crucified God* and *The Trinity and the Kingdom*. In fact, he argues that Barth's doctrine of the Trinity prevents him from perceiving the Trinitarian theology of the cross or the resurrection. I will show that this is simply not the case.

implies that we may speak with confidence of God as the God of the living, because God is himself the living God—Father, Son and Holy Spirit.

In short, according to Karl Barth, the *subject* and *basis* of Christ's resurrection is the triune God. Tracing these two themes—the Trinitarian grammar of Easter and its corresponding Trinitarian ground—in Barth's mature theology is the primary task of this book. In order to properly execute this interpretive task, we must first assess the state of the question in Barth research. What, if any, connection has been drawn by Barth's interpreters between Christ's resurrection and the doctrine of the Trinity?

The State of the Question

A survey of the literature on Karl Barth shows that attention is only beginning to be focused on the relationship between resurrection and Trinity in his theology. Studies of Barth's understanding of Christ's resurrection have moved through three basic phases. It is crucial to note at the outset that the later phases do not ignore the concerns of the earlier phases, but rather reframe them in terms of a new central question.

The earliest phase focused on the question of the *historicity* of the resurrection. As early as 1933, Walter Künneth criticized Barth for having an insufficiently historical view of the Easter event.[5] In English-language reception, the works of Richard R. Niebuhr and Van A. Harvey are representative of this phase.[6] Both figures criticized Barth for placing the resurrection event outside of history, though the latter noted Barth's later shift toward historicity.[7] Investigations of this sort have continued in recent decades.[8]

---

5. Walter Künneth, *Theologie der Auferstehung* (Munich: C. Kaiser, 1933). Even earlier, Rudolf Bultmann argued against Barth that appearance reports in 1 Corinthians 15 were intended by Paul as historical "proofs" of Christ's resurrection in *Faith and Understanding* (Philadelphia: Fortress Press, 1969), 83–86. Since he shared Barth's judgment that such proofs are misguided, Bultmann's challenge remained only at the exegetical level. Later, Wolfhart Pannenberg elevated this exegetical critique of Barth in his attempt to rehabilitate the systematic significance of the historical probability of Christ's resurrection in *Jesus–God and Man* (Philadelphia: Westminster, 1968), 88–99.

6. Richard R. Niebuhr, *Resurrection and Historical Reason* (New York: Scribner's, 1957); Van A. Harvey, *The Historian and the Believer: The Morality of Historical Knowledge and Christian Belief* (Urbana, IL: University of Illinois Press, 1966), 153–59. A similar criticism aimed at Barth's early theology can be found in James D. Smart, *The Divided Mind of Modern Theology: Karl Barth and Rudolf Bultmann, 1908–1933* (Philadelphia: Westminster, 1967).

7. V. A. Harvey, *The Historian and the Believer*, 153–59. Gerald O'Collins identifies Barth's supposed turn from dialectic to analogy in 1931 as the cause of this shift in "Karl Barth on Christ's Resurrection," *Scottish Journal of Theology* 26:1 (1973): 85–99. O'Collins's reliance on this now-defunct account of Barth's development dilutes an otherwise insightful essay.

The limitation of this phase of interpretation was its tendency to abstract Barth's understanding of Christ's resurrection from its broader dogmatic context. Questions concerning the historicity of the resurrection are not irrelevant, especially since Barth often places his discussion of Christ's resurrection within the larger debate concerning "faith and history." But such historical questions cannot be adequately answered without understanding more fully the theological meaning and significance of Easter.

Despite this general trend toward abstraction, an important dogmatic question arose during this phase of reception: What is the relationship between resurrection and revelation? It is common in Barth interpretation to assert that his doctrine of Christ's resurrection is over-determined by his doctrine of revelation, and then to identify this over-determination as the cause of his insufficiently historical view of the Easter event.[9] This claim is half right. On the one hand, Barth certainly assigns a revelatory function to Christ's resurrection, and did so throughout his career.[10] On the other hand, that Barth *reduces* resurrection to a function of revelation can only reasonably be asserted of his earlier theology.[11] Furthermore, the causal link between this reduction and the non-historical character of Easter is suspect, for even in the earlier stages of his development Barth asserted the corporeality of Christ's resurrection.[12]

Nevertheless, the complex relationship between resurrection and revelation remains an important question for Barth research. Although answering this question is not the purpose of this book, I will have occasion to

8. Peter Carnley, *The Structure of Resurrection Belief* (Oxford: Clarendon, 1987), 132–43.

9. For example, W. Pannenberg, *Jesus–God and Man*, 111. This critique fits within a larger trend of seeing Barth's theology as one grand reduction of Christianity to its epistemic aspects, exemplified most brazenly by Gustaf Wingren, *Theology in Conflict* (Edinburgh: Oliver and Boyd, 1958). A far subtler version of this critique can be found in Hans W. Frei's early suggestion that Barth's early theology suffered from an epistemological monophysitism. This charge is the centerpiece of Mike Higton's account of Frei's reception of Barth in *Christ, Providence & History: Hans W. Frei's Public Theology* (New York: T&T Clark, 2004).

10. Evidence in support of this claim is provided throughout this book.

11. Most famously, the tangent/circle passage in Karl Barth, *The Epistle to the Romans*, translated by Edwyn C. Hoskyns (London: Oxford University Press, 1933), 30: "The Resurrection is the revelation: the disclosing of Jesus as the Christ, the appearing of God, the apprehending of God in Jesus. . . . In the Resurrection the new world of the Holy Spirit touches the old world of the flesh, but touches it as a tangent touches a circle, that is, without touching it. . . . The Resurrection is therefore an occurrence in history. . . . But inasmuch as the occurrence was conditioned by the Resurrection . . . the Resurrection is not an event in history at all." See also ibid., 202–7.

12. Ibid., 203: "the concrete, corporeal person of the risen Jesus." The bodily character of Christ's resurrection is more emphatic in the original: "der leiblich, körperlich, persönlich Auferstandene," Karl Barth, *Der Römerbrief* (Zürich: Evangelischer Verlag, 1922), 183.

address it insofar as the concept of revelation looms large *both* in Barth's doctrine of Christ's resurrection *and* in his doctrine of the Trinity. Systematically, the three doctrines together form a triangle in which the interpretation of one draws on the other two. But this triangle does not fall from the sky; it emerges over the course of Barth's development. First, during his early period (for example, *The Epistle to the Romans* and *The Resurrection of the Dead*), Barth interpreted Christ's resurrection in terms of his emerging doctrine of revelation. Second, during the development of his dogmatic prolegomena, Barth employed a reciprocal interpretation of the doctrines of the Trinity and revelation, each influencing the interpretation of the other.[13] Third, and finally, in his mature theology Barth completed the triangle by unfolding Christ's resurrection and the doctrine of the Trinity in light of each other. Although this last connection is my focus, I will not ignore the revelatory aspect of Easter highlighted by the first phase of Barth interpretation.

The first major interpreter to break from the narrowly historical focus of the first phase of reception and locate Barth's doctrine of Christ's resurrection in its broader dogmatic context was Berthold Klappert. In two early works, Klappert directed his attention to the differentiated unity of cross and resurrection.[14] In so doing, he initiated the second phase in the reception of Barth's doctrine of Christ's resurrection, which was *soteriological* in focus. Klappert has effectively shown that Barth's mature understanding of Christ's resurrection includes a revelatory aspect, but is not reduced to it. Christ's resurrection is a distinct event from the cross, in which God enacts his verdict on Jesus Christ and us in him. This verdict concerns the work of the cross, and so is united with it. According to Klappert's interpretation of Barth, the rich meaning of Christ's resurrection can be seen only in its differentiated unity with his crucifixion.

Although my focus is different from his, Klappert's work provides two crucial insights relevant for discerning Barth's Trinitarian theology of Christ's

---

13. Karl Barth, *The Göttingen Dogmatics*, Vol. 1 (Grand Rapids: Eerdmans, 1991), §5; idem., *Die Christliche Dogmatik in Entwurf* (Munich: Chr. Kaiser Verlag, 1927) §9–13; idem, *Church Dogmatics*, Vol. I, Part 1 (2nd ed.; Edinburgh: T&T Clark, 1975), §8–12, hereafter cited as *CD* I/1.

14. Berthold Klappert, *Diskussion um Kreuz und Auferstehung: Zur gegenwärtigen Auseinandersetzung in Theologie und Gemeinde* (Wuppertal: Aussaat Verlag, 1967), 105–44; idem., *Die Auferweckung des Gekreuzigten: Der Ansatz der Christologie Karl Barths im Zusammenhang der Christologie der Gegenwart* (Neukirchen-Vlyun: Neukirchener Verlag, 1971). Cf. his later summation and development, "Die Auferweckung des Gekreuzigten," in *Auferweckung Jesu, Auferweckung der Toten, Auferweckung der Welt: Karl Barths Theologie aufnehmen und weiterdenken*, ed. Berthold Klappert and Michael Weinrich (Herrenalb: Evangelische Akademie Baden, 1989), 7–22.

resurrection. First of all, the differentiated unity of cross and resurrection is Barth's point of entry for developing the Trinitarian grammar of Christ's resurrection, at least in *CD* IV/1.[15] As Klappert puts it, "The doctrine of the Trinity according to Barth explicates the relationship between the cross and resurrection; it is the taking up of the differentiated relationship of the cross and resurrection into the concept of God."[16] Secondly, Klappert highlights Barth's distinction between the raising (*Erweckung*) of Jesus Christ and his own arising (*Auferstehung*).[17] This distinction aids in the identification of the distinct modes in which the triune persons participate in the Easter event. Although this book moves beyond Klappert in the exploration of this theme, his initial contribution must be acknowledged.

In German scholarship, Klappert's soteriological approach has been followed by Tilman Schreiber in his survey of modern theological interpretation of Rom. 4:25.[18] In English-speaking Barth research, David Mueller draws heavily on Klappert's interpretation.[19] The soteriological lens also shapes the recent work of R. Dale Dawson, who exposits Barth's theology of the resurrection in terms of the movement of the crucified and risen Christ to us.[20] Dawson's work has enriched the discussion by identifying "movement" or "transition" as the unifying theme of Barth's various discussions of Christ's resurrection. Whereas Klappert's early work focused almost exclusively on *CD* IV/1, Dawson explores the role of Christ's resurrection throughout *CD* IV/1-3, in addition to two earlier texts. Although I will critique Dawson's analysis throughout this book, I concur with his basic thesis that, for Barth, the soteriological function of Easter consists in its being Christ's own transition from his life history to us in our sphere.

In the context of its broad soteriological focus, Dawson's work also refers briefly to the Trinitarian aspects of the resurrection. As such, he participates in the emerging third phase in the reception of Barth's doctrine of Christ's resurrection, which is *Trinitarian* in focus. Such a turn is inevitable, since for Barth the question of the purpose of Christ's resurrection is intertwined with

---

15. See ch. 2, "The Trinitarian Grammar of the Raising of Christ."
16. B. Klappert, *Die Auferweckung des Gekreuzigten*, 306.
17. Ibid., 291–93, 391–95.
18. Tilman Schreiber, *Die Soteriologische Bedeutung der Auferweckung Jesu Christi in gegenwärtiger systematischer Theologie* (Frankfurt am Main: Peter Lang, 1998), 117–32.
19. David Mueller, *Foundation of Karl Barth's Doctrine of Reconciliation: Jesus Christ Crucified and Risen* (Lewiston, NY: Edwin Mellen, 1990).
20. Richard Dale Dawson, *The Resurrection in Karl Barth* (Hampshire: Ashgate, 2007). For an extended summary and analysis of Dawson, see my review in *Koinonia Journal* 19 (2007): 125–29.

the question of the identity of the God who acts in this event. So by asking the "who" question, the third phase does not leave behind the "why" question of the second phase, but rather includes it and gives it a clearer and more secure ground.

Unfortunately, Dawson's argument falters with respect to this topic because it inadequately addresses the Trinitarian pattern of Barth's overarching structure and his commitment to God's self-correspondence in the economy of salvation. Dawson notes Barth's references to the Father and the Spirit in connection with Christ's resurrection, but critiques Barth for insufficiently differentiating the triune persons in the Easter event. In his desire for greater differentiation, Dawson moves toward treating the triune persons as multiple agents to whom discrete acts are attributed.[21] Although he has every right to pursue independent justification for this line of thought, it departs significantly from Barth's own doctrine of the Trinity and therefore obscures Barth's unique contribution to a Trinitarian theology of Christ's resurrection. The multiple aspects of the Easter event around which Barth organizes his reflections are not divided among the persons of the Trinity; rather, the Father, Son and Holy Spirit participate in each aspect of the Easter event in a mode that corresponds to their eternal relations.

Three additional scholars interact with Barth in their explorations of the relationship between Christ's resurrection and the doctrine of the Trinity: Sarah Coakley, Eugene Rogers, and Paul Molnar. The work of each has been an important impetus for my constructive interest in a Trinitarian theology of Easter. However, all of these authors bring their own Trinitarian presuppositions to Barth's texts without adequately attending to the kind of relationship Barth himself discerns between Christ's resurrection and the Trinity.

In an influential essay, Sarah Coakley identifies the Christian practice of prayer as a source for the doctrine of the Trinity. Drawing on biblical and patristic texts, Coakley shows how the practice of praying to the Father, on the basis of incorporation into the risen Christ, through the Spirit of adoption by whom the Father raised the Son, functions as the experiential starting point for the development of the doctrine of the Trinity.[22] Although Barth does not share Coakley's interest in an experiential basis for the doctrine of the Trinity, his Trinitarian theology of Christ's resurrection bears a formal

---

21. Dawson, *The Resurrection in Karl Barth*, 215–27.

22. Sarah Coakley, "Why Three? Some Further Reflections on the Origins of the Doctrine of the Trinity," in *The Making and Remaking of Christian Doctrine: Essays in Honour of Maurice Wiles*, ed. Sarah Coakley and David A. Pailin (Oxford: Clarendon, 1993), 29–56.

resemblance to hers. Unfortunately, Coakley does not address Barth's positive contribution, because she has already relegated him to a different "type" of Trinitarian theology.[23]

In his constructive pneumatology, Eugene Rogers takes the resurrection of Jesus as his starting point.[24] Before treating the role of the Spirit at key points in Jesus' life, Rogers first treats the role of the Spirit in the Father's raising of Jesus from the dead. The Trinitarian grammar of this event casts light on the previous events of Jesus' life, such as the annunciation, baptism, and transfiguration.[25] Again, Barth makes a similar move, inasmuch as he identifies these events as precursors to Christ's resurrection that make sense only in its light.[26] These same events are cited as instances of the work of the Spirit in the life of Jesus Christ.[27] But Rogers criticizes Barth for not giving sufficient autonomy to the Spirit, and so misses out on Barth's contribution to a Trinitarian theology of Christ's resurrection.[28]

Lastly, Paul Molnar uses Barth to advance his thesis that a proper doctrine of the incarnation is the necessary presupposition for a proper doctrine of Christ's resurrection.[29] Much of what Molnar says about Barth's doctrine of resurrection is basically correct. For instance, he is right that Jesus Christ does not become divine upon being raised, but is revealed to be the Son of God he already was. However, in his elucidation of this claim, Molnar appeals to his own reading of Barth's doctrine of the Trinity instead of addressing the explicit connection made between Christ's resurrection and the doctrine of the Trinity in *CD* IV/1–3.

---

23. Ibid., 33–35. Coakley categorizes Barth (along with Rahner) within the revelational type of trinitarian theology. This is of course totally accurate, especially with regard CD I/1-2. But it is not the whole story.

24. Rogers takes as the starting point of his constructive pneumatology the resurrection of Jesus, cf. Eugene F. Rogers Jr., *After the Spirit: A Constructive Pneumatology from Resources outside the Modern West* (Grand Rapids: Eerdmans, 2005), 75–97.

25. Ibid., 98–199.

26. Cf. Karl Barth, *Church Dogmatics*, Vol. I, Part 2 (Edinburgh: T&T Clark, 1956), 114, hereafter cited as *CD* I/2; Karl Barth, *Church Dogmatics*, Vol. III, Part 2 (Edinburgh: T&T Clark, 1960), 478–80, hereafter cited as *CD* III/2; Karl Barth, *Church Dogmatics*, Vol. IV, Part 2 (Edinburgh: T&T Clark, 1958), 135–41, hereafter cited as *CD* IV/2.

27. Cf. *CD* I/2, 199; Karl Barth, *Church Dogmatics*, Vol. IV, Part 1 (Edinburgh: T&T Clark, 1956), 308–9, hereafter cited as *CD* IV/1.

28. E. Rogers, *After the Spirit*, 19–23, 29–32. Cf. also idem., "Eclipse of the Spirit in Karl Barth," in *Conversing with Barth*, ed. John C. McDowell and Mike Higton (Hampshire: Ashgate, 2004), 173–190.

29. Paul D. Molnar, *Incarnation and Resurrection: Toward a Contemporary Understanding* (Grand Rapids: Eerdmans, 2007), 1–44.

In light of these recent explorations, it is high time for a thoroughgoing analysis of Barth's Trinitarian theology of Easter. This book aims to fill this gap through close readings of selected texts from *CD* IV/1–3. These close readings will substantiate my thesis that, according to Karl Barth, the subject and basis of Christ's resurrection is the triune God.

The Twofold Thesis

What does it mean to say that the triune God is the subject and basis of Christ's resurrection? The meaning and significance of this claim comes to light when it is heard as the answer to a more basic question: Why the resurrection? For what purpose did the Easter event occur? Barth's basic answer is that the resurrection of Jesus Christ took place *for us*. God was pleased not only to fulfill the covenant in the life history of Jesus Christ, but also to declare its fulfillment in our sphere so that we may participate in it in a manner appropriate to our condition. Christ's resurrection is the divinely enacted transition by which we come to participate in our reconciliation.

The polemical point of Barth's argument is that the transition from Christ to us is not a human work. How does Jesus Christ move from his sphere to ours? Not by our own ingenuity or activity, but by God acting for us in the resurrection of Jesus Christ. In order to maintain this point, Barth goes out of his way to identify the divine subject at work in this act. It is here that the doctrine of the Trinity comes into play, for the task of identification requires an explication of the Trinitarian grammar evoked by the Easter event.[30]

Who acts in the Easter event? In the first instance, God the Father acts, initiating a new history beyond the cross by raising Jesus Christ from the dead. In the history that issues forth from this initiating act, Jesus Christ himself is the one who arises in the power of the Holy Spirit. And viewed from either side, we have to do with the one living God-man, Jesus Christ. So there are not three subjects at work here, but the one God in his threefold self-differentiation as Father, Son, and Holy Spirit. Thus, from every angle, the true God is truly at work in the Easter event.

That Barth so explicates his doctrine of Christ's resurrection according to this Trinitarian grammar is the first side of my thesis, that is, that the subject of

---

30. For the notion of a "Trinitarian grammar" governing our God-talk, I am indebted to Ingolf U. Dalferth, *Der auferweckte Gekreuzigte: Zur Grammatik der Christologie* (Tübingen: Mohr Siebeck, 1994), 200–236. Dalferth is insistent on the resurrection of Jesus Christ as the only means by which we can speak this way (ibid., 38–84), though the focus of his exposition is on the Trinitarian grammar of God at work in the cross of Christ.

Christ's resurrection is the triune God. To understand the second side, we must return to Barth's answer to the question of Easter's purpose. If the transition from Christ to us is a divine work, then it follows that this transition is grounded solely in God. God was not compelled to do this for us, but was pleased to do this for us. And in his being and acting for us, God does not contradict himself but corresponds to himself. Here again the doctrine of the Trinity comes into play, for it is the *triune* God who corresponds to himself in this event. The triunity of God manifest in the Easter event corresponds to the triune God himself. In this sense, the triune God himself is the *basis* of Christ's resurrection.

In pursuing this line of thought, Barth engages in creative re-conceptualizations of the doctrine of the Trinity. Such re-conceptualizations are a consequence of his decision to think through the Trinitarian ground of Easter from the perspective of its Trinitarian grammar. In asking after the basis of Christ's resurrection in the triune life of God, Barth does not depart from the plane of history, but rather takes with utter seriousness the idea that God is truly at work in this event. Therefore, the two sides of my thesis belong together. Easter's Trinitarian grammar points to its Trinitarian ground; Easter's Trinitarian ground is perceived only in its Trinitarian grammar. That the triune God is the subject of Christ's resurrection implies that God alone is its basis; that the triune God is the basis of Christ's resurrection underscores that God truly is its subject.

So, in its more detailed form, *my twofold thesis is that Barth (1) explicates the doctrine of Christ's resurrection in terms of a unique Trinitarian grammar, and (2) grounds the event of Christ's resurrection in the eternal triune being of God*. Both sides of this thesis work together to answer the question of the identity of the one who acts for us in the Easter event, which in turn answers more fully the question of its purpose. In his being and acting for us, the triune God remains faithful to himself.

The Threefold Argument

Since they belong together, I will trace both sides of my thesis through each part-volume of *CD* IV/1–3. This means that my twofold thesis will be advanced by a threefold argument. The three steps of the argument correspond to the three central chapters of the book, each of which focuses on the "transitional" discussion of each part-volume: "The Verdict of the Father" (§59.3), "The Direction of the Son" (§64.4), and "The Promise of the Spirit" (§69.4). The Trinitarian titles of these subsections might mislead one to think that Barth divides the works of the Trinity in order to describe them independently.

But this is precisely what Barth avoids. Instead, he develops God's triune self-differentiation from the perspective of three aspects of Christ's resurrection: Jesus Christ was *raised*, *arises*, and is *present*.[31] For Barth, the resurrection of Jesus Christ is one complex event that includes all three aspects.

These aspects correspond to the themes of each part-volume of IV/1–3: Jesus Christ was raised for our justification; Jesus Christ arises to be for us and give to us a sanctifying direction; and Jesus Christ was, is, and will be present with us as we fulfill our missionary vocation. Barth's mature Trinitarian theology of Easter emerges out of a consideration of each of these three aspects in turn. It is thus embedded in the complex structure of *CD* IV/1–3, and too much would be lost in an attempt to remove his thoughts from their surrounding context. So, I consider a threefold argument that follows Barth's own threefold structure to be the best approach.

What is this threefold argument? First, I consider the Easter event from the perspective of the *raising* of Jesus Christ. Befitting the christological motif of the humiliated Son of God in *CD* IV/1, Barth appropriates the raising of Jesus Christ to *God the Father*, but in a way that does not exclude the distinctive participation of Jesus Christ and the Holy Spirit. Jesus Christ was raised as God's free, gracious verdict for us. The basis for the Son's receiving this free grace in time is the eternal movement of grace given by the Father to the Son in the Spirit. This Trinitarian grammar and ground of the raising of Jesus Christ assures us of the utter graciousness of God's justification of us in Christ.

This first step raises a question: Is Jesus Christ only receptive in the Easter event? Is he not also active? So my second step is to view Easter from the perspective of Jesus Christ's own *arising*. Befitting the christological motif of the exalted Son of Man in *CD* IV/2, Barth speaks of the exalted human Jesus acting in his own arising by the power of the *Holy Spirit*. The Holy Spirit mediates between the risen Christ and us. The basis of the Spirit's mediation between the risen Christ and us is the Spirit-mediated partnership of the Son with the Father. This Trinitarian grammar and ground of Jesus Christ's arising highlights the concrete confidence with which we follow the sanctifying direction of the Son given to us in and by the Holy Spirit.

Though not contradictory, these first two perspectives stand in stark contrast with one another. The third step of my argument is to set forth their unity, which for Barth is teleologically established. I set forth this teleological

---

31. I.e., *Auferweckung*, *Auferstehung*, and *Parusie*. Cf. Berthold Klappert, "Die Rechts-, Freiheits- und Befreiungsgechichte Gottes mit dem Menschen: Karl Barths Versöhnungslehre (*KD* IV/1-3)," *Evangelische Theologie* 49:5 (1989): 460–78, esp. 462.

unity by viewing Easter from the perspective of Jesus Christ's risen *presence*. Befitting the christological motif of the glorious mediator in *CD* IV/3, Barth appropriates Christ's parousia to the living *Jesus Christ*. Jesus Christ as both true God and true human was, is, and will be present as the one who came before. The intermediate form of this presence in the promise of the Spirit is no less than the first or final forms. This threefold parousia of the one Jesus Christ is formally analogous to the perichoresis of the triune God. And this ever-new coming of Jesus Christ is materially grounded in the triune God's self-communicative being. The triune God is eloquent and radiant, ever ready to share himself. This Trinitarian grammar and ground of Christ's risen presence assures us that the call of Jesus is truly the call of God, and that we may obey this call with bold humility, for Jesus Christ himself is on the move with us.

After unfolding this threefold argument in support of my twofold thesis, I conclude with some constructive reflections on Barth's Trinitarian theology of Christ's resurrection. These reflections are both retrospective and prospective. Retrospectively, I consider Barth's earlier doctrine of the Trinity from *CD* I/1 in light of the concept of God operative in these materials from *CD* IV/1–3. Understanding the revealed God as the resurrected God fleshes out Barth's highly formal doctrine of the Trinity in *CD* I/1. I thereby show that the connection discerned between Christ's resurrection and the Trinity enriches the exposition of both doctrines.

Prospectively, I consider how we might think with and beyond Barth about the being-in-act of the resurrected God. What are the implications of the claim that the triune God is antecedently fit for resurrection? God's eternal readiness for resurrection consists in his triune life. This claim entails a deepening of the sense in which God is the living God. The eternal livingness of God as a fellowship of persons is God's readiness to share his own life with creatures in time. In other words, the living God *is* the God of the living.

The primary contribution of this study, however, is its careful analysis of the Trinitarian grammar and ground of Christ's resurrection as it comes to expression in *CD* IV/1–3. It is time to turn to the first aspect of this analysis.

2

The Verdict of the Father and the Generation of the Son

Who raised Jesus Christ from the dead? The simple answer is "God." But for those who confess the deity of Jesus Christ, this simple answer alone will not do. On the one hand, the deity of Jesus Christ seems to entail that he raised himself from the dead. But then, was he really dead if he could raise himself? On the other hand, we could further specify that God *the Father* raised Jesus Christ. But then, is Jesus Christ not fully God if he is excluded from the act of resurrection? What is needed is an account of the triune God at work in the initiating act of Easter: one that takes seriously the identification of God the Father as the one who raised Jesus Christ, yet without consequently denying the unity of God or the deity of Jesus Christ. Barth provides such an account in "The Verdict of the Father" (*CD* IV/1, §59.3).

The thesis of this chapter is that (a) Barth strictly appropriates the act of raising Jesus Christ to God the Father, yet in a way that does not exclude the distinctive participation of Jesus Christ and the Holy Spirit, and (b) according to Barth, in this act the triune God corresponds to himself, that is, God the Father's raising of Jesus Christ is grounded in the Father's eternal generation of the Son. These two claims together underscore that Easter is an act of free grace; it is grounded in nothing but the movement and act of grace that takes place in God himself. Such a Trinitarian theology of the raising of Jesus Christ, with its *patrological* focus, takes the first step in the development of the overall thesis of this book: that the triune God is the subject and basis of Christ's resurrection.

The Transition of the Humiliated Son of God

In order to understand Barth's Trinitarian doctrine of Christ's resurrection, we must place it in the context of Barth's doctrine of reconciliation. Within the structure of *CD* IV/1–3, the subsections devoted to Christ's resurrection perform a *transitional function* and bear a *Trinitarian form*. I will substantiate this claim by first briefly surveying the place of Christ's resurrection within the structure of Barth's doctrine of reconciliation in general. Then I will discuss the transitional function of §59.3 within *CD* IV/1 in particular. The purpose of these remarks is to place the systematic analysis of the remainder of this chapter within its proper literary context.

THE TRANSITIONAL SUBSECTIONS OF IV/1–3

Barth's doctrine of reconciliation is developed over four part-volumes. The first three are structured along parallel lines, with five sections (or "paragraphs") in each part-volume. Barth builds this threefold structure through a unique coordination of three traditional christological loci: the two natures, the threefold office, and the two states. The five sections within each volume correspond to traditional loci as well: Christology, hamartiology, soteriology, ecclesiology, and the Christian life.[1] The ordering is at points peculiar to Barth, and the material exposition is thoroughly revised from his christocentric standpoint. On account of this standpoint, it should come as no surprise that the christological sections at the head of each part-volume are by far the largest and exercise perspectival control over the remaining topics.

Of particular interest is where Barth places his doctrine of Christ's resurrection. The final subsection of each christological section is dedicated to a reflection on Christ's resurrection. At first glance, this appears quite traditional and thus unremarkable. Where else would one treat Christ's resurrection than at the end of Christology before turning to other topics? It must be granted that Barth is following the linear narrative form of Scripture and the Creed by proceeding from Christ's incarnation through his death to his resurrection. But we must not let this smooth narrative shape obscure the architectonic function of these subsections.

The function of these subsections is transitional.[2] Barth places his discussion of Christ's resurrection where he does in order to speak of Christ's transition to us. Topically, Barth transitions from Christology proper to its anthropological effects and consequences (sin, ecclesiology, etc.).[3] On account of his radical

---

1. Eberhard Jüngel describes, charts, and discusses the structure of Barth's doctrine of reconciliation in *Karl Barth, a Theological Legacy*, trans. Garrett E. Paul (Philadelphia: Westminster, 1986), 46–51.

2. The transitional function of Christ's resurrection is R. Dale Dawson's central interpretive thesis in *The Resurrection in Karl Barth* (Burlington, VT: Ashgate, 2007). Jüngel also notes the significance of these "transitional concepts" in *Karl Barth*, 50.

3. *CD* IV/1, 284: "But before we enter on this series of further problems . . . we must engage in a kind of transitional discussion. . . . What is the connexion between these new problems and our previous

christocentrism, Barth regards such a transitional discussion as necessary. He has developed his Christology and soteriology in such a way that one cannot avoid wondering whether there is any room left for us. The life history of Jesus Christ *is* the history of reconciliation. He "took our place."[4] In him the covenant between God and humanity is fulfilled. What could possibly come after such a finished, perfect work?

In the light of the risen Jesus Christ we see that God wills a further history beyond this fulfillment of the history of the covenant. At Easter, Christ's life of obedience unto death is opened up to us. The risen Christ himself makes room for us. He supplies his own transition to us, so that we are not left to our own devices, trying to bridge the ugly ditch between history and faith on our own.[5] His living self-attestation makes possible our attestation of him. Bearing witness to this opening up—this transition—is the function of Barth's subsections on Christ's resurrection.[6]

Over the course of IV/1–3, Barth develops this same basic transitional argument from three different perspectives. In each subsection, he develops the transitional argument in a manner congruent with the christological motif of the part-volume in which it is found. So, in IV/1, Barth speaks of Christ's resurrection as the *Verdict* of the Father, corresponding to the judicial language of the first form of the doctrine of reconciliation. In IV/2, Barth describes Christ's resurrection as the *Direction* of the Son, corresponding to the moral focus of the second form of the doctrine of reconciliation. In IV/3, Barth discusses Christ's resurrection as the *Promise* of the Spirit, corresponding to the teleological orientation of the third form of the doctrine of reconciliation. In

---

questions and answers? How are we going to proceed to build on this christological basis? . . . With what right can we speak of our sin, of our justification, of ourselves as a community and of our faith, in the light of what Jesus Christ is and has done for us? How does He come to us or we to Him?"

4. *CD* IV/1, 273. Here Barth summarizes the fourfold "for us" of "The Judge Judged in Our Place" (§59.2).

5. Barth alludes to and occasionally names Lessing in the context of these transitional discussions.

6. Joseph Mangina is formally correct when he identifies "participation" as the theme of Barth's transitional discussions in *Karl Barth on the Christian Life: The Practical Knowledge of God* (New York: Peter Lang, 2001), 51–89. However, his material account of Barth's understanding of participation is skewed. He claims that Barth "found himself compelled to abandon their [his liberal teachers'] anti-metaphysical prejudices" (83). The truth is Barth remained anti-metaphysical throughout his theological development, and his understanding of participation in the risen Christ is decidedly anti-metaphysical, insofar as the mode of our participation is *witness*: we share in the risen Christ's own active self-attestation. For more on the meaning of participation in Barth, see Adam Neder, *Participation in Christ: An Entry in Karl Barth's Church Dogmatics* (Louisville: Westminster John Knox, 2009). Neder's critiques of Mangina are insightful and persuasive (ibid., 97, 114).

each case, the transitional subsection moves the argument from Christology proper to its anthropological/ecclesial consequences by bearing witness to Christ's resurrection.[7]

However, unlike the preceding Christological subsections, *the transitional discussions of Christ's resurrection bear a Trinitarian form*. Instead of a dialectical inversion of Christological themes (for example, "The Way of the Son of God into the Far Country" vs. "The Homecoming of the Son of Man"), we find a Trinitarian pattern: the Verdict of the *Father*, the Direction of the *Son*, and the Promise of the *Spirit*. In fact, this is the only instance of Trinitarian parallelism in the sectional titles of *CD* IV. This is not meant to imply that these are the only relevant Trinitarian texts within Barth's doctrine of reconciliation, but it does indicate that these are major resources for understanding Barth's mature doctrine of the Trinity.

This Trinitarian parallelism is not mere window dressing. It highlights the Trinitarian structure of Barth's doctrine of Christ's resurrection. Read together in light of this parallelism, the common thesis of all three subsections is that the subject and basis of the transition from Christ to us is the triune God. The grammar of the risen Christ's transition to us is Trinitarian, and the ground of this transition is the triune God who corresponds to himself in this act.

The Trinitarian form of Barth's argument in these subsections supports the transitional function of Christ's resurrection within the doctrine of reconciliation. By identifying the triune God as the subject and basis of the act of transition, Barth removes any sense in which we are left to our own devices in trying to bridge the gap between Christ and us. In other words, Christ's transition to us is a work of *grace*. The Trinitarian grammar and ground of Christ's resurrection underscores this soteriological point.

BEYOND-THE-CROSS: THE PROBLEM OF TRANSITION IN §59.3

Now that we have discussed the transitional function and Trinitarian form of Christ's resurrection within *CD* IV as a whole, let us turn to §59.3 in particular. The whole of §59.3 is dedicated to answering one main question: Is there room for us sinners after the conversion of the world that took place on the cross? Is there a "genuine beyond" the crucifixion, one that includes us without canceling the seriousness of the cross?[8] The short answer is yes. Because God

---

7. Barth signals the structural significance of these transitional discussions in his overview of the doctrine of reconciliation by organizing his discussion of the anthropological side of reconciliation ("The Being of Man in Jesus Christ," §58.2) around these three concepts: verdict (pp. 93–99), direction (pp. 99–107), and promise (pp. 108–22).

raised Jesus Christ from the dead, there is a genuine beyond-the-cross event, one that makes room for us without overturning what took place on Good Friday. On Easter, the humiliated Son of God was revealed and justified by God the Father and comes to us in the power of the Holy Spirit.

Barth expands this answer by deriving from Easter five conditions of a genuine beyond-the-cross event: it must be (1) an act of *God*, (2) a *new* act of God, (3) an act positively *related* to the act of crucifixion, (4) an event *in space-and-time*, and (5) an act *united* with the cross as an event within the one history of Jesus Christ. Barth organizes §59.3 around these five points, showing how Christ's resurrection meets each of these conditions.

Since Barth has derived these conditions from the actuality of this particular event, his argument seems to lack suspense.[9] However, the movement of thought over the course of the five points is full of tension, as he *begins by stressing the sharp differentiation between cross and resurrection before moving to their deep unity*. Barth argues that the raising of Jesus Christ is a free act of divine grace, not a necessary sequel to the cross. So the suspense and even surprise of Easter morning is highlighted in Barth's exposition, even while the overall trajectory of his argument points toward the interconnection and unity of cross and resurrection.[10]

---

8. *CD* IV/1, 297. Barth's question in this subsection is a critical appropriation of the modern faith and history question. The real problem is the confrontation between our true, reconciled being in Jesus Christ crucified and our sinful being. In the modern period, this problem takes the form of the problem of faith and history. Barth takes seriously this "problem of time," or "Lessing's problem," but regards it as an evasion of the real problem when considered abstractly. Barth signals the distinction between the real problem and this evasion by the line break on page 323 of *Die Kirchliche Dogmatik*, Band IV, 1 (Zürich: Theologischer Verlag Zürich, 1980), hereafter *KD* IV/1. This line break is unfortunately missing in the standard English translation (*CD* IV/1, 294). Despite this distinction, however, Barth does not simply set aside the problem of faith and history as a pseudo-problem, as suggested by R. D. Dawson in *The Resurrection in Karl Barth*, 96–98. Rather, Barth *sublates* the problem: he affirms its relevance, negates its evasiveness, and transposes its temporal aspect into the higher problem of transition. For Barth's use of the Hegelian pattern of sublation, cf. George Hunsinger, *How to Read Karl Barth: The Shape of His Theology* (New York: Oxford University Press, 1991), 98.

9. In fact, this is a common pattern in Barth's theology, both within particular subsections and over the course of large blocks of material. Barth often briefly introduces the solution at the head of an argument in order to develop the problem on its basis. He then proceeds to develop the solution in detail. This pattern of thought is as an expression of his christocentric methodology.

10. The differentiated unity of cross and resurrection is the central theme of Klappert's analysis of §59.3 in *Die Auferweckung des Gekreuzigten: Der Ansatz der Christologie Karl Barths im Zusammenhang der Christologie der Gegenwart* (Neukirchen-Vlyun: Neukirchener Verlag, 1971), 287–397.

It is important to stress this movement of thought because it corresponds to the Trinitarian grammar operative in this subsection.[11] Barth begins with the differentiation between cross and resurrection, in the context of which he appeals to the differentiation between the Father and the Son. As Barth moves to the positive relation and unity of cross and resurrection, he appeals to the unity of the Father and the Son in the Spirit. Barth's Trinitarian theology of Easter thus serves his overall transitional argument. Consequently, the Trinitarian reflections of §59.3 are not merely "tacked on" to an unrelated argument, but are incorporated into the structure of Barth's movement of thought.

The point of departure in this movement of thought manifests the *patrological focus* of §59.3. God the Father raised Jesus Christ from the dead, the Son participating in this act only as the object and recipient of the Father's grace. Such a patrological focus befits the Christology of IV/1: the way of the obedient Son of God led to death, and so God the Son in his humiliation stands in need of God the Father's act to release him from death. In other words, the Trinitarian form of §59.3 serves its transitional function within the structure of IV/1. Keeping this context in mind, let us now turn to an analysis of Barth's Trinitarian grammar of the raising of Jesus Christ.

The Trinitarian Grammar of the Raising of Christ (§59.3)

Who is the subject of Christ's resurrection? For Barth, the first answer is "God the Father." Christ is the one who *was raised*. Thus in §59.3 Barth speaks first of the raising of Jesus Christ by God the Father, and only secondarily of Christ's own arising. In my exposition, I will begin by discussing at length the sense and significance of appropriating the initiating act of Easter to God the Father. Then I will turn briefly to the sense in which both Jesus Christ and the Holy Spirit participate in this act.[12] The purpose of this section is to substantiate the

---

11. This movement of thought fits a Trinitarian pattern identified by Eberhard Busch in *The Great Passion: An Introduction to Karl Barth's Theology* (Grand Rapids: Eerdmans, 2004), 44: "In the dogmatics Barth views each of the themes he addresses as an aspect from which to reflect on the being of God in his Word and work. He structures his train of thought, with a certain freedom and yet with a recognizable constancy, with a three-step sequence, in both small and large contexts. This threefold step is obviously an implication of the way he understands the doctrine of the Trinity. As a rule he speaks first of the subject of the divine Word and work, then of the act, and finally of the goal. Again and again his train of thought seeks to correspond to God's movement to humanity, to his turning to humanity and of humanity, in order to disclose himself to the human and the human to him." The first three points of §59.3 correspond roughly to Busch's three-step structure: (1) subject: God the Father raised Jesus Christ; (2) act: God declares his verdict concerning the cross; and (3) goal: Jesus Christ is present with his community in the time between the times. Although I do not follow this pattern, this rough correspondence corroborates my analysis of §59.3.

claim that *Barth strictly appropriates the act of raising Jesus Christ from the dead to God the Father, but in a way that does not exclude the distinctive participation of Jesus Christ and the Holy Spirit.* This claim is significant for two reasons: (1) it shows that Barth does in fact have a Trinitarian grammar of Christ's resurrection,[13] and (2) it sets the stage for the argument of the third major section of this chapter, concerning the Trinitarian ground of the raising of Jesus Christ.

God the Father

In the first instance, the subject of Christ's resurrection is God the Father. It is important for my overall argument that Barth *begins* by appropriating Christ's resurrection to God the Father. Positively, this is the proper starting point because all acts of God are *initiated* by the Father. We are not speaking of the Father in abstraction from the Son and the Spirit, but as the source of the divine act of resurrection. Negatively, if one were to begin with the activity of Jesus Christ, then reference to the action of God the Father on Jesus Christ is rendered superfluous. This is one of the weaknesses of the traditional view that Christ's resurrection was logically necessary due to his deity. Barth blocks the docetic tendency of this view by appropriating the initiating act of Easter to God the Father. The depth of the incarnate Son's obedience unto death is manifest in this: he stands in utter need of God the Father's gracious act of raising him from the dead.

There are three dogmatic reasons why Barth appropriates the raising of Jesus to God the Father. The first is that Easter is an exclusively *divine* act initiated by God the Father. The second is the *newness* of God's act of raising. The third is the *creative* character of Christ's resurrection. The first two reasons are laid out in Barth's first two points of §59.3, respectively. The third reason is a recurring theme throughout §59.3.

How does this Trinitarian form of Barth's doctrine of the raising of Jesus Christ serve its transitional function? Barth's appeal to the Trinitarian differentiation of Father and Son serves to emphasize the differentiation between cross and resurrection. The initiative of God the Father in the act of raising corresponds to the *revelatory* function of Christ's resurrection. The

---

12. In anticipation of ch. 3, it is worth noting the inversion of the movement of thought between §59.3 (from God the Father to Jesus Christ in the Holy Spirit) and §64.4 (from Jesus Christ through the Holy Spirit to God the Father).

13. *Pace* Jürgen Moltmann, who claims that Barth's doctrine of the Trinity prevents him from perceiving the Trinitarian relations operative in the Easter event, in *The Trinity and the Kingdom* (Philadelphia: Fortress Press, 1993), 61–65, 83–90, 139–44.

newness of God the Father's act of raising corresponds to the *juridical* character of Christ's resurrection. Easter's connection to creation corroborates the previous two points as well as supports the temporal and historical aspects of Barth's argument. God the Father raised the crucified Christ in order to reveal himself in him, to pronounce his verdict upon him, and to confirm himself as Creator and Lord. These aspects of Christ's resurrection as a distinct act that follows his crucifixion are intensified and explicated by appropriating this act to God the Father.

RESURRECTION AS REVELATION

According to Barth, the raising of Jesus Christ was a divine act of revelation. The revelatory function of the resurrection distinguishes it from the crucifixion. Christ's resurrection from the dead is an act of *God*, whereby God reveals himself in Jesus Christ. Easter is the primal revelation. The obedience of the Son of God that was fulfilled on Good Friday has been revealed on Easter. Whereas the former is an act of God with a component of human action, the latter is an act of God alone. In order to develop this point, Barth draws on the Trinitarian grammar of Easter. It is God *the Father* who raises his Son Jesus Christ from the dead, initiating a new history beyond the cross. Since (a) the Father is the initiator of divine revelation, and (b) Christ's resurrection is the primal revelation, then (c) God the Father is rightly spoken of as the initiator of Christ's resurrection. This move substantiates my claim that Barth attributes the act of raising Jesus Christ to God the Father.

Barth's first point in §59.3 is that "the raising of Jesus Christ . . . is . . . an act of *God*."[14] Per his usual pattern of thought, Barth begins with the divine *subject* who acts in the event under investigation.[15] Of course, to say that the raising of Jesus is an act of God does not set it apart from any other event worthy of theological study. The raising of Jesus shares with the "preceding event of the cross" its character as an act of God.[16] In fact, this was the whole point of the preceding subsections: that God himself acts in Jesus Christ's life of obedience unto death (§59.1), and thereby executes his gracious judgment (§59.2). Like the cross before it, the subject of Christ's resurrection is God.

---

14. *CD* IV/1, 330, translation revised and original German emphasis restored; cf. Karl Barth, *Die Kirchliche Dogmatik*, Band IV, 1 (Zürich: Theologischer Verlag Zürich, 1980), 330, hereafter cited as *KD* IV/1.

15. E. Busch, *The Great Passion*, 44: "As a rule he speaks first of the subject of the divine Word and work."

16. *CD* IV/1, 300.

What differentiates the cross and resurrection is not whether God was the acting subject, but whether God was the *sole* acting subject. The raising of Jesus, unlike his death, is a work performed solely and exclusively by God, without any accompanying human action. The crucifixion was exclusively ordained by God, but it was fulfilled with the participation of human agents.[17] Not so the resurrection. The resurrection was ordained *and fulfilled* by God alone: "The happening on the third day which followed that of Golgotha is the act of God with the same seriousness, but it is unequivocally marked off from the first happening by the fact that it does not have in the very least this component of human willing and activity. Not merely in purpose and ordination, but in its fulfillment, too, it is exclusively the act of God."[18] This difference in agency—an act of God with a human component on the one hand and an exclusively divine act on the other—constitutes the first and decisive difference between the cross and the resurrection.[19] As we shall see, this difference cannot be coherently asserted without recourse to the Trinitarian grammar of Easter.

Having begun by asserting this difference, Barth then substantiates his assertion. *The resurrection of Jesus Christ is an exclusive act of God because it is the revelation of God in Jesus Christ.*[20] Here is Barth's argument in a nutshell: since (a) resurrection is revelation, and (b) revelation is an act of God alone, therefore

---

17. *CD* IV/1, 300: "As the judgment of God, the event of Golgotha is exclusively the work of God. Its fulfillment is ordained by God even in detail. But all the same it has a component of human action—both obedient and good on the one hand and disobedient and evil on the other."

18. *CD* IV/1, 300.

19. Barth compares this exclusivity to the work of creation, a point to which I will return below (cf. "Resurrection as New Creation")

20. This is Barth's second and decisive reason. Prior to this, he notes a true but inadequate reason. This reason is anthropological: dead people don't *do* things. The dead are not subjects who can perform acts. "An event which continues the being of man after death cannot be the result of the will and activity either of the man himself or of other men. To be dead means not to be. Those who are not, cannot will and do, nor can they possibly be objects of the willing and doing of others. ἀνάστασις ἐκ νεκρῶν is not one possibility of this kind with others. Where it takes place, *God* and God *alone* is at work" (*CD* IV/1, 301).But this anthropological reason for attributing the raising of Jesus exclusively to God (the Father) is inadequate. In fact, to entertain the implications of this human impossibility for too long could easily slip into natural theology, albeit of a negative sort. To speak of human impossibility is not the same as speaking of divine possibility, "for to talk of that which is impossible to man is not by a long way to speak of God" (*CD* IV/1, 301). Barth does not deny the truth contained in this line of thought, especially if it is a truly *theological* anthropology of resurrection. But the anthropological reason must not compete with the strictly theological reason: that divine self-revelation is by definition an exclusively divine act. For an account of the subjectivity of the Father in the Easter event that relies more on this anthropological argument, see Hans Urs von Balthasar, *Mysterium Paschale* (Edinburgh: T&T Clark, 1990), 203–17.

(c) resurrection is an act of God alone.[21] The logic of this argument is *prima facie* valid. What may not be so obvious is the truth of its premises. Within the immediate context, Barth offers a brief explanation of and substantiation for these two premises.

The revelatory function of Christ's resurrection emerges from his reading of the New Testament. According to Barth's interpretation of the narrative logic of the Gospels, God himself was present and active in Jesus Christ and so was revealed in him, but the apprehension of this revelation was not mediated to the apostles until the forty days of Easter. Barth draws on the simple exegetical observation that the Easter appearance stories are *revelations*, and argues that they reveal not only who he is but also who he was, casting light on the previously hidden reality of God in him. All anticipations of this apprehension (for example, the transfiguration on Mount Tabor, Peter's confession at Caesarea Philippi, the baptism of Jesus in the Jordan) are exceptions that prove the rule.[22]

The identification of revelation as an exclusive act of God also emerges from Barth's reading of the New Testament. In the Easter narratives, Jesus Christ's self-revelation does not rely on the human agency or ingenuity of his apostles. Rather, Jesus calls them by name, opens their eyes, and even knocks them off their horses. It was not until the element of human willing was removed, as it was in the resurrection, that a genuine and trustworthy revelation could be received: "In a strange way this perception was unattainable by the disciples as long as they had the opportunity for it, as long as it seemed to be attainable, as long as the happening still had that component of human willing and action, and could to that extent be accepted and understood by them."[23] Revelation in its most basic form is an exclusive act of God, and the most basic form of revelation is Christ's resurrection.

So, since resurrection is revelation, and since revelation is an exclusive act of God, then resurrection is an exclusive act of God. Although I have recapitulated Barth's brief supporting evidence for the two premises of this

---

21. *CD* IV/1, 302: "The perception was mediated to them when on the third day, Easter Day, He came amongst them again in such a way that His presence as the man He had been (had been!) was and could be exclusively and therefore unequivocally the act of God without any component of human will and action; that it was and could be understood by them only and exclusively as such, exclusively and therefore unequivocally as the self-attestation of God in this man without any co-operation of a human attestation serving it."

22. *CD* IV/1, 302. In this context, Barth mentions only Peter's confession, but these three events are consistently cited together (cf. *CD* I/2, 114; *CD* III/2, 478–80; *CD* IV/2, 135–41).

23. *CD* IV/1, 302.

argument, it would be misleading to think that the evidence supplied in this context exhausts the whole of Barth's support for these premises. Why? Because these premises can be found among the basic constellation of convictions Barth came to during his break from theological liberalism that he retained throughout his career.[24] Thus the full substantiation of these premises can only be found in Barth's work as a whole. The expression of these convictions within "The Verdict of the Father" is representative, and so for our purposes we can be satisfied with a presentation that stays within this context.

There are two important implications of the fact that Barth introduces the concept of revelation to support his claim that the resurrection is an exclusive act of God. First, it shows that Barth continued to identify revelation as a crucial function of resurrection. Even as he sought to overcome his earlier tendency to reduce resurrection to a function of revelation, Barth never displaced the revelatory character of Christ's resurrection.[25] Second, it shows that Barth remained committed to the irreducible subjectivity of God in his revelation. God truly reveals himself in Jesus Christ without being made into a mere object of knowledge to be "read off" the history of Jesus of Nazareth.[26] God's irreducible subjectivity in his revelation was protected by means of a thoroughgoing eschatological interpretation of Easter during Barth's Romans II period.[27] But from the *Göttingen Dogmatics* forward, Barth deployed the

---

24. Both themes (the irreducible subjectivity of God in his revelation and the resurrection as the primal revelation) saturate both the first and second editions of Barth's Romans commentary, as well as other writings from this early period. See the evidence supplied by Bruce L. McCormack, in *Karl Barth's Critically Realistic Dialectical Theology: Its Genesis and Development 1909–1936* (Oxford: Clarendon, 1995), 161, 198, 212, and 251–58.

25. Over the course of his career, Barth sought to overcome his earlier reduction of resurrection to a function of revelation. As he puts it, the resurrection "was not . . . something merely formal and noetic" (*CD* IV/1, 301). Christ's resurrection is not merely the noetic counterpart to the cross (*CD* IV/1, 304). Christ's resurrection is both noetic and ontic; it has a formal and material side. These sorts of lines are certainly aimed at Rudolf Bultmann, with whom Barth is engaged in "an intensive, although for the most part quiet, debate" throughout IV/1 (*CD* IV/1, ix). But it must be recalled that many of Barth's critiques of Bultmann are also directed against his earlier theology, e.g., his self-critical reflections in *Church Dogmatics*, Vol. II, Part 1 (Edinburgh: T&T Clark, 1957), 634–36, hereafter cited as *CD* II/1. However, this self-critique does not imply that Barth rejects the revelatory function of Christ's resurrection. Revelation remained an important function of Christ's resurrection from the beginning of Barth's break from liberalism until the day he died. There was significant development here, but development along a consistent trajectory.

26. Bruce McCormack, *Orthodox and Modern: Studies in the Theology of Karl Barth* (Grand Rapids: Baker Academic, 2008), 28–29.

27. Per the developmental paradigm advanced by Bruce McCormack in *Karl Barth's Critically Realistic Dialectical Theology*, 21–22; noted also in idem, *Orthodox and Modern*, 29–31.

doctrine of the Trinity in his argument for the subjectivity of God in his revelation.[28] God is the initiator, act, and result of revelation, that is, Father, Son, and Holy Spirit. So it is fitting that in §59.3, after appealing to the concept of revelation, Barth turns to a Trinitarian analysis of Christ's resurrection.

The deity of God in his Easter revelation calls for a Trinitarian analysis. For Barth, God the Father is the initiator of divine revelation. So if Christ's resurrection is the primal form of divine revelation, then God the Father is the initiator of Christ's resurrection. The initiating act of Easter, the *raising* of Jesus Christ, is rightly appropriated to God the Father. This appropriation does not exclude the distinctive participation of the Son and the Spirit, for the raising of Christ does not exhaust the richness of the Easter event. Christ also *arises* and is *present* to the end of the age. But the initiating act of this manifold event rests wholly with God the Father.

This assertion appears in the final fine-print paragraph of Barth's first point, where he restates in Trinitarian terms the claim that the raising of Jesus Christ is an act of God. But Barth does not simply apply a ready-made doctrine of the Trinity to Easter. In fact, Barth warns against a careless application of Trinitarian dogma to the subject of the resurrection: "we must also be careful how to handle the thought (which is *correct* not merely in the sense of later Trinitarian theology) that Jesus Christ as the Son of God was associated with the Father as the Subject of His own resurrection. The New Testament does not put it in this way."[29] Note that Barth does not outright reject the participation of the Son of God in his resurrection—a point I will return to later. But he does place a stern warning here against a careless application of the Trinitarian dogma to the raising of Jesus Christ.

Instead of such careless Trinitarian theologizing, Barth develops an exegetical argument for appropriating the raising of Jesus Christ to God the Father. Barth begins by citing Gal. 1:1 and Rom. 6:4 as underlining the fact that "the Subject of the resurrection is not simply θεός, according to the regular usage, but θεός πατήρ."[30] These are by no means the only New Testament

---

28. Again per McCormack's paradigm; cf. *Göttingen Dogmatics*, §5; *Christliche Dogmatik*, §9; CD I/1, §8.

29. CD IV/1, 303, original German emphasis restored (KD IV/1, 334).

30. CD IV/1, 303. Barth does not identify any references for the "regular usage," though there is little disputing that the raising of Jesus is consistently attributed to "God" in the New Testament. He is probably not referring to the Easter narratives in the Gospels, which make few references to God the Father's raising of Jesus, focusing rather on Jesus' own agency in his self-disclosure. Instead, he is likely referring to Paul's regular usage along with that of other NT epistles, and perhaps also the pattern of the speeches in the book of Acts. For more on the dogmatic significance of identifying "God" in the New

texts that attribute the raising of Jesus to God the Father; rather, they are representative of a larger pattern. However, Barth's selection of texts from Galatians and Romans is not incidental. *Church Dogmatics* IV/1 is controlled by the juridical metaphor, so it befits the context to cite texts from the Reformers' favorite epistles.[31]

By contrasting texts that identify simply "God" as subject with those that identify "God the Father" as subject, Barth indicates that Christian proclamation from its inception cannot avoid some kind of differentiation between God as the one who raised Jesus Christ from the dead and the Son of God as the one who was raised in Jesus Christ. Simply speaking of an undifferentiated "God" in this case will not do; further specification is required. The theological task set by such texts is to develop this specified differentiation with clarity and consistency.

Barth takes up this task by first addressing some problematic passages. Barth cites two Johannine texts that seem to attribute Christ's resurrection to himself (John 10:18; 11:35). He argues that (a) these texts can be interpreted in a sense that does not contradict those that attribute his raising to God the Father, and (b) these texts must be interpreted in dialectical juxtaposition to other texts (Johannine and otherwise) that place Jesus Christ within the sphere of God the Father's raising while still attributing the act of raising wholly to the latter.

Barth cites three such texts: John 5:26; Rom. 1:4; and Philippians 2. John 5:26 shows that the life the Son has in himself is in fact "*given* to him by the Father," who has life in himself.[32] Romans 1:4 says Jesus Christ "in His resurrection from the dead by the power of the Holy Spirit ... was characterized, designated, declared to be the Son of God."[33] Accordingly, Jesus' status as the Son of God is declared in his resurrection, and yet he is not the subject of this declaration. Barth emphasizes that the verb for "designated" (ὁρισθείς) is in the passive voice. Finally, and most decisively, Philippians 2 sets in clear contrast the Son's self-emptying and self-humbling unto death on the one side, and God's exalting of him and giving to him the name above every

---

Testament as the Father, see Karl Rahner, "Theos in the New Testament," *Theological Investigations*, Volume I (London: Darton, Longman & Todd, 1961), 79–148.

31. Of course, these references could simply come from Barth's immersion in Galatians and Romans as he prepares for his forthcoming doctrine of justification (§61). But, as we shall see below ("Resurrection as Justification"), Barth deploys juridical concepts in his doctrine of Christ's resurrection. So these texts are selected not only because they attribute the raising of Jesus to the *Father*, but also because they point to the *verdict* pronounced by the Father in raising Jesus from the dead.

32. *KD* IV/1, 334, emphasis original.

33. *CD* IV/1, 303.

name on the other. Barth places emphasis on the word "God" (*Gott*) in verse 9 as the acting subject of Christ's exaltation, and on the verb "given" (*geschenkt*), for which he supplies the Greek word (ἐχαρίσατο), with its connotations of grace, as indicating Christ's position as the recipient of God's grace.[34]

In light of the significance of the first stanzas of the Philippian hymn in "The Way of the Son of God into the Far Country" (§59.1), it is fitting that Barth would complete the christological section of IV/1 with a reference to the final stanzas of that hymn. Such fittingness is not only a matter of formal symmetry, but also a material consequence of the Christology developed in §59.1. Since the mystery of the deity of Jesus Christ is that the true God became truly human and died as such, it follows that "the one whole Jesus Christ, very man and very God, was dead and buried."[35] This means that not only as man, but also as God, we must speak of Jesus Christ as dead and buried and so standing in need of God the Father's gracious act of resurrection.[36]

God the Father's act of raising Jesus Christ is not Barth's only word on the subject, but it is the certainly the first word. It is fitting that this would be the first Trinitarian move Barth would make, given that his first point about Easter is that it is the basic form of revelation and therefore an exclusively divine act of revelation. As such, the initiative of Easter lies wholly with God the Father. But all this talk of the activity of God the Father is not intended to exclude talk of Jesus Christ as the subject of his resurrection. I will develop this idea below.[37] At this point, it is necessary to see the purpose of Barth's appropriation of the act of raising Jesus Christ to God the Father: Barth prohibits docetism by appropriating the initiating act of Easter to God the Father. In Christ's death, all possibilities for further action are removed. But God the Father acts in raising him from the dead. All subsequent action on the part of the risen Jesus Christ and us with him is based on the initiating act of God the Father.

Why does Barth so emphasize the subjectivity of God the Father in this context? The short answer is *grace*.[38] According to Barth, the free grace of Easter

---

34. *KD* IV/1, 334.

35. *CD* IV/1, 303. "Gestorben und begraben war der eine ganze Jesus Christus, wahrer Mensch und wahrer Gott" (*KD* IV/1, 334).

36. Earlier in his career, Barth did appropriate the raising of Jesus Christ to God the Father: "God the Father acts on Him and through Him by raising Him from the dead" (*CD* I/1, 387). However, he did so only with reference to "the man Jesus of Nazareth" (ibid.). What is new in IV/1 is the claim that God the Father raised Jesus Christ in his divine-human unity.

37. See "The Receptivity of the Son."

38. *CD* IV/1, 304: "The comprehensive relevance of the resurrection, its redemptive significance for us, depends upon its being what it is described in the New Testament, God's free act of grace."

can only be expressed in terms of this Trinitarian grammar. God's free grace is shown in that the Father raises his Son Jesus Christ from the dead. Humanity's receptivity of divine grace is shown in that Jesus Christ did not raise himself but was raised by God the Father. This sets up the argument of a later section concerning the ontological ground of Christ's resurrection: God the Father's act of free grace is grounded in the movement and action of grace within the triune God. But before we turn to this matter, I must further explicate Barth's Trinitarian grammar of the raising of Jesus Christ.

RESURRECTION AS JUSTIFICATION

The raising of Jesus Christ was not only a divine act of revelation, but also a *new* divine act of *justification*. When understood in the light of its juridical character, the resurrection is further distinguished from the crucifixion. Christ's resurrection from the dead is a *new* act of God, in which God freely justified himself, his Son Jesus Christ, and us in him. When developing this distinction in terms of the juridical rubric operative throughout *CD* IV/1, Barth continues to draw on the Trinitarian grammar of Easter. It is God the *Father* who acts justly in raising his Son Jesus Christ from the dead. This is set in contrast to the crucifixion, which was the fulfillment of the loving obedience of the *Son* in his relation to the Father. In order to advance his overall transitional argument, Barth *differentiates* the resurrection from the cross by expositing the *juridical* character of Christ's resurrection along *Trinitarian* lines. This move further substantiates my claim that Barth appropriates the act of raising Jesus Christ to God the Father.[39]

Why does Barth turn from revelation to justification? Scripture, of course, leads him to discuss the raising of Jesus Christ as our justification: "he was raised for our justification" (Rom. 4:25). But why does he turn to justification at this point in his argument? Barth believes that the judicial character of Christ's resurrection more clearly differentiates Christ's resurrection from his crucifixion. Although revelation remains a leading motif for describing Christ's resurrection, it does not exhaust the meaning of Easter. Resurrection ought not to be reduced to a function of revelation.[40] As "an autonomous, new act of God," Christ's resurrection is "not, therefore, the noetic converse of [the cross]; nor is it merely the revelation and declaration of its positive significance and

---

39. Gerald O'Collins says regarding Barth's doctrine of Christ's resurrection that "penal substitution theology requires relegation to the museum of theology" ("Karl Barth on Christ's Resurrection," *Scottish Journal of Theology* 26:1 (1973): 95). I consider Barth's use of juridical language to conceptually re-describe not only Christ's death but also his resurrection as evidence that forensic categories can be adapted and expanded rather than merely set aside.

relevance."[41] Barth does not deny this revelatory function, but he is concerned that a reductively noetic account of the resurrection would not clearly differentiate cross and resurrection as distinct *acts* of God.[42]

The newness of the resurrection as an act distinct from the cross comes most clearly into view when discussing its juridical character. Both the death and resurrection of Jesus Christ are acts of justice. But they are two distinct acts of justice, the one following the other. The resurrection follows as God's answer to, confession of, and verdict on the crucifixion.[43] The cross is the question to which the resurrection is the *answer*: "in raising Jesus Christ from the dead . . . [God] answered the question which in Mark and Matthew forms the last words of the Crucified."[44] The righteousness of Christ's life was hidden in his death but *confessed* in his resurrection: God "recongised [*sic*] and proclaimed not merely the innocence but the supreme righteousness and holiness, the incomparable goodness of the work of Him who gave Himself up to death in pure obedience."[45] The resurrection was God's *verdict* on the Son in his way of obedience unto death. By means of these three concepts (answer, confession, and verdict), Barth aims to set forth the judicial character of the raising of Jesus Christ in its differentiation from his death.

What is of interest for our purposes is that Barth develops this judicial account in terms of the Trinitarian grammar of Easter. The differentiation of cross and resurrection as distinct acts of divine justice is cast in terms of the logic of appropriations. The resurrection is appropriated to God the Father, while the cross is appropriated to God the Son. Both acts bear the formal character of justice, but each in its own way in correspondence to the differentiation between the Father and the Son. The raising of Jesus Christ from the dead "had formally the character of an act of justice on the part of God the Father in his relation to Jesus Christ as His Son."[46] As an act of the Father in his relation to

---

40. This was a danger in Barth's earlier theology, and is a danger Barth detects in Bultmann—whose name has not yet been mentioned in §59.3, but with whom Barth is already "in intensive, although for the most part quiet, debate" (*CD* IV/1, vii).

41. *CD* IV/1, 304.

42. They are certainly related, even united, as the execution of the one great history of God with us. But within this unity a differentiation must be acknowledged, and acknowledged first, so that the resurrection is not regarded as a logically necessary consequence of the cross. Resurrection is a *free* act of God; this is Barth's constant refrain.

43. Answer (*Antwort*), Confession (*Bekenntnis*), Verdict (*Urteil*): these three concepts are emphasized in the German original (*KD* IV/1, 336).

44. *CD* IV/1, 307.

45. *CD* IV/1, 307.

46. *CD* IV/1, 305.

the Son, the resurrection stands in contrast to the crucifixion, which was "an act of justice on the part of the Son in His relation to God the Father."[47] So the crucifixion and resurrection of Jesus Christ are comparable to each other in their formal character as acts of justice, but they are differentiated in terms of the Trinitarian relations between the Father and the Son.

It is crucial to note that the raising of Jesus Christ is not appropriated to God the Father in the abstract, but to God the Father *in his relation to Jesus Christ his Son*. This is important because it keeps Barth from excluding Jesus Christ's distinct mode of participation in the act of raising, a point to which I will return below. Nevertheless, the differentiation is stark: Easter was God the Father's "free act of divine grace," whereas the obedience fulfilled on Good Friday was God the Son's "free act of love."[48] The one God acts justly in the Son's love and the Father's grace. The doctrine of the Trinity operates here as the "deep grammar" of the differentiation between cross and resurrection as acts of divine justice. The upshot of this line of reflection is Barth's insistence on appropriating the act of raising Jesus to God the Father.

I have been focusing on the differentiation between cross and resurrection, and rightly so, since this is Barth's main point in the material at hand. But there is another crucial aspect to Barth's judicial account of resurrection: *the threefold justification of Jesus Christ, humanity, and God himself that takes place on Easter*. The center and heart of the Easter gospel is that God justified Jesus Christ. This is good news for us because all were justified in him. And this good news is secure because, first and foremost, God justified himself. Barth summarizes these three dimensions of God's Easter verdict in the final paragraph of his second point:

> To sum up, the resurrection of Jesus Christ is the great verdict of God, the fulfillment and proclamation of God's decision concerning the event of the cross. . . . In this [acceptance of the act of the Son of God] the resurrection is the justification of God himself, of God the Father, creator of heaven and earth, who has willed and planned and ordered this event. It is the justification of Jesus Christ, His Son, who willed to suffer this event, and suffered it to the very last. And in His person it is the justification of all sinful humans, whose death was decided in this event, for whose life there is therefore no more place. In the resurrection of Jesus Christ, his life and with it their life

---

47. *CD* IV/1, 305.
48. *CD* IV/1, 305.

has in fact become an event beyond death: "Because I live, you shall live also" (Jn. 14:19).[49]

Grammatically speaking, there are three objects of the divine justification enacted in the raising of Jesus Christ from the dead: Jesus Christ, humanity, and God himself. God justified Jesus, God justified all humanity in him, and God justified himself.

Of particular interest to us is this third, self-referential justification, on account of its implicit Trinitarian grammar. The antecedent of the reflexive pronoun is not Jesus Christ, but God the Father. Elsewhere, Barth uses self-referential language to speak of Jesus Christ in his resurrection revealing himself as Lord. But in this judicial context, Barth speaks of God the Father as the one who justifies. In raising his Son Jesus Christ from the dead, God justified himself as Creator and Lord of the creature[50] and as the Father of his Son. This self-referential aspect of the divine justification enacted in the raising of Jesus Christ once again brings God the Father's activity to the foreground.

Again, this appropriation to the Father is not made in abstraction from his relation to the Son. In fact, it is precisely God the Father's "faithfulness as the Father of this Son" that is disclosed in Christ's resurrection.[51] Even as God the Father justifies himself, he does so in explicit relation to his Son Jesus Christ. Furthermore, the Holy Spirit makes his first appearance in this context as God in his freedom to give life.[52] So, Barth's Trinitarian account of the threefold justification that took place in the Easter event is further evidence that Barth strictly appropriates the act of raising Jesus Christ from the dead to God the Father, but in a way that does not exclude the distinctive participation of Jesus Christ and the Holy Spirit.

I have shown in this discussion of the juridical character of Easter that Barth seeks to advance his transitional argument by indicating that Christ's resurrection is a genuine beyond-the-cross event inasmuch as it is a *new* act of God. The newness of this act comes into view most clearly when exposited in terms of the forensic metaphor operative throughout IV/1, that is, Easter is God's *verdict* on Jesus Christ's way of obedience unto death. Barth develops

---

49. *CD* IV/1, 309, translation revised (*KD* IV/1, 340–41).

50. *CD* IV/1, 308: "He justified Himself . . . first in the revelation of His faithfulness as the Creator and Lord of heaven and earth and all men, to whom . . . He has spoken a second Yes which creates and gives them new life: a Yes . . . which was the gracious confirmation of His own original will to create and His act of creation."

51. *CD* IV/1, 308.

52. See "The Holy Spirit" below.

this judicial differentiation of cross and resurrection in terms of the *Trinitarian* grammar of Easter: God the Father justified his Son Jesus Christ and himself in him, confirming the Son's obedience and revealing his faithfulness as the Father of this Son.

By Barth's own lights, such an account of Christ's resurrection raises an important question: Did God have to do this? Was it necessary that God justify himself?[53] The question inevitably arises in an account like Barth's, where God himself is the reflexive object of God's acts. Surely God does not have to justify us. But is God in some sense compelled to justify himself by raising his Son Jesus from the dead? I will return to this question later in this chapter ("The Trinitarian Ground of the Raising of Christ (§59.3)"), for it is precisely by following this line of inquiry that we move from Easter's Trinitarian grammar to its ontological ground in the triune God. But before pursuing this line of inquiry, we must first have the full Trinitarian grammar before us.

Resurrection as New Creation

Before turning to the distinct participation of Jesus Christ and the Holy Spirit in God the Father's act of raising Jesus, it is worth noting a third aspect of the Father's appropriation. In addition to the deity and newness of the initiating act of Easter, there is a third reason why Barth appropriates the raising of Jesus to God the Father: the *creative* character of resurrection. Just as the work of creation is appropriated to God the Father,[54] so the work of resurrection is also appropriated to God the Father.

There are three aspects to this creative character, which correspond to Barth's first three points in §59.3. The first is the analogy between creation and resurrection as exclusively divine acts. The second is God's justification of himself as Creator in Christ's resurrection. The third is God's creation of a new time between the times that is oriented toward the coming new creation. In all three aspects, Barth appropriates both creation and resurrection to God the Father, but in a way that does not exclude the distinctive participation of Jesus Christ and the Holy Spirit.

(1) Barth makes explicit reference to the analogy between creation and resurrection under his first point: "*Like creation*, it [the happening on the third day] takes place as a sovereign act of God, and only in this way."[55] The point of

---

53. *CD* IV/1, 306: "Was this necessary?"
54. Karl Barth, *Church Dogmatics*, Vol. III, Part 1 (Edinburgh: T&T Clark, 1958), 49, hereafter cited as *CD* III/1.
55. *CD* IV/1, 300, emphasis added.

similarity between the two is the absolute sovereignty with which God executes them. There is no creaturely co-agency in either the creation of the world or the raising of Jesus. Creaturely participation enters the picture in the history that commences with these acts, but in their inception they are exclusively divine acts. This exclusivity is indicated by the appropriation of these acts to God the Father. As originating events, creation and resurrection are both analogous to the Father's eternal generation of the Son. So it is fitting that we speak of creation and resurrection as acts of God the Father, though, following the logic of Barth's reception of the appropriations doctrine, not to the exclusion of God the Son or God the Spirit.[56]

According to Barth's version of the appropriations doctrine, it is not a nameless λόγος ἄσαρκος (discarnate Word) who participates in God the Father's external works, but rather Jesus Christ himself in his eternally willed divine-human unity.[57] In the case of creation, this Trinitarian logic funds Barth's claim that creation is the external basis of the covenant. Christ participates in the work of creation *teleologically*, as the reason and basis of God's creating. In the case of resurrection, this Trinitarian logic funds Barth's claim that the raising of Christ is an act of utterly free grace. Christ participates receptively, as the object of God the Father's act of raising. Despite these differences in mode, Christ does participate in God's acts of creating and raising. In both cases, Christ participates in a manner peculiar to his divine-human unity, and so the appropriation of creation and resurrection to God the Father is not a mere word game but an unsubstitutable ascription to the first person of the Trinity.[58]

The analogy between creation and resurrection in Barth's theology has been noted before.[59] The usual reason for pointing out the analogy is to highlight the unique sense in which both are "historical." Creation and resurrection are both historical in the sense of being events in space and time. Yet they are not historical in the sense of being the results of creaturely processes. They are free acts of God without creaturely cooperation. So it is

---

56. *CD* III/1, 49–59.

57. *CD* III/1, 50–56.

58. The language of unsubstitutable identity ascription comes from Hans W. Frei's early christological experiment, *The Identity of Jesus Christ: The Hermeneutical Bases of Dogmatic Theology* (Eugene, OR: Wipf and Stock, 1997), 174. Although I am taking considerable license in using this language to talk of God the Father's act of creating, I take solace in the fact that such ad hoc use of concepts would not bother Frei.

59. E.g., Kathryn Tanner, "Creation and Providence," in *The Cambridge Companion to Karl Barth*, ed. John Webster (Cambridge: Cambridge University Press, 2000), 120.

fitting that both God's work of creation and God's act of raising Jesus are borne witness to by means of the genre of saga, which can set forth the spatio-temporality of these unique events without treating them as the consequences of historical causality.[60]

This aspect of the analogy is certainly important. But this formal similarity in terms of genre is based on a material similarity in terms of the subject matter itself. The point of Barth's generic observation is not merely to resolve the problem of faith and history, but more basically to testify to the irreducible subjectivity of God. In these crucial moments in the history of God with us, God acts alone. Creation and resurrection are thus both acts of God's free grace. That is Barth's point. My point is that in both cases Barth deploys a Trinitarian grammar of the event in order to make his point: in the first instance, we must speak of these events as acts of God the Father, who is the initiator of divine activity.

As with any analogy, the element of dissimilarity is as important as the element of similarity. The language here is explicitly analogical: Christ's resurrection is "*like* creation."[61] Creation and resurrection are distinct works of God. For all their interconnection, they are not strictly identical.[62] In the case of the analogy between creation and resurrection, the crucial element of dissimilarity is that *ex nihilo* applies to the former but not to the latter. In his mature theology, Barth never speaks of the raising of Jesus as an act of creation out of nothing.[63] Although it is an exclusive act of God the Father with no component of human action, it nevertheless happens to a creature with a prior history of human action. Jesus' prior history does not produce his resurrection—this delimitation is the point of Barth's appropriation to the Father. But God the Father's act of raising does happen to the subject of this human history. So the event of resurrection, unlike the event of creation, is an event with a past.[64] And so creation, which is out of nothing, and resurrection,

---

60. *CD* III/1, 78.

61. *CD* IV/1, 300, emphasis added.

62. Cf. *CD* III/1, 42–48, where Barth strongly warns against collapsing creation and covenant, even though they belong to each other.

63. In fact, Barth's only use of the *ex nihilo* clause in §59.3 is found in his critique of Bultmann, who according to Barth treats the creation of faith in the disciples as a *creatio ex nihilo*, instead of as founded on its object, the risen Jesus Christ.

64. Of course, creation also has a "past," but it is the past of the pre-temporal election of Jesus Christ. It is even a "human" past, in that the content of pre-temporal election is God the Son's self-identification with the man Jesus. But creation does not have a past in a chronological, mundane sense. The raising of Jesus Christ does have this sort of past: the past of Jesus of Nazareth. It is concerning *this* Jesus that resurrection takes place.

which follows the life history of Jesus, bear this important dissimilarity.⁶⁵ Within this dissimilarity, however, the crucial similarity of their appropriation to God the Father remains.

(2) But there is more than just an analogy between creation and resurrection. Christ's resurrection is not only *like* the work of creation, but it also *concerns* the work of creation. The raising of Jesus Christ is God the Father's justification of himself as the Creator and Lord of his good creation. Barth develops the justificatory purpose of Christ's resurrection with special reference to God as Creator.⁶⁶ In raising Jesus Christ, God the Father justified his work of creation, and therefore justified himself as Creator.

On Easter, God shows himself to be faithful to himself as the Creator. God has not given up on his creature or on himself as Creator. Barth states that God "primarily justified Himself. He did this first in the revelation of His faithfulness as the Creator and Lord of heaven and earth and all men . . . He has spoken a second Yes which creates and gives them new life: a Yes which He did not owe to them, but which He willed to speak, and which was the gracious confirmation of His own original will to create and His act of creation."⁶⁷ Barth goes on to speak of a "higher level" of God's self-justification: God's faithfulness to himself as the Father of the Son. I will return to this higher level in the section "The Trinitarian Ground of the Raising of Christ (§59.3)." At this point, it is enough to observe that God's justification of himself as the Creator evokes a

---

65. This element of dissimilarity is important to emphasize, especially in light of the current trend toward applying the *ex nihilo* clause to resurrection. See, e.g., Craig Keen, "Holy, Holy, Holy: The World Need Not Have Been," *Wesleyan Theological Journal* 44:1 (Spring 2009): 200–218; Brian Robinette, "The Resurrection in Retrospect: A Response to Recent Criticisms of Creatio Ex Nihilo," presentation at the Annual Meeting of the American Academy of Religion, Nov. 9, 2009. Keen in particular is right to highlight the apocalyptic character of Christ's resurrection, especially in contrast to those who tend to reduce Christ's resurrection to an affirmation of the creaturely order as such, e.g., Oliver O'Donovan, *Resurrection and Moral Order: An Outline for Evangelical Ethics*, 2nd ed. (Grand Rapids: Eerdmans, 1994), 31–52. However, it seems sufficient to speak of creation and resurrection as *analogous*, to avoid reducing the doctrine of creation out of nothing into code language for the resurrection of the dead.

66. This should come as no surprise, since Barth develops his understanding of the goodness of creation with special reference to the doctrine of justification. Cf. *CD* III/1, §42.3, "Creation as Justification." God's declaration that his work of creation is good is not made in the abstract but points forward to his work of justification in Jesus Christ. God's work of justification in Jesus Christ is therefore understood as the fulfillment of God's original covenantal intention for his creation. Trevor Hart observes this important connection between the doctrines of creation and justification in *Regarding Karl Barth: Toward a Reading of His Theology* (Downers Grove, IL: InterVarsity, 1999), 49–53. Hart does not, however, develop the consequences of this connection for Barth's doctrine of Christ's resurrection.

67. *CD* IV/1, 308.

Trinitarian grammar. Since the creation of the world is appropriated to God the Father, the raising of Jesus Christ as God's justification of himself as Creator is fittingly appropriated to God the Father as well.

(3) There is a third and final aspect to the creative character of Christ's resurrection. In addition to the analogical and the justificatory aspects, there is an eschatological aspect to the creative character of Easter. In raising his Son Jesus Christ from the dead, God creates a new time between the times that is oriented toward the coming new creation.[68]

This eschatological aspect emerges in the context of Barth's third point in §59.3, in which he develops the positive relationship between the crucifixion and resurrection of Jesus Christ. Here Barth shifts his attention from the initiating act of God the Father's raising of Jesus Christ to the ongoing act of the risen Jesus Christ in the power of the Spirit. Jesus Christ is the Lord of the church, directing its attention in recollection and expectation. By the authority of the Spirit, the church recollects Jesus Christ in his past as the crucified one, which has been made present in him as the risen one, and expects him in his future as the coming one, which is already present in him as the risen one.[69]

Despite this emphasis on the present activity of the risen Christ, Barth's earlier appropriation of the raising of Christ to God the Father performs an important function in this argument. God the Father, to whom creation is fittingly appropriated, acts as the one who creates this new time between the times. "This temporal togetherness of the Jesus Christ of Good Friday and the Jesus Christ of Easter Day as *created* by the divine verdict is the basis of life for men of all ages."[70] The verdict of the Father is no mere legal fiction; it is a creative verdict. God the Father graciously raised his Son Jesus Christ from the dead so that we may participate in his self-attestation as God's new creation. The time of Christ's presence by his Spirit—the time of the church between the times—is created by God's act of raising Jesus Christ. Therefore, the new creation that dawns on Easter morning is fittingly appropriated to God the Father.

---

68. George Hunsinger is right to categorize Barth's doctrine of Christ's resurrection under "the eschatological view," for the presence of the future in the risen Christ is a recurrent theme in all of Barth's numerous treatments of Christ's resurrection throughout the *Church Dogmatics*. "The Daybreak of New Creation: Christ's Resurrection in Recent Theology," *Scottish Journal of Theology* 57:2 (2004): 163–81. I will return to this eschatological aspect in greater detail in ch. 4.

69. This nexus of claims shows that the basic idea behind the "threefold parousia" is already up and running in IV/1, even though Barth has not yet made the explicit terminological innovation. See ch. 4, "The Trinitarian Grammar of Christ's Parousia (§69.4)."

70. *CD* IV/1, 316, emphasis added.

This eschatological aspect is the third and final reason why Barth appropriates Christ's resurrection in its creative character to God the Father. On account of the analogical, justificatory, and eschatological aspects of its creative character, Barth appropriates the initiating act of Easter to God the Father. These reasons together corroborate the case made above in connection with the revelatory and juridical meanings of Easter. The raising of Jesus Christ is not only an exclusively divine act of revelation and a new divine act of justification, but also a creative act of God as analogous to the original act of creation, as God's justification of himself as Creator, and as the creation of a new time between the times. In light of all this, Barth appropriates the act of raising Jesus Christ to God the Father.

Jesus Christ

I have been arguing throughout this section that Barth strictly appropriates the raising of Jesus Christ to God the Father, but in a way that does not exclude the distinctive participation of Jesus Christ and the Holy Spirit. The emphasis has been on the first clause of this claim. The focus here is God the Father. In the remaining chapters, I will focus much more on the Son and the Spirit. However, already in "The Verdict of the Father" (§ 59.3) we encounter the role of the Son and the Spirit in the transition effected by Christ's resurrection.

This inclusion should come as no surprise, because Barth does not think of the triune persons as three autonomous agents among whom works can be divided. Instead, Barth thinks of the triune God acting in a differentiated unity. In this, he follows the tradition. Yet he follows it in his own way, as he speaks decisively of the eternal triune relations being repeated in the temporal work of God. Barth's version of the doctrine of appropriations does not relegate the relations to eternity alone. Rather, Barth appropriates a work to a person in his relation to the other persons.[71] In the case of Easter, Barth appropriates the raising of Jesus Christ to God the Father *in his relation to the Son in and with the Holy Spirit*. I have indicated this relation above, but now must explicate it directly. Once we have this full Trinitarian grammar of the raising of Christ before us, we can then follow Barth in asking after the ground of this aspect of the Easter event in God's triune life.

What is the mode of Jesus Christ's participation in his resurrection? In order to answer this question, Barth makes a crucial distinction between the

---

71. Eberhard Jüngel has shown that Barth's doctrine of appropriations underscores the *concreteness* of God's triune self-differentiation, so that the relations between the persons are expressed through God's act of corresponding to himself in his works. See *God's Being Is in Becoming: The Trinitarian Being of God in the Theology of Karl Barth* (Edinburgh: T&T Clark, 2001) 47–53.

initiating act of Easter and the *ongoing* act of Easter.[72] Barth expresses this conceptual distinction in terms of a terminological distinction between the raising (*Erweckung*) of Jesus Christ and his own arising (*Auferstehung*).[73] Since both terms can be translated "resurrection," the difference between them is difficult to render in English.[74] However, Barth's grammatical pattern is

---

72. It is crucial to recall that for Barth, the term "resurrection" in its expansive sense includes everything *from* the events of the forty days, *to* the final return of Jesus Christ, *through* the presence of Christ with the church in the time between the times. Barth develops the perichoretic unity of these three forms of Christ's risen presence in *CD* IV/3, §69.4, which I will discuss in ch. 4, "The Trinitarian Grammar of Christ's Parousia (§69.4)." But Barth already asserts this expansive sense of resurrection in §59.3: "meaning by His resurrection (*Auferstehung*) . . . the whole of His *parousia* as it began with the Easter events and will be completed as the end of all time, but equally His living present in which in the time between the Once and the One Day He is now concealed in God for us, being present and active in the work of Holy Spirit, but also on earth, in history, in our very midst" (*CD* IV/1, 342; *KD* IV/1, 378).

73. Barth borrows this terminological distinction from Heinrich Vogel. Here is Barth's description of Vogel's argument: "The *arising* (*Auferstehung*), the being-alive of the one who was dead and buried, his new presence and action on the one hand, and his *reawakening* (*Erweckung*) from the dead on the other hand, are not easily interchangeable concepts, wherein he himself would be thought as the acting subject one time and God (the Father) at another time. Thus the case has been recently shown by H. Vogel (*Gott in Christo* 1951, S. 739 f.)" (*KD* IV/1, 334). Berthold Klappert highlights this distinction in his classic treatment of §59.3 in *Die Auferweckung des Gekreuzigten*, 291–93, 391–95. He has also shown how the distinction operates throughout *CD* IV/1–3 in "Die Rechts-, Freiheits- und Befreiungsgechichte Gottes mit dem Menschen: Karl Barths Versöhnungslehre (*KD* IV/1–3)," *Evangelische Theologie* 49:5 (1989): 460–78. David Mueller has picked up on Klappert's earlier insights in *Jesus Christ Crucified and Risen*, 336–67. More recently, R. Dale Dawson has made this distinction a centerpiece of his interpretation and critique of Barth in *The Resurrection in Karl Barth*, 118–23, 211–15. My use of this distinction focuses solely on its function within Barth's *Trinitarian* theology of Easter. In this I am indebted to some insightful comments made by Klappert (*Auferweckung des Gekreuzigten*, 306), although I go beyond him in my interpretation and development of this theme.Because this distinction looms so large in the secondary literature on Barth's theology of resurrection, it is worth noting that Barth's use of the distinction is not identical to Vogel's. Barth deploys the distinction to highlight the *freedom* of the raising of Jesus Christ as an act of God the Father's *grace*. Vogel deploys the distinction to incorporate both the ontic and noetic aspects of Easter, in *Gott im Christo: Ein Erkenntnisgang durch die Grundprobleme der Dogmatik* (Berlin: Lettner, 1951), 737–44. Barth and Vogel engaged in an ongoing debate over eschatology regarding the relationship between its ontic and noetic aspects. Vogel critiqued Barth for reducing eschatology to mere revelation. Barth's repeated refrain was that the revelatory character of the eschaton did not exclude ontic transformation, but that revelation was the *mode* of this transformation. See Karl Barth, *Letters 1961–68*, ed. Jürgen Fangmeier and Heinrich Stoevesandt (Grand Rapids: Eerdmans, 1981), 128–29, 147–48. Now it is easy to see how Vogel's use of the *Erweckung/Auferstehung* distinction underwrites his distinction between the ontic and (merely) noetic aspects of eschatology. It is hard to imagine that Barth is uncritically adopting Vogel's distinction; rather, he is adapting it to his own purposes.

consistent: Jesus Christ is never the active subject of his raising (*Erweckung*). Rather, he is either the passive subject or the object of this verb ("Jesus Christ was raised" or "God the Father raised Jesus Christ"). Only of his arising (*Auferstehung*) does Barth speak of Jesus Christ as an active subject (Jesus Christ "arose," "arises," "is risen").

This distinction makes possible a clear statement of the mode of Jesus Christ's participation in his own resurrection. God the Father alone was the acting subject of the initiating act of Easter: the raising of Jesus Christ from the dead. *Jesus Christ participates in this act only as the object and recipient of God the Father's act.* Secondarily, and on this basis, we can go on to say that Jesus Christ is the acting subject of the ongoing act of Easter: Jesus Christ arose from the dead, shows himself to his disciples, and is risen as the present head of his community. "But the facts themselves tell us decisively that the event of Easter has to be understood primarily as the *raising* [*Erweckung*] which happens to Jesus Christ, and only secondarily and (actively) on that basis as His *arising* [*Auferstehung*]."[75]

So there are two distinct modes in which Jesus Christ participates in the Easter event. In the first instance, Christ is "the one who was raised"[76] by God the Father. Only secondarily is Christ the one who arises and reveals himself. Now this second mode of Christ's participation in his resurrection is important to Barth. In fact, it commands his attention through the third point of §59.3, which is by far the longest and by his own admission the "decisive"[77] point in this subsection. But the *orderly differentiation* between the receptive and active subjectivity of Jesus Christ in his resurrection is crucial to note, for it expresses the Trinitarian grammar of Easter. The initiating act of Easter flows *from* the first person of the Trinity *to* the second person of the Trinity. Only subsequently is the second person the active subject of Easter as an ongoing act.

Barth highlights this orderly differentiation by correlating voice and tense. On one side, he correlates the passive voice with the past tense: Jesus Christ *was* raised. On the other side, he correlates the active voice with the present tense:

---

74. *Erweckung* carries connotations of being awakened, whereas *Auferstehung* carries connotations of an uprising. These connotations are relevant in certain contexts (e.g., the play on words with regard to the "awakening" of faith by the "awakened" Jesus Christ, CD IV/1, 748; KD IV/1, 836). However, I prefer to translate both terms using English cognates of "to resurrect," precisely because the substantive point of the terminological distinction is that they are two aspects of the one complex event that is the resurrection of Jesus Christ.

75. CD IV/1, 303, translation revised (KD IV/1, 334).

76. CD IV/1, 305.

77. CD IV/1, 309.

Jesus Christ *is* risen. Observe Barth's grammar: "It is one thing that He '*rises again*' [*aufersteht*] and shows Himself (ἐφανερώθη) to His disciples as the One raised again [*erweckte*] from the dead (Jn 21:14). Quite another thing is the act of this *resurrection* [*Auferweckung*]. He shows Himself to be alive to His disciples (Ac. 1:3), but He *lives*, after He (ἐξ ἀσθενείας) was crucified, ἐκ δυνάμεως θεοῦ (2 Cor. 13:4). 'The God of peace has brought him again from the dead' (Heb. 13:20)."[78] On one side, Jesus Christ was raised—a passive and past verb. On the other, Jesus Christ rises again, shows himself, and lives—all present and active verbs. The correlation of voice and tense indicates the chronological precedence of the passive before the active voice. This chronological precedence corresponds to the logical precedence of God the Father as the one who raised Christ from the dead.

The chronological precedence of the passive voice enables Barth to incorporate the subjectivity of Jesus Christ into his account of Easter without undermining a strict appropriation of the act of raising to God the Father. Jesus Christ was raised; God the Father raised him. That's the Trinitarian grammar of the initiating act of Easter in a nutshell. This grammar also corresponds to the judicial character of Christ's resurrection: "He Himself, Jesus Christ, the Son of God made man, was justified by God in His resurrection from the dead."[79] Jesus Christ was justified; God the Father justified him. God the Father was the subject of the act of raising Jesus Christ from the dead. Jesus Christ was the subject of this act only in a passive sense.

It is important to note also that by this account Barth rules out any strict sense in which Jesus Christ raises himself. He rejects the traditional formula that Jesus Christ (as God) raised himself (as man). Barth emphatically states, "No, not simply as man, but even as the Son of God Jesus Christ is here [in his resurrection] simply the One who takes and receives, the recipient of a gift, just as in His death on the cross it is not only as man but as the Son of God that He is wholly and only the obedient servant."[80] Barth certainly does not deny Christ's deity. Rather, he takes it as an implicate of the Son's union with Jesus of Nazareth that, *even in his true deity*, Jesus Christ participates in the initiating act of his resurrection *only as one who receives* from the Father.

Barth avoids the traditional reflexive formula for at least two reasons. First, he is concerned about its potential *docetism*.[81] If the Son raises himself, then the Son did not really taste death. If Barth's argument in "The Way of the

---

78. *CD* IV/1, 303, original German emphasis restored (*KD* IV/1, 334).
79. *CD* IV/1, 305–6.
80. *CD* IV/1, 304.

Son of God into the Far Country" (§59.1) succeeds, then God the Son truly experienced death on the cross. If he was sufficiently alive to then subsequently raise himself from the dead, then he was not really dead. "The one whole Jesus Christ, very man and very God, was dead and buried."[82]

Second, Barth is concerned about the *freedom* of God's justifying act of resurrection. If the deity of Jesus Christ in some sense logically necessitates his resurrection, the freedom of God's grace is undermined.[83] Of course, there is an important sense in which Christ's resurrection is "necessary," in that the triune God has determined himself to be with us both from and to all eternity. But this is not the logical necessity of the kind at work in, for example, Athanasius's understanding of Christ's death and resurrection.[84] So, for these reasons, Barth avoids the traditional pattern of Jesus Christ as God raising himself as man.

But the point of this present discussion is not to highlight what Barth rules out, but what he rules in. Barth does speak of Jesus Christ's active subjectivity as the Lord of his new time with us as the risen one.[85] In fact, later in §59.3 this becomes the dominant note, and remains so in §64.4 and §69.4, which I will treat in subsequent chapters. But the high note of the present activity of Jesus Christ to us and with us will not be heard aright if the bass note of his utter reliance on the grace of God the Father is not heard first. The utter receptivity of the Son in his resurrection accompanies Barth's appropriation of the raising of Jesus Christ to God the Father.

---

81. Barth detects a docetic tendency in Vogel's use of the *Erweckung/Auferstehung* distinction, inasmuch as Jesus Christ as the passive subject of his being-raised might imply that he is merely "impotent" rather than truly and complete dead (*CD* IV/1, 303). This is why Barth strictly appropriates the raising of Jesus Christ to God the Father, and regards this initiating act as logically prior to Jesus Christ's own arising, which as his own act of self-manifestation is dependent on the prior act of God the Father.

82. *CD* IV/1, 303.

83. Although he endorses Barth's rejection of the traditional reflexive formula, Dawson criticizes Barth for speaking of the resurrection as unnecessary. Dawson suggests that the *Erweckung/Auferstehung* distinction could be used to speak of the resurrection as the completion of Christ's obedience unto death, and as such necessary to the work of reconciliation. On this view, the Son as passive to the Father's raising is the final step in his passion (*The Resurrection in Karl Barth*, 211–15). Although this is an interesting proposal in its own right, it seems to undermine the very point of Barth's use of the raising/arising distinction, which is to deny that the initiating act of resurrection is in any sense the *work* of Jesus Christ, but rather a free act of the Father's *grace* upon him. This line of thought is central to Barth's contribution to a Trinitarian theology of Christ's resurrection, and gets lost in an attempt to render Christ's resurrection the necessary completion of reconciliation.

84. For Athanasius, the resurrection necessarily follows the death of Christ on account of his incarnation. See *On the Incarnation of the Word*, §20, §26, and §32.

85. *CD* IV/1, 309–333, esp. 313–14.

Now Barth does not develop this Trinitarian grammar only for the sake of setting parameters for faithful speech. He is interested in that, but not only that. The grammar itself points toward the ontological ground of Easter. Jesus Christ as the recipient of God the Father's act of raising leads Barth to discuss the prior movement of grace in the triune God. But before turning directly to this discussion, let me complete my analysis of the Trinitarian grammar by identifying the role of the Holy Spirit in the raising of Jesus Christ.

THE HOLY SPIRIT

Who is the subject of Christ's resurrection? In the first instance, Barth appropriates the raising of Jesus Christ to God the Father alone. This appropriation does not exclude the distinctive participation of Christ in the Easter event, first as a passive subject who receives the Father's act of raising, and only secondarily and on this basis as an active subject who arises to reveal himself. Furthermore, Barth's appropriation to God the Father does not exclude the distinctive participation of the Holy Spirit. God the Father raised Jesus Christ *by the Holy Spirit*, that is, in the life-giving, glory-revealing freedom of the Spirit.

In the context of God the Father's raising of Jesus Christ, the Holy Spirit is *God in his life-giving freedom*: "The Holy Spirit is . . . outside the Trinity, in His work as Creator and Reconciler of the world: God Himself as the One who creates life in freedom, who gives life from the dead, thus making His glory active in the world."[86] The raising of Jesus Christ according to the New Testament takes place by the Holy Spirit. Barth supports this exegetical claim by citing a series of texts: 1 Tim. 3:16; Rom. 1:4; 1 Pet. 3:18; Rom. 6:4; 2 Cor. 13:4; Col. 2:12; and Rom. 8:11.[87] Grammatically speaking, in these passages the Spirit is identified as both the "means" by which God (the Father) raised Jesus Christ from the dead and as himself the "subject" of the act of raising. The Spirit is thus both the freedom with which God the Father raised Jesus Christ and is God himself exercising this freedom.

Barth understands the biblical reference to the Spirit specifically in terms of *God in his freedom to reveal himself*. After discussing the revelatory function of God's Easter self-justification, Barth says, "This helps us to understand an important characteristic in the New Testament view of the raising of Jesus

---

86. *CD* IV/1, 308.

87. For an exegetical discussion of some relevant texts, see Scott Brodeur, *The Holy Spirit's Agency in the Resurrection of the Dead: An Exegetico-Theological Study of 1 Corinthians 15,44b–49 and Romans 8,9–13* (Rome: Pontificia Università Gregoriana, 1996).

Christ, that as a free work demonstrating and revealing the grace of the Father it took place by the *Holy Spirit*."[88] In other words, God the Holy Spirit is God in his mode of being-revealed.[89] The content of the Spirit's work in the Easter event is, unsurprisingly for Barth, revelation. And the determination of the Spirit's work in the Easter event is, again unsurprisingly, freedom. God is free in his being-revealed. This point not only coheres with Barth's doctrine of the Trinity, but also fits the context of §59.3, which emphasizes the freedom of God in the resurrection of Jesus Christ.

Interestingly, Barth experiments with the thought that the work of the Holy Spirit in the life of Jesus is the ground for the necessity of his resurrection from the dead. Barth says that if the resurrection was a necessity, then this would be way to think it through.[90] But he quickly rejects this line of thought, citing some New Testament passages that highlight the freedom of the Spirit (John 3:8; 2 Cor. 3:17). He concludes that "when we speak of the Spirit, *per definitionem* we do not speak of a necessary but of a *free* being and activity of God."[91]

However, there is a special sense in which reference to the Spirit entails a necessity. It is not that the Spirit's work in the life history of Jesus Christ necessitates the raising of Christ, which is a free act rooted solely in God's good pleasure. That the Spirit is involved only confirms the freedom of this act: "The fact that Jesus Christ was raised from the dead by the Holy Spirit and therefore justified confirms that it has *pleased* God to reveal and express Himself to the crucified and dead and buried Jesus Christ in the unity of the Father with the

---

88. CD IV/1, 308, original German emphasis restored.

89. CD I/1, §8 and §12.1.

90. It might be tempting to follow this track beyond Barth, using the doctrine of the Trinity as the grammar of freedom and necessity in God. Along these lines, we could say that the Father in relation to the rising Son is God in his (protological) freedom, and that the Spirit in his relation to the rising Son is God in his (teleological) necessity. Although Dawson does not put it this way, he also expresses interest in developing Barth's suggestion (*The Resurrection in Karl Barth*, 226). There is a hint of truth here, inasmuch as it gets at Barth's unique understanding of divine freedom in the context of the overall temporal structure of his doctrine of Christ's resurrection. However, to develop this line much further would be to obscure Barth's contribution to a Trinitarian theology of Christ's resurrection. Barth shows that one can think of the triune God as a self-differentiated single subject and still develop the Trinitarian grammar of Christ's resurrection. For all his development over the *Church Dogmatics*, Barth never turns his back on his commitment to the single subjectivity of God. Consequently, personal properties are appropriate only with reference to genetic relations, not with reference to divine perfections such as freedom. Thus the freedom of God cannot be attributed to the Father alone. The Spirit is also God in his freedom, but in a different mode of being, that is, the mode of self-glorification, of being-revealed.

91. CD IV/1, 309, original German emphasis restored (KD IV/1, 340).

Son and therefore in the glory of the free love which is His essence."[92] But, given that it was in fact the triune God's good pleasure to reveal his glory in Jesus Christ beyond his death, this free revelation will necessarily include the Spirit's life-giving work: "a revelation and expression which as such—and where the Spirit of God blows, where the Holy Spirit is at work, this does take place necessarily—must consist in the merciful work of creating the καινότης ζωῆς (Rom. 6:4) of this One who is dead, in His presentation and exhibition as the One who is alive for evermore."[93] That God is Spirit means that his will to reveal is effective. If God has chosen to glorify himself, then nothing stands in his way—not even death.

Barth's discussion of the Holy Spirit's role in the raising of Jesus Christ serves primarily to underscore the freedom of God the Father in the initiating act of Easter. But the new light cast by this discussion is that the ongoing history of Easter *follows necessarily* from this initial free act. As a living subject, the risen Jesus Christ acts freely, but he does so in the "authority of the verdict of the Holy Spirit."[94] This same Spirit authorizes the community of Jesus Christ to declare along with him the reconciliation accomplished in him. This living proclamation is not an afterthought but the very purpose for which God the Father raised Jesus Christ. God the Father's raising of Jesus Christ was not a private affair between them, but was necessarily an outgoing act aimed toward the risen Christ's self-attestation in the power of the Spirit.

In order to highlight the free grace of God the Father, Barth has emphasized the *distinction* between the initiating act of Easter and its ongoing history, that is, between God the Father's raising of Jesus Christ and his own arising. But this distinction does not mean there is not a deep connection and even *unity* between them. It is fitting that the Holy Spirit, who unites the Father and the Son, unites these two aspects of the one event of Christ's resurrection.[95]

CONCLUSION: FROM APPROPRIATIONS TO OPERA AD EXTRA

Who is the subject of Christ's resurrection? First and foremost, *God the Father* raised his Son Jesus Christ as a free and gracious act of revelation, justification, and new creation. In the first instance, *Jesus Christ* participated in God the Father's act only as the one who was raised. Secondarily, and on this basis,

---

92. *CD* IV/1, 309, original German emphasis restored (*KD* IV/1, 340).

93. *CD* IV/1, 309.

94. *CD* IV/1, 320.

95. We will return to the unity of these two aspects in the one event of Jesus Christ's living presence in ch. 4.

Christ arises, revealing himself to his own. Finally, God the Father raised Jesus Christ by the *Holy Spirit*, who is God in his life-giving freedom to be revealed, and consequently confessed by authorized witnesses. This is the Trinitarian grammar of the raising of Jesus Christ as it comes to expression in §59.3. "It was, as we saw, the *gracious* act of God in a perfectly exemplary form, given that even the Son of God as such was active only as recipient, God the Father alone the agent, God the Holy Spirit alone mediating His action and revelation."[96]

Does this account entail that there are three subjects of Christ's resurrection? No. Barth begins by emphasizing the differentiation between the persons of the Trinity in order to advance his transitional argument. But he does not end there. Barth's fifth and final point in §59.3 is the unity of Jesus Christ in his death and resurrection.[97] Barth supports this point by deploying the Trinitarian axiom that the external works of the triune God are indivisible. This axiom does not mean the works of the triune persons are indistinguishable. If that were so, then the appropriations developed over the course of §59.3 would amount to a meaningless word game. But this axiom does mean that these appropriations do not strictly divide the works of God among the triune persons. Instead, the distinctions between God the Father, Jesus Christ, and the Holy Spirit in the Easter event are internal to the one act of the triune God. Barth's movement of thought from appropriations to *opera ad extra* serves his point that God the Father is the subject of Christ's resurrection, but in a way that includes rather than excludes the distinctive participation of the Son and the Spirit.

To what extent is all this true? To what extent does the triune God manifest in the Easter event correspond to the triune God in himself? To what extent, then, is the triune God not only the subject but also the *basis* of Christ's resurrection? To these questions we now turn.

The Trinitarian Ground of the Raising of Christ (§59.3)

The thesis of this present section is that, according to Barth, God corresponds to himself in the raising of Jesus Christ from the dead. The purpose of setting forth this correspondence is to show the extent to which the triune God is the sole ground of Easter. This act is free, but it is not capricious. According to Barth, the raising of Jesus Christ is grounded in a movement and action in God himself—a movement and action of free and pure grace, given *by* the Father *to* the Son *in* the Spirit. In the Easter event, God is revealed as the God who *gives*

---

96. *KD* IV/1, 393, emphasis original.
97. *CD* IV/1, 342–47.

grace, the God who *receives* grace, and the God who *maintains his unity* in this self-differentiated movement and action.[98]

In what follows, I will set forth the distinct roles of each triune person in this intra-divine movement. In doing so, I am admittedly smoothing out and systematizing the Trinitarian discourse embedded in §59.3. However, such a systematic mode of presentation is appropriate, for it clarifies Barth's own position and identifies areas for further development and expansion.

The Grace of the Father

The New Testament identifies the one who raised Jesus Christ from the dead as God the Father. In virtue of his commitment to divine self-correspondence, Barth takes this identification seriously as a witness to an act that takes place in God himself. The raising of Jesus Christ is not merely appropriated to God the Father in the sense that it could have just as easily been appropriated to any other triune person. Rather, this appropriation points to a personal property: the Father alone gives grace to the Son. This self-differentiated movement and action in God himself is the basis of God the Father's raising of Jesus Christ in time.

Barth's point of entry into this Trinitarian basis is the *freedom* of God. As I have already shown, Barth appropriates the raising of Jesus Christ to God the Father by means of an exegesis of several relevant New Testament

---

98. With its emphasis on God's self-correspondence, this section is a development of Jüngel's brief description of the Trinitarian structure of Christ's resurrection in Barth: "In giving himself away God does not give himself up. But he gives himself away because he will not give up humanity. The Son of God who is united with the Son of Man, the Son of God as man, is certainly *dead*. This dead man cannot make himself alive. Here Barth thinks in strictly anti-docetic terms. That even in death God's being *remains* a being in becoming is not the work of the Son of God who died as man. But God's being remains a being-in-*act* only in the constantly new acts of *God's self-affirmation*. And so God's persistence in his historicity in the face of the death of Jesus Christ is a new act also. In the face of the death of the Son of God who died as man, 'God's being *remains* in becoming' means the *new* act of the resurrection, which happens to the Son of God and with him to the man Jesus. In saying *Yes* to the dead Son of God, God also said *Yes* to humanity, indeed, with the *same Yes*. In that here *God corresponds to himself* anew, he also brings *humanity* anew *into correspondence with God*. For in the resurrection of Jesus Christ humanity is given a share in the being of God that asserts itself against death. But as grace this sharing, too, belongs to God's being-in-act. And it belongs to God's *being* to *become* the God of every person" (*God's Being Is in Becoming*, 102–3, emphasis original). I would concur with this description. However, Jüngel says little more than this, instead giving the lion's share of his attention to God's self-correspondence in the death of Jesus. Such attention is not misplaced, but it requires the supplementary discussion of God's self-correspondence in the resurrection of Jesus Christ. This book provides that supplementary discussion by extending Jüngel's insights beyond him.

passages.⁹⁹ This appropriation functions in Barth's argument to underscore that the resurrection is "an act of divine grace which follows the crucifixion but which is quite free."¹⁰⁰ As a free act of divine grace, the raising of Jesus Christ from the dead has no ground other than God himself.¹⁰¹

Barth substantiates this assertion by referring to Phil. 2:9 and Heb. 5:10. According to Phil. 2:9, "The name which is above every name is *given* to Him."¹⁰² According to Heb. 5:10, Jesus Christ is "greeted and addressed (προσαγορευθείς) by God as a High Priest 'after the order of Melchizedek'"—not a hereditary priesthood but a free and spontaneous designation by God the Father.¹⁰³

Barth acknowledges that, alongside this line of texts, the New Testament also states that Christ's resurrection "had to happen" and was "according to the Scriptures."¹⁰⁴ Barth cites Luke 24:26; Acts 17:3; John 20:9; 1 Cor. 15:4; and Acts 2:25ff. as instances of this line of thinking. Barth does not wish to deny the biblical sense in which the resurrection of Jesus Christ had to happen. He does wish to avoid, however, the specter of necessity that hovers over the doctrine of Christ's resurrection when such passages are taken as one's point of entry.¹⁰⁵ So

---

99. See "God the Father" above.

100. *CD* IV/1, 303.

101. The fact that the freedom of God is Barth's point of entry is important for at least two reasons. First of all, it indicates that Barth does not escape the sphere of history in his inquiry into the Trinitarian basis of Easter, but rather underscores its historicity by identifying its basis in the prior historicity of God's own triune life. Nathan Kerr has criticized Barth on the grounds that basing the resurrection in God departs from the contingency of history, in *Christ, Apocalyptic, and History: The Politics of Christian Mission* (Eugene, OR: Cascade, 2009), 79–89. It must be acknowledged that the sort of contingency that Kerr wants differs from Barth's highly teleological concept of history. Nevertheless, it is a mistake to interpret Barth's move from the Trinitarian grammar of Easter to its Trinitarian ground as a *departure* from history, precisely because the move is aimed against accounts that render necessary Christ's resurrection.Secondly, the reference to divine freedom also blocks the misunderstanding that the triune God's eternal fitness for resurrection entails that Christ's resurrection is necessary for God to be God. As Barth says, the raising of Christ is "free even in its innermost divine basis" (*CD* IV/1, 305). Paul Molnar has raised this concern in his review of Dawson in *International Journal of Systematic Theology* 11:2 (April 2009): 240–43. Although Dawson opens himself up to the charge of rendering the resurrection necessary, developing Barth's insights concerning God's self-correspondence in the Easter event should not be rejected outright as leading to a "collapse of the immanent into the economic Trinity" (43), for the purpose of asking after Easter's ground in God is to crowd out all competing grounds.

102. *CD* IV/1, 303, original German emphasis restored (*KD* IV/1, 334).

103. *CD* IV/1, 303.

104. *CD* IV/1, 304.

105. Taking these texts as one's point of entry is especially problematic when combined with a sort of "incarnational" thinking in which the cause of Christ's resurrection is his deity. This critique coincides

Barth takes the passages that emphasize divine freedom in the raising of Jesus Christ as his point of entry, and then interprets the passages that emphasize the necessity of Easter in light of them.

Barth sets down the following hermeneutical rule: "this 'had to' does not mean that in this event God was acting any the less freely than in the giving of His Son or in the divine act of obedience of the Son even to the death of the cross."[106] The particular truth of the "had to" and the "according to the Scriptures" must not be denied: the raising of Jesus Christ took place "according to the continuity of the divine will and plan."[107] But these passages must not be taken as asserting an absolute logical necessity of the resurrection on the basis of Christ's divine identity or the merit of his obedience on the cross.[108] "His resurrection did not follow *from* his death, but sovereignly *on* his death."[109]

Does this sovereign freedom of God imply that the raising of Jesus Christ was capricious? Is Barth making an appeal to sheer divine omnipotence? No! Although there is no logical necessity, there is a logical *connection* between Christ's death and his resurrection: "Its only logical connection with it was that of the sovereign and unmerited faithfulness, the sovereign and free and constantly renewed mercy of God."[110] The "only" in this quote points to the freedom of God's grace in raising Jesus: there is no external necessity binding God to act in this way. Yet the claim of a logical connection between crucifixion and resurrection rooted in the faithfulness of God points to the basis of Christ's resurrection in God himself. In the raising of Jesus Christ, God is faithful to himself. God corresponds to Godself in this act.

Barth develops this divine basis by speaking in terms of *a movement and action in God himself*: "Certainly in the resurrection of Jesus Christ we have to do with a movement and action which took place not merely in human history

with Berthold Klappert's point that Barth does not think in a traditional "incarnational" way in *Versöhnung und Befreiung: Versuche, Karl Barth knotextuell zu verstehen* (Neukirchen-Vluyn: Neukirchener Verlag, 1994), 143–44. Instead, Barth thinks in a "reconciliational" way, in which God and humanity come together in Jesus Christ precisely in his obedience unto death. On this account, the resurrection can be thought through as a new act of God that happens *to* the dead Jesus Christ, without denying his deity.

106. *CD* IV/1, 304.
107. *CD* IV/1, 304.
108. A classic argument for the former, "incarnational" necessity of Christ's resurrection can be found in Athanasius, *On the Incarnation*, §20, §26, and §32. A classic argument for the latter, "meritorious" necessity of Christ's resurrection can be found in Thomas Aquinas, *Summa Theologica* III, q. 53, a. 4.
109. *CD* IV/1, 304, original German emphasis restored (*KD* IV/1, 335).
110. *CD* IV/1, 304. This statement coheres with the general thrust of Barth's earlier discussion of the constancy of God in *CD* II/1, 490–522.

but first and foremost in God himself."[111] And, just as when he inquired into the basis of Christ's obedience unto death in §59.1, this parallel inquiry leads to the doctrine of the Trinity. The freedom with which God the Father raised Jesus Christ is not the arbitrary freedom of an obscure omnipotent God, but rather the freedom of the triune God, the freedom of the divine love. It therefore fits Barth's larger pattern of thought that he extends his previous argument concerning the gracious act of God the Father into the immanent Trinity.

Although complex, Barth's argument concerning the Trinitarian ground of the initiating act of Easter is clear: if Jesus Christ's obedience unto death is grounded in the obedience of the Son, then God the Father's raising of Christ from the dead is grounded in *the grace of the Father*.

> We must not be afraid of the apparently difficult thought that, just as in God Himself (as we have seen), in the relationship of the Son to the Father (the model of all that is demanded from man by God), there is a pure *obedience*, subordination and subjection, the historical goal of which is the death of Jesus Christ, so also in the relationship of the Father to the Son (the model of all that is given to man by God) there is a free and pure *grace* which as such can only be received, the historical fulfillment of which is the raising of Jesus Christ.[112]

Can there be a movement of grace in God himself? Barth admits the difficulty of this train of thought. He begins with the phrase, "We must not be afraid of the apparently difficult thought."[113] We must certainly agree with Barth that it is difficult to think of a movement of grace in God himself. We might be afraid of such an assertion. Is this assertion not a metaphysical abstraction from the history of Jesus Christ against which Barth has warned us many times? If this were so, we would have every reason to fear. But Barth tells us not to fear. He is not going "behind" Jesus Christ, but rather taking seriously the basic Christian confession that Jesus is Lord.[114] The true deity of Jesus Christ means that what we say about him we may and must say about God. The movement revealed in the raising of Jesus Christ is none other than the very movement of God himself. Therefore, the difficulty of this thought is only "apparent."[115] It is created by our

---

111. *CD* IV/1, 304.

112. *CD* IV/1, 304, revised translation and original emphasis restored (*KD* IV/1, 335).

113. *CD* IV/1, 304.

114. This confession is Barth's consistent starting point in his earlier exposition of the doctrine of the Trinity (*Göttingen Dogmatics*, 110–30; *Christliche Dogmatik*, 171–214; *CD* I/1, 384–489). This confession is also the starting point of the argument in §59.1 (*CD* IV/1, 160).

prior assumptions about God. If we take our bearings from Jesus Christ, then we will learn how to speak not only of obedience in God but also of grace in God. This is a great mystery, but it need not be a great difficulty.

obedience, subordination and subjection, the historical goal of which is the death of Jesus Christ."[116] This explicit reference is crucially important here, because Barth admittedly does not develop the Trinitarian ground of the raising of Jesus Christ in §59.3 with the length and detail found in his discussion of the Trinitarian ground of Christ's obedience unto death in §59.1. However, the explicit reference to §59.1 indicates that the conclusions of that argument are relevant in this context.

Barth could not make the parallel more explicit: *just as* there is obedience in God, *so also* there is grace in God.[117] This explicit parallelism shows that Barth does not think of the Trinitarian ground of the raising of Jesus Christ as a minor matter in contrast to the Trinitarian ground of Christ's obedience unto death. Rather, Barth takes it that the complex argument regarding the obedience of the Son in §59.1 need not be rehearsed, but can simply be carried over into the distinct but related context of the grace of the Father fulfilled in the raising of Jesus Christ from the dead. Therefore, Barth's claims in §59.1 apply to §59.3, *mutatis mutandis*.[118]

In his application of the conclusions of §59.1 to the raising of Jesus Christ, Barth inverts the direction of the Trinitarian relation. Instead of speaking of the relationship of the Son to the Father, as in §59.1, Barth turns his attention to the relationship of the Father to the Son in §59.3. This inversion is a matter of perspective.[119] Barth does not shift to a consideration of the Father in the abstract, but to a consideration of the Father's act of relating to the Son. This inversion befits the patrological focus of §59.3, which in turn befits the christological motif of humiliation in IV/1.[120]

---

115. *CD* IV/1, 304.

116. *CD* IV/1, rev. (*KD* IV/1, 335).

117. *KD* IV/1, 335: "wie es . . . so auch . . ."

118. The parallelism between §59.1 and §59.3 is the insight that drives Adam Eitel's analysis of Barth's doctrine of Christ's resurrection in "The Resurrection of Jesus Christ: Karl Barth and the Historicization of God's Being," *International Journal of Systematic Theology* 10:1 (January 2008): 36–53. Barth answers not only *Quo iure Deus homo*, but also "*Quo iure resurrectio Dei*" (46). My disagreements with Eitel's argument are matters of detail and not at all with this perceptive insight.

119. The perspectival character of this inversion is important to remember, for Barth speaks of both persons in both subsections. In §59.1, the corollary to the Son's obedience is the Father's command. In §59.3, the corollary to the Father's grace is the Son's *receptivity*—a point to which we will return in "The Receptivity of the Son" below.

120. See "Beyond-the-Cross: The Problem of Transition in §59.3" above.

In accordance with this inverted perspective, Barth shifts from the *obedience* of the Son to the *grace* of the Father. Just as there is pure obedience in the relation of the Son to the Father, so also there is "free and pure *grace*"[121] in the relation of the Father to the Son. This shift constitutes the crucial difference between the Trinitarian ground of Christ's death and the Trinitarian ground of Christ's resurrection: whereas the cross is grounded in the obedience of the Son, the resurrection is grounded in the grace of the Father. Despite its boldness, Barth considers this claim to be the straightforward implication of the New Testament's identification of God the Father as the subject of the raising of Christ. Since God the Father acts with free grace in raising his Son Jesus, and since God corresponds to himself in his acts, then it follows that in God himself there is a movement of free and pure grace from the Father to the Son. Easter's Trinitarian grammar leads directly to its Trinitarian ground.

What Barth has uncovered in this line of thought is the ontological basis of Christ's resurrection in the triune God. There is no independent logical necessity guaranteeing that the raising of Jesus Christ follows his obedience unto death. But in light of its occurrence, we can identify its basis in God: the Father's act of relating to the Son. This basis is free, but it is not capricious. It befits the "logic" of God's own life. The Father eternally begets the Son and the Son eternally loves the Father. Just as the eternal Son-Father relationship supplies the basis for the obedience of the Son in time, so also the eternal Father-Son relationship supplies the basis for the grace of the Father in time. The Father gives and the Son receives. The Father alone begets the Son in eternity, and so it is fitting that the Father alone raises the Son in time. A movement of grace takes place in God himself and, only on that basis, also in the Easter event. In other words, *the eternal generation of the Son is the basis of the Easter verdict of the Father*.[122]

Barth has admittedly gone out on a limb in positing a movement of grace in God. To speak of God being gracious toward us is one thing; to speak of God being gracious in himself is quite another. The doctrine of the Trinity helps to make sense of this language, inasmuch as it teaches us how to speak of the Father's act of relating to the Son. But to specify this relationship in terms of grace strains credulity. Does not grace mean the condescension of God to that which is *not* God? Furthermore, does not grace mean the condescension of God

---

121. *CD* IV/1, 304.

122. Dawson has criticized Barth for not taking "the next step to extend the parallel of the Father's work in the resurrection into the intratrinitarian dynamic of the Father's eternal begetting of the Son" (*The Resurrection in Karl Barth*, 216). I am arguing that Barth has in fact taken this very step, just without the explicit use of the traditional terminology.

to that which is in *rebellion* against God? Does positing a movement of grace in God require the concomitant positing of sin in God?

In reply to this objection, we must attend to the *analogical* character of Barth's language in this context.[123] The movement and action of grace in God is "pure."[124] This movement of grace is not simply identical with the grace by which God reconciles sinners to himself. Rather, this movement is the "model of all that is given to man by God."[125] The Father-Son relationship in God is not simply identical with the Creator-creature relationship or the Reconciler-sinner relationship. Instead, the Father-Son relationship is the *model* for these relationships. As such, it is appropriate to speak of a movement of grace in God, but only if this is understood as the *pure* grace whereby the Father gives himself wholly to the Son.[126]

The analogical character of this language highlights the proper distinction between the movement of grace in God and the event of Easter. But Barth's emphasis in this context is on the *positive relationship* between the grace of the Father and its historical fulfillment. The raising of Jesus Christ from the dead is the historical *Vollzug* (fulfillment, outworking, execution) of the movement and action of grace that takes place first and foremost in God himself.[127]

Fulfillment does not mean that God needs to raise Jesus in order to be or become triune. It is precisely the specter of necessity that Barth intends to supplant by his discussion of the innermost divine basis of Easter. But, at the

---

123. The analogical character of this language should come as no surprise, insofar as it is an explication of the doctrine of the Trinity. Already in *CD* I/1, Barth readily admits that even "begotten" is only a figure of speech, so that we "can say it only in such a way that on our lips and in our concepts it is untruth. . . . Nevertheless, in naming God thus we are expressing the truth, His truth" (*CD* I/1, 433). "Grace" in God is obviously analogical, but so is "begotten."

124. *CD* IV/1, 304.

125. *CD* IV/1, 304.

126. In *CD* II/1, Barth speaks not only of God's grace toward us but also of God's grace in himself. The analogical character of this language is especially emphatic: "The form in which grace exists in God Himself and is actual in God is in point of fact hidden from us and incomprehensible to us" (357). The incomprehensibility of the form of grace in God himself does not contradict, but determines and delimits, its being revealed: "But in this mystery it is actually revealed and operative as God's being and action in our midst" (357). Therefore, the incomprehensible form of grace in God is the basis of the grace God manifests toward us: "Because He who is Father, Son and Holy Spirit is from eternity to eternity the center and source of all unity and all peace, therefore He must be the origin and essence of that which we know as grace in such a very different form" (358). Despite its different historical and literary context, this line of thought is compatible with Barth's talk of "pure grace" in God in §59.3. In both cases, Barth speaks of the grace that is in God as pure: "It is manifest in the pure love and grace which binds the Father with the Son and the Son with the Father by the Holy Spirit" (358).

127. *CD* IV/1, 304; *KD* IV/1, 335.

same time, Barth does not intend to diminish the significance of Easter for God by identifying its basis in a primary and pure movement in the triune God. Rather, this movement and action in God is *aimed toward* its historical fulfillment. Just as the aim or goal (*Ziel*) of the Son's eternal obedience to the Father is his obedience unto death on the cross, so also the aim or goal of the Father's eternal grace given to the Son is his raising of Jesus Christ from the dead.[128] The raising of Christ from the dead is the historical fulfillment of the triune God's eternal will not to be God alone, but God-with-us. God puts his inner triune life on display so that we may know and confess him as the one he is for us.

The raising of Jesus Christ is not, then, a mere mirror of some otherworldly movement, nor does Barth remove Easter from time altogether.[129] Rather, God the Father's raising of Jesus Christ in time *corresponds* to the grace the Father gives to the Son in eternity. This self-correspondence is utterly free. There is no basis requiring God to act in this way other than his own free decision to work out his pure triune movement on the plane of human history. But on the basis of God's free decision, the relationship of the Father to the Son is genuinely repeated and reenacted on that plane.

Barth speaks of this self-correspondence in terms of divine *faithfulness*. In the Easter event, the triune God is faithful to himself. By justifying himself in the raising of Jesus Christ, the Father is faithful to the Son: "He did it in the revelation of His faithfulness as the *Father* of this *Son*, in the revelation of the love with which He loved Him from all eternity and all along His way into the far country."[130] The eternal love and faithfulness of the Father for the Son is revealed in God the Father's raising of Jesus Christ from the dead. God is faithful to himself in the Easter event.[131]

---

128. Christ's death as the *Ziel* (aim, goal, end) of the Son's relation to the Father and Christ's raising as the *Vollzug* (fulfillment) of the Father's relation to the Son stand in precise parallel relation in this passage (*KD* IV/1, 335). Unfortunately, the former clause is missing in the standard English translation (*CD* IV/1, 304).

129. This is exactly the aforementioned concern Kerr raises against Barth's grounding of Easter in God's eternal being (*Christ, Apocalyptic, and History*, 79–89). As an internal criticism of Barth, I do not see the problem. Barth's talk of a prior movement and act in God is an assertion of the historicity of God's being, and therefore precisely not a departure from but an affirmation of the concreteness of history. As an external criticism, however, Kerr is right that the understanding of history he wants (i.e., as radically contingent) is not found in Barth, for whom the concept of history is determined protologically and so teleologically. On this count, I simply do not share with Kerr the collateral commitments that lead him to this criticism.

130. *CD* IV/1, 308, emphasis restored from original German (*KD* IV/1, 339).

God's act faithfulness to himself is utterly *free*. "His whole eternal love would still have been His even if He had acquiesced in His death as the Judge who was judged, if His mission had concluded at that ninth hour of Good Friday, if it had been completed with His fulfilling and suffering in His own person the No of the divine wrath on the world."[132] Barth not only asserts this freedom to limit our claims on God's faithfulness, but also draws from this assertion the following counterfactual claim: "But then . . . it would have been without witnesses, without participants, because without proclamation, without outward confirmation and form, concealed in the mystery of the inner life and being of the Godhead."[133]

Barth draws this counterfactual claim not to protect an arbitrary divine will, but to highlight the fulfillment of God's eternal purpose in raising Jesus Christ: "It *pleased* God, however, to justify Himself, that is, to reveal and give force and effect to His faithfulness and love in this supreme sense, by an ὁρίζειν (Rom. 1:4) of His Son which the disciples of Jesus could see and hear and grasp, and which was ordained to be publicly proclaimed."[134] The final clause is especially telling: "which was ordained (*bestimmtes*) to be proclaimed."[135] The faithfulness and love of the Father for the Son was ordained—or "determined"—to be revealed. According to Barth, the triune God determines himself to be known. This divine *self-determination* is the positive meaning of divine freedom. The Father freely wills to put on display in our sphere his eternal faithfulness to his Son. It pleased the living God to be the God of the living.

---

131. By identifying God in his triunity as the basis of Christ's resurrection, my reading of Barth differs from Eitel's in "The Resurrection of Jesus Christ." I do not find sufficient evidence in this context that Barth thinks God eternally self-differentiates himself on the basis of a logically prior decision to undergo resurrection in time. Rather, Barth identifies God's eternal self-differentiation as the antecedent condition of both the eternal decision for and the temporal execution of the raising of Jesus Christ. Nevertheless, Eitel is right to see a historicizing move in Barth's reflections in §59.3, for Barth insists that this eternal self-differentiation is eternally *aimed toward* and so *fulfilled by* the raising of Jesus Christ. In other words, God's triunity is logically but not ontologically prior to God's covenantal decision, for both occur in eternity.

132. *CD* IV/1, 308.

133. *CD* IV/1, 308.

134. *CD* IV/1, 308, emphasis added. Generally speaking, counterfactuals function in Barth's theology not as assertions of logical necessities abstracted from history but as thought experiments to aid the explication of the meaning and purpose of God's free acts in history. For a striking example, see *CD* IV/1, 734–39.

135. *CD* IV/1, 308.

What does this entail? Though free, Christ's resurrection is not an afterthought to his crucifixion. Revelation is not external to reconciliation. God's justification of himself before us is the outworking of God's right in himself. The revelation effected in the raising of Jesus Christ is the fulfillment of God's eternal decision: "He willed to give His eternity with Him and therefore to Himself an earthly form. He willed to give the inner and secret radiance of His glory an outward radiance in the sphere of creation and its history. He willed to give to His eternal life space and time. And that is what He did when He called Jesus Christ to life from the dead."[136] This will of God is free. He did not have to do it. But he did do it. And so, on the basis of the actuality of God's revelation, we can say that God willed from all eternity to reveal his grace in the Easter event. By raising Jesus Christ from the dead, God the Father corresponds to himself as the one who gives grace to the Son.

I have laid out the divine basis of the raising of Jesus Christ in terms of the grace of the Father. But what about the Son? In what sense does God the Son also correspond to himself in being raised by God the Father?

The Receptivity of the Son

According to Barth, the raising of Jesus Christ is grounded in a movement of grace in God. This movement is triune: the Father gives grace to the Son in the Spirit. In accordance with the patrological focus of §59.3, Barth speaks of this movement primarily from the perspective of the Father's relation to the Son: the Father gives grace to the Son. However, Barth also speaks of this movement from the perspective of the Son's relation to the Father: the Son *receives* grace from the Father. And so we come to the second aspect of the Trinitarian ground of the raising of Jesus Christ: the receptivity of the Son.

In discussing the Trinitarian grammar, I noted that the appropriation of the raising of Jesus Christ to God the Father did not exclude the distinct mode in which Jesus Christ participated in this event. In the first instance, Jesus Christ was associated with God the Father as the one who was raised. As a free act of grace, Jesus Christ did not raise himself but was raised by another: God the Father. Only in a secondary and dependent sense does Jesus Christ himself arise, coming to his own to reveal himself. The Trinitarian grammar and ground of this second sense will move to the foreground in chapter 3. Here, our concern is with the divine basis of his being-raised.

For Barth, the receptivity of Jesus Christ to the activity of God the Father is not relegated to his humanity in abstraction from his deity. Rather, Jesus

---

136. *CD* IV/1, 308.

Christ himself, in the unity and totality of his being as the incarnate Son of God, died and was raised by God the Father. Following his signature pattern of thought from actuality to possibility, Barth asks after the basis of this receptivity in God himself. Jesus Christ, not only as a man, but also as the very Son of God, participated in his being-raised as the *object* and *recipient* of the grace of God the Father.

Barth develops his understanding of the unique mode of the Son's participation in his resurrection by comparing and contrasting it with his death: "Certainly in the raising of Jesus Christ we have to do with a movement and action which took place not merely in human history but first and foremost in God Himself, a movement and action in which Jesus Christ as the Son of God had no less part than in His humiliation to the death of the cross, yet only as a pure *object* and *recipient* of the *grace* of God."[137] Both the death and resurrection of Jesus Christ are events in which the Son of God participates. However, his mode of participation differs in each. Whereas the death of Christ is the historical outworking of the obedience of the Son, the raising of Christ is the historical outworking of the receptivity of the Son.[138] The Son is not only obedient to the Father's command, but also the object and recipient of the Father's grace. And he is this not only in human history, but first and foremost in the movement and action that takes place in God himself.

To speak of the basis of the raising of Jesus Christ in the Son's receptivity elicits ontological puzzles similar to those encountered in the context of Barth's discussion of the Son's obedience in §59.1. How can it be that there is receptivity in God? Surely God is gracious in himself before he is gracious to us. But is God also receptive to grace in himself? Barth says yes. The whole of his theology is directed against the assumptions that render this thought puzzling. God is in himself as he reveals himself to us. The center of God's revelation is Jesus Christ in his death and resurrection. At this center we see both a command-obedience relationship and grace-receptivity relationship. Although such relationships in God seem odd to us given our theological assumptions, they do in fact befit the true, living God, who in himself is a self-differentiated movement. In other words, God is the triune God, and therefore it is possible to speak of receptivity within God himself.

---

137. *CD* IV/1, 304, translation revised and original German emphasis restored (*KD* IV/1, 335).

138. In describing the Son's mode of participation in the initiating moment of Easter, Barth shies away from "passivity" because it "approximates to a suspiciously docetic view of what is meant by death" (*CD* IV/1, 303). This is what he fears in Vogel's use of the raising/arising distinction. There is certainly a passive element to the Son's obedience fulfilled in his death (*CD* IV/1, 244–56). But with regard to the raising of Jesus Christ, Barth prefers the language of "receptivity."

In order to speak rightly of the Son's receptivity, we must once again acknowledge the *analogical* character Barth's language in this context. He specifies that the Son's receptivity is pure: it is "a movement and action in which the Son of God has no less part than in His humiliation to the death of the cross, yet only as a *pure* object and recipient of the grace of God."[139] Barth is not speaking of just any receptivity, but of the unique receptivity of God the Son. The pure receptivity of the Son in God is both like and unlike creaturely receptivity. Negatively, this means that the Son's receptivity is pure in contrast to the impurity of receptivity as we experience it in human history. Even our reception of God's free and pure grace by faith is impure in comparison with the purity of the Son's reception of the Father's eternal gift of life.[140] Positively, this means that the receptivity of the Son is the genuine receptivity that grounds all true receptivity in human history. In being raised from the dead by the grace of the Father, the Son corresponds to himself as "the One who takes and receives."[141] And the human reception of God's grace by faith is modeled after the Son's pure receptivity in God himself as enacted in the Easter event.[142]

Having acknowledged the analogical character of this language, one might still object to the apparent subordinationism of Barth's position. Does talk of the Son's receptivity place him in a position of unequal deity vis-à-vis the Father? Surely Jesus Christ as human only receives what God the Father gives him in raising him from the dead. But is not Jesus Christ as God the acting subject of his resurrection without qualification? Is this not a necessary consequence of his true deity? Barth says no. The true deity of Jesus Christ entails that we must learn from him the truth of deity. And in him we see that there is receptivity in God. It is as the recipient of the Father's grace that the Son participates in his own raising: "No, not simply as man, but even as the Son of God Jesus Christ is here simply the One who takes and receives, the recipient of a gift."[143] This does not entail a denial of his true deity because "the fact that as very God and very man He is worthy of the divine gift of new life from the dead does not alter in the slightest the fact that He did not take this new life but that it was

---

139. *CD* IV/1, 304, emphasis added.

140. Barth often engages in the dialectical "purification" of concepts. To cite only two instances: he defines God's eternity as "pure duration" (*CD* II/1, 608), and he says that he has been "thinking and speaking in pure concepts of movement" in his re-translation of the traditional christological "phenomenology into the sphere of a history" (*CD* IV/2, 106). Here Barth's indebtedness to Hegelian thought forms is self-evident.

141. *CD* IV/1, 304.

142. *CD* IV/1, 304: "the model of all that is given to man by God."

143. *CD* IV/1, 304.

given to Him."[144] It is precisely in his receptivity of the Father's grace that Jesus Christ shows himself to be not only human but also the Son of God.

Although his talk of grace and receptivity in God is an innovation, there is a sense in which Barth is simply extending a line of argument as old as the fourth century. The opponents of Nicea thought that generation was unbecoming of God, and so the Son could not be equal in deity to the Father. Athanasius argued that the Son's generation implies no inequality precisely because it is eternal, and so describes a personal distinction within God that has always been true of God.[145] The later distinction between *ousia* and *hypostasis* only aids this line of argument, inasmuch as generation speaks only to the hypostatic distinctions, not the common divine *ousia* that is shared without reserve. This line of argument could be extended to the receptivity of the Son without much controversy: as eternally begotten from the Father, it is fitting for God the Son to receive.

However, there is an important sense in which Barth's thinking differs from this line of argument against subordinationism. This line takes it for granted that the generation of the Son establishes an eternal relating that is abstracted from the life history of Jesus Christ in time. Therefore, one must on the one hand attribute all that does not befit God in the life of Christ to his humanity, and on the other attribute all that appears divine to his deity. This habit of thought is deeply embedded in the tradition, despite breakthroughs at many points along the way.[146]

This is not Barth's habit of thought. In fact, he is quite critical of it: "We obscure and weaken the character of resurrection as a free pure act of divine grace (in contrast to the character of His death on the cross suffered in obedience), if appealing to His divine sonship we describe it as His own action and work."[147] Instead of attributing receptivity to Christ's humanity alone, Barth regards Christ's receiving of new life in time as corresponding precisely to the Son's receptivity of the Father's grace in God himself. He reaches this conclusion not by abstracting the Father-Son relation from Christ's resurrection, but by thinking after God's correspondence to Godself in the Easter event. Only in the light of the Son's eternal act of self-identification with the man Jesus can we see that there belongs in God himself the movement of grace and receptivity. So, for Barth, it is the eternality of Jesus Christ in

144. CD IV/1, 304.

145. This is a central claim of Athanasius's *Orations against the Arians*.

146. This pattern of thought recurs throughout Athanasius's *Orations against the Arians*, and remains a central feature of the tradition thereafter, most (in)famously in the *Tome of Leo*.

147. CD IV/1, 304.

his divine-human unity that blocks subordinationism.[148] This is why Barth does not shy away from correlating the Father-Son relationship with the God-human relationship "in the relationship of the Son to the Father (the model of all that is demanded from man by God) . . . [and] in the relationship of the Father to the Son (the model of all this is given to man by God)."[149] Jesus Christ's reception of new life from God the Father in time is the exact representation (Heb. 1:3) of God's eternal self-differentiation as Father and Son.

THE UNITY OF THE SPIRIT

According to Barth, the free divine act of raising Jesus Christ from the dead is grounded in a movement and action in God himself—a movement and action of free and pure grace given *by* the Father *to* the Son. The triune God corresponds to himself in the initiating act of Easter. The differentiation manifest at Easter corresponds to God's own eternal self-differentiation.

But by so positing a movement of grace in God, does Barth undermine the unity of God? No, for God is not only the God who gives grace and the God who receives grace, but also the God who *maintains his unity* in this self-differentiated movement and action—God the Holy Spirit. I have already discussed the role of the Spirit in the Trinitarian grammar of the initiating act of Easter.[150] What remains to be seen is how far and in what sense God the Spirit corresponds to himself in the Easter event.

Now, admittedly, pneumatology does not play as large a role in the Trinitarian ground of Easter as developed in §59.3 as it does in §64.4. So we should not be too disappointed that a full doctrine of the Spirit does not emerge in this context. However, we may at this point ask why the Spirit does not become a major theme here. The short answer: context. The picture of the Holy Spirit in §59.3 fits the Christology of IV/1: Jesus Christ, the Lord as Servant. The downward, self-humbling movement of the Son of God is in the foreground in IV/1. A "downward" perspective on the Trinity thus corresponds to this christological motif. The movement is from the Father who sends his obedient Son into the far country and raises him up by sheer grace. There is

---

148. Barth sets forth thorough exegetical, historical, and dogmatic arguments for this claim in *Church Dogmatics*, Vol. II, Part 2 (Edinburgh: T&T Clark, 1957), 94–145, hereafter cited as *CD* II/2. In this context, Barth supplies a lengthy citation from Athanasius as a precursor to the claim that the Son of God in his unity with the man Jesus is the subject of election (*CD* II/2, 108–10). However, it must be acknowledged that this insight does not determine the whole of Athanasius's theology the way it does for Barth.

149. *CD* IV/1, 304.

150. See "The Holy Spirit" above.

a before and after in God, both in the command and obedience fulfilled in Christ's death and in the grace and reception fulfilled in Christ's resurrection. In this triune movement, the Spirit is God maintaining his unity in the midst of this deep differentiation within himself. As Barth puts it, "The Holy Spirit . . . is within the Trinity: God Himself maintaining His unity as Father and Son, God in the love which unites Him as Father with the Son, and as Son with the Father."[151] Because the "downward" christological vector prevails in IV/1, it befits the context that Barth introduces the Spirit into an already developed differentiation between Father and Son.

As the eternal unifier of the Father and Son, God the Holy Spirit corresponds to himself in the initiating act of Easter. God the Father's raising of Jesus Christ "took place by the Holy Spirit."[152] Since the Holy Spirit is the bond of union between the Father and the Son in God, it is fitting that the Holy Spirit is the bond of union between God the Father and the risen Jesus Christ.[153]

This move is an extension of Barth's "Augustinian" pattern of thought regarding the third person of the Trinity. In Barth's theology generally, the Holy Spirit is God as he maintains the faithfulness and love of the union of Father and Son.[154] This pattern remains operative throughout Barth's development, though it is certainly not the only such pattern.

Barth deploys this pattern in terms of his own understanding of God's *self-correspondence*. The Spirit's act of uniting Father and Son is not just a solution to the conceptual puzzle of unity and difference in the Godhead. Rather, the eternal unity of the Father and the Son in the Holy Spirit is revealed in the Easter event. God the Father's raising of Jesus Christ by the Holy Spirit is the "revelation of His faithfulness as the Father of this Son."[155] Because the Holy Spirit eternally unites the Father with the Son, it is fitting that the revelation

---

151. *CD* IV/1, 308. As we shall see in ch. 3, Barth keeps this broadly Augustinian pneumatology in "The Direction of the Son," but turns it on its head. Barth *begins* with God the Spirit as the Lord of the occurrence in God by which God the Son in his exalted majesty partners with God the Father in his humble mercy. This Spirit-directed occurrence in God is the ground of both the coincidence of humiliation and exaltation in the life history of Jesus and of the directive fellowship of the risen Christ toward us in the Spirit. This dialectical inversion of the Trinitarian grammar and ground befits the christological motif of IV/2, i.e., the "upward" movement of the exaltation of the Son of Man.

152. *CD* IV/1, 308.

153. The Holy Spirit also corresponds to himself by mediating the ongoing action of the risen Jesus Christ as the head of his body, the church (*CD* IV/1, 309–333). Barth's development of the Trinitarian basis of this aspect of the Spirit's work appears in §64.4, and so will be treated in ch. 3.

154. *CD* I/1, §12. Cf. Daniel L. Migliore, "Vinculum Pacis: Karl Barths Theologie des Heiligen Geistes," *Evangelische Theologie* 60:2 (Jan 2000): 131–52.

155. *CD* IV/1, 308.

of God's faithfulness to himself as the Father of Jesus Christ "took place by the Holy Spirit."[156] So, the triune God—Father, Son, and Holy Spirit—corresponds to himself in the Easter event.

Up to this point in my analysis, I have emphasized the *differentiation* between the Father and the Son, and therewith the *freedom* of the Father's grace. Does this reference to the eternal unity of the Father and the Son in the Holy Spirit render the raising of Jesus Christ necessary? Does the Spirit compel the Father to raise the Son? Barth says no. God the Holy Spirit is by definition free: "When we speak of the Spirit, *per definitionem* we do not speak of a necessary but of a *free* being and activity of God."[157] The unity of the Spirit is not an abstract principle but the living unity of the Father and the Son. The unity of the Spirit does not entail that God is somehow forced to perform the work of resurrection, but that the triune God is true to himself in this work. "The fact that Jesus Christ was raised from the dead by the Holy Spirit and therefore justified confirms that it has *pleased* God to reveal and express Himself to the crucified and dead and buried Jesus Christ in the unity of the Father with the Son and therefore in the glory of the free love which is His essence."[158] God's essence is his act of free love that takes place between the Father and the Son in the Spirit. Thus the triune God corresponded to himself when he freely chose to reveal himself in the raising of Jesus Christ.

This discussion shows that Barth's grounding of the initiating act of Easter in the differentiation between the Father who gives grace and the Son who receives grace does not undermine the unity of God, for God is the Spirit who eternally and essentially unites the Father and the Son. We have once again followed Barth's movement of thought in §59.3 from differentiation to unity, this time in terms of the inner life of God as the unity of the Father and the Son in the Holy Spirit.

But by this reference to the inner life of God, we do not depart from the sphere of God's work for us. *Barth thinks toward the unity of God's being by thinking after the unity of God's work.* Barth's reference to the unity of the Spirit is not an application of a principle, but a witness to an event. This event is the one history of the covenant fulfilled in Jesus Christ, crucified and raised for us. For all his attention to the differentiation between the crucifixion and the resurrection, Barth's final word in §59.3 is their *unity* in the person of Jesus Christ.

---

156. *CD* IV/1, 308.
157. *CD* IV/1, 309, original German emphasis restored (*KD* IV/1, 340).
158. *CD* IV/1, 309, original German emphasis restored (*KD* IV/1, 340).

Barth clearly states that his emphasis throughout §59.3 has been on the differentiated relationship between crucifixion and resurrection: "We have so far spoken of two different acts of God and therefore only of the 'relationship' (*Zusammenhang*) between them."[159] Barth's first two points asserted that the raising of Jesus Christ was an act of *God*, which was *new* and so distinct from his death. Barth's third point developed the complex differentiated *relationship* between these two acts. These three points are central to Barth's transitional argument in §59.3.[160] Barth's discussion of the triune ground of Easter serves this transitional argument. The differentiated relationship between cross and resurrection is grounded in the differentiated movement of grace in God. God the Father raised Jesus Christ in fulfillment of the free grace of the eternal Father that the eternal Son can only receive.

But Barth ends on a note of unity: "The time has now come when we must use a stronger term [than 'relationship']. . . . For these are not two acts of God, but one. The two have to be considered not merely in their relationship but in their *unity* (*Einheit*)."[161] After asserting the unity of the death and resurrection of Jesus Christ, Barth makes the following rich statement of explanation: "It is the *one* God who is at work on the basis of His *one* election and decision by and to the *one* Jesus Christ with the *one* goal of the reconciliation of the world with Himself, the conversion of men to Him."[162] Barth does not speak of God's oneness in abstraction from the act in which the Son of God became incarnate for us as a human subject in partnership with God the Father in the unity of the Holy Spirit. In this oneness of God in his work, we see the oneness of God himself.

Barth can assert the oneness of God in this work without undermining God's self-differentiation because he does so in explicitly Trinitarian terms: "We have thought of the resurrection of Jesus Christ as the gracious work of God the *Father*. But this work of grace is wholly and utterly the answer to the work of obedience of the *Son* fulfilled in His self-offering to death. This work of grace and this work of obedience as the act of God the Father, Son and Holy Spirit are one work."[163] Just as the differentiation between the death and resurrection of Christ is grounded in the differentiation between the Father and the Son, so

---

159. *CD* IV/1, 342 (*KD* IV/1, 378). It is again worth recalling that no commentator has set forth this emphasis of Barth's as well as Berthold Klappert in *Die Auferweckung des Gekreuzitgten*.

160. Barth refers to his fourth and fifth points as formal amplifications of the main argument developed in his first three points (*CD* IV/1, 333).

161. *CD* IV/1, 342, original German emphasis restored (*KD* IV/1, 378).

162. *CD* IV/1, 342, original German emphasis restored (*KD* IV/1, 378).

163. *CD* IV/1, 342–43, original German emphasis restored (*KD* IV/1, 378).

also the unity of the death and resurrection of Christ is grounded in the unity between the Father and the Son *in the Holy Spirit*.[164]

This brief pneumatological discussion concludes the exposition of the Trinitarian ground of the raising of Jesus Christ. According to Karl Barth, the initiating act of Easter is grounded in a movement and action of free and pure grace in God himself, given *by* the Father *to* the Son *in* the Spirit. In the raising of Christ, God is revealed as the God who *gives* grace, the God who *receives* grace, and the God who *maintains his unity* in this self-differentiated movement and action.

The Significance of a Trinitarian Theology of the Raising of Christ (§61.2)

By grounding the initiating act of Easter solely in the triune God, Barth testifies to the fact that the raising of Jesus Christ was totally and completely an act of God's free grace. This is good news for us. Barth's Trinitarian theology of the raising of Jesus Christ is not merely an intriguing theoretical exploration, but a matter of supreme practical significance. In this fourth and final section of chapter 2, I will discuss this significance as it comes to expression in the remainder of *CD* IV/1.

My central claim in this section is that, for Barth, *the Trinitarian grammar and ground of the raising of Jesus Christ guarantees the graciousness of justification*. Because the transition effected in the raising of Jesus Christ is grounded in nothing but the free grace of the triune God, the justification of humanity that took place in him is a divine *actuality*. Therefore, we may have *assurance* in the grace of God for us in the raised Jesus Christ. Identifying this significance serves two functions. First, it corroborates our account of Barth's Trinitarian theology of the raising of Christ. Second, it replies to the potential objection that the ontological ground of Easter set forth above distracts from the practical proclamation of the gospel by showing how it underscores the assurance of faith.

---

164. Barth goes on to speak briefly of the unity of God in his work as "the unity of an irreversible sequence" (*CD* IV/1, 346; cf. also 343), which is "established teleologically" in the one decision of God (*CD* IV/1, 346). Barth states the teleological character of this unity in explicitly Trinitarian terms: "The *way of God* the Father, Son and Holy Spirit, the way of the true God, is *not* a cycle, *not* a way of eternal recurrence, in which the end is a constant beginning" (*CD* IV/1, 345, original German emphasis restored [*KD* IV/1, 381]). The teleological character of the unity of Jesus Christ in his resurrection and its ground in the purposive perichoresis of God is developed at greater length in *CD* IV/3, and so will be treated thematically in ch. 4.

Barth indicates the significance of his Trinitarian theology of the raising of Jesus Christ throughout §59.3. Because it is an act of the triune God, the transition effected in Christ's resurrection is an act of pure grace. "The comprehensive relevance of the resurrection, its redemptive significance for us, depends upon its being what it is described in the New Testament, God's free act of grace."[165] The graciousness of Christ's resurrection is grounded in the Trinitarian movement of grace and receptivity in God himself. There is free grace in God: "the event of Easter [is] a free act of grace, free even in its innermost divine basis."[166] Because there is free grace in God, there is free grace for us in the raising of Christ.

Although he indicates this significance for Christian proclamation and practice throughout §59.3, Barth does not develop it in great detail. For this, we will have to turn to his doctrine of justification. The basic direction of Barth's doctrine of justification can be found within his Christology (§59). Jesus Christ himself is our justification: the obedience of the Son established the judgment of God that is revealed in his resurrection by the grace of God the Father. In raising Christ, God justifies himself, his Son Jesus Christ, and us in him. However, Barth waits until the doctrine of justification proper (§61) to develop this line of thought in detail.

What is of particular interest for this study is Barth's explicitly Trinitarian deployment of the concepts of divine acting and receiving when developing his understanding of the alien righteousness of Jesus Christ in §61.2, "The Judgment of God." I will focus on this subsection, and especially its final ten pages, in order to identify the practical significance of Barth's Trinitarian theology of the raising of Christ.[167]

Barth develops his doctrine of justification under four headings: (1) the Problem of the Doctrine of Justification, (2) the Judgment of God, (3) the

---

165. *CD* IV/1, 304.

166. *CD* IV/1, 304–5.

167. The significance of Christ's resurrection for the remaining topics of IV/1 rests in its transitional function. Attention to the remaining topics (sin, justification, ecclesiology, etc.) is made possible by the risen Christ's transition to us and our sphere. This general significance is well documented in the secondary literature. Furthermore, there are a number of specific references to this significance throughout IV/1. For example, sin as pride is revealed by the risen light of the Son's obedience (§60.1), the Holy Spirit is defined as the awakening (*erweckende*) power in which the awakened Jesus Christ comes to his church (§62.1), the time of the community as that which is between the first and final parousia of the risen Jesus Christ (§62.3), and faith is understood as an awakening (§63.1; note the "awakening" wordplay, *KD* IV/1, 826). All these examples fit the well-known logic of transition. What is less well known is the significance of the *Trinitarian* form of Barth's doctrine of resurrection for the remainder of IV/1. This comes most clearly into view in §61.2.

Acquittal of Man,[168] and (4) Justification by Faith Alone. Within this fourfold structure, the subsection concerning "The Judgment of God" (§61.2) is foundational.[169] Here Barth makes his basic christocentric move: our justification is an actuality in the death and resurrection of Jesus Christ. Barth adopts the Reformation doctrine of the alien righteousness of Christ, but adapts it to his own "actualized" Christology.[170] The "alienness" of our righteousness in Christ is thought through in terms of the particular history of God with us in Christ. He is our righteousness as the stranger who comes to us from beyond the grave, one in whom our righteousness has been totally and perfectly accomplished.[171]

Barth draws directly on his Trinitarian theology of Easter in discussing the alien righteousness of Jesus Christ. He does so because he understands justification as a *divine participation* in our situation. The alienness of Christ's righteousness is ultimately the alienness of God's own activity. What makes God's judgment a righteous judgment is God's self-substitution for us. What has taken place concretely in Christ is the "divine participation in," the "divine intervention for," and the divine identification with us and our situation.[172] God acts here to establish our right before him. How does God in Christ do this? It is a twofold act. "On the one side the justification of man in Jesus Christ is the destruction of his wrong and his own setting aside as the doer of that wrong."[173]

---

168. "Acquittal" is more preferred as a translation for *Freispruch* (*KD* IV/1, 634) than "pardon," as the standard English translation has it (*CD* IV/1, 568). "Acquittal" also better reflects Barth's material position on the doctrine of justification.

169. Under the first heading, Barth discusses the preliminary formal questions concerning the status and function of the doctrine. Under the third heading, Barth describes the acquittal of humanity as the history of the transition from humanity's past as sinner toward humanity's future as forgiven sinner and child of God who awaits an inheritance in hope. Under the fourth and final heading, Barth describes the justified human in terms of the humility of faith.

170. Barth's adaptation of the Reformation heritage is explored in Bruce L. McCormack, "*Justitia Aliena*: Karl Barth in Conversation with the Evangelical Doctrine of Imputed Righteousness," in Bruce L. McCormack, ed., *Justification in Perspective: Historical Developments and Contemporary Challenges* (Grand Rapids: Baker Academic, 2006), 167–96.

171. George Hunsinger draws explicitly from Barth when he argues that "Christ's being in act involves a perfect work (*opere perfectus*) that is also a perpetual operation (*operatione perpetuum*). The perpetual operation adds nothing new in content to the perfect work, which by definition needs no completion. Yet it belongs to the perfect work's perfection that it is not merely encapsulated in the past" (*Let Us Keep the Feast: The Eucharist and Ecumenism* [Cambridge: Cambridge University Press, 2008], 16). This distinction captures well the function of Christ's resurrection in Barth's doctrine of justification, for Easter is the *transition* from Christ's perfect work to his perpetual operation.

172. *CD* IV/1, 551.

173. *CD* IV/1, 552.

"On the other side, the justification of man in Jesus Christ is the establishment of his right, the introduction of the life of a new man who is righteous before God."[174] In the twofold act of the death and resurrection of Jesus Christ, God himself acts to justify humanity. It is in this sense—as a twofold act of God in Christ—that our righteousness is alien.

At this point in his argument, Barth picks up on two lines of thought from §59.3. First, he asserts the "differentiation and unity," the "indissoluble relationship," and "the irreversible sequence" of these two acts.[175] These concepts are central to Barth's transitional argument: Jesus Christ was raised for us as a genuine beyond-the-cross event. This transition is the event of our justification.[176]

Second, Barth also picks up the Trinitarian form of the transitional argument in §59.3. In accordance with the leading motif of IV/1, Barth attributes this twofold act to the Son of God. "On this [first and negative] side we have to do with a definite *action* of the Son of God."[177] "On this second and positive side of our justification as it has taken place in Jesus Christ, we are dealing with something specific which has *happened* to Him, the Son of God, in His unity with our fellow-man Jesus of Nazareth."[178] The Son of God in his divine-human unity both acts and receives in the event of our transition from sin and death to righteousness and life.

By so reiterating the Son's acting and receiving as the foundation of our justification, Barth not only underlines the extent of his commitment to the Trinitarian thought pattern of §59.3, but also and more importantly deploys this thought pattern to advance his main point in §61.2: that the justification of humanity is not a "purely external"[179] activity of God, for "the justification of man has a meaning for God Himself."[180] Barth concludes the argument of §61.2 by asking after this meaning.[181] His answer reveals the practical significance of his Trinitarian theology of Christ's resurrection as it comes to expression in IV/1.

---

174. *CD* IV/1, 554.

175. *CD* IV/1, 557–58. Note the Chalcedonian pattern at work here.

176. The concept of transition becomes prominent in §61.3 (e.g., *CD* IV/1, 573 and 591).

177. *CD* IV/1, 552, original German emphasis restored (*KD* IV/1, 616).

178. *CD* IV/1, 555, original German emphasis restored (*KD* IV/1, 619).

179. *CD* IV/1, 559.

180. *CD* IV/1, 560.

181. There is a line break on page 624 of *KD* IV/1, signaling that this question is the theme of the final portion of §61.2. This line break is unfortunately missing in the standard English translation (*CD* IV/1, 559).

What does justification mean for God himself? Barth first answers the question schematically: "In this work of the justification of unrighteous man God also and in the first instance justifies Himself."[182] After this schematic answer, Barth asks a characteristic question: "But to what extent is it true that in our justification God does also and in the first instance justify Himself?"[183] Barth's answer unfolds in four points. The first is the presupposition, while the remaining three progress sequentially in ascending order of significance.

The presupposition is that only the *living* God can justify himself. "It can be true only on the presupposition that God as God is in Himself the living God, that His eternal being of and by Himself has not to be understood as a being which is inactive because of its pure deity, but as a being which is supremely active in a positing of itself which is eternally new."[184] Barth goes on to say, "His immutability is not a holy immobility and rigidity, a divine death, but the constancy of His faithfulness to Himself continually reaffirming itself in freedom. His unity and uniqueness are not the poverty of an exalted divine isolation, but the richness of the one eternal origin and basis and essence of all fellowship."[185] On what ground does Barth say such things of God? "The fact that according to His revelation God is the triune God means that He is in Himself the living God."[186] So, the triunity of God is the necessary presupposition of God's self-justification. The point of making explicit this presupposition is to indicate that God's work of justifying us has "its basis . . . in the life of God Himself."[187]

But Barth aims not only to identify this presupposition of God's work of justification, but also to indicate the depths of God's involvement in our situation. So he presses on by asking, "But what does it mean and to what extent does it actually happen that in this occurrence God in the first instance justifies Himself?"[188] First of all, God justifies himself as the *Creator*.[189] Second, and at

---

182. *CD* IV/1, 561.

183. *CD* IV/1, 561.

184. *CD* IV/1, 561. Barth is alluding to the arguments of *CD* II/1, §28, "The Being of God as the One Who Loves in Freedom."

185. *CD* IV/1, 561. Barth is alluding to the arguments of *CD* II/1, §31, "The Perfections of the Divine Freedom."

186. *CD* IV/1, 561.

187. *CD* IV/1, 562.

188. *CD* IV/1, 562.

189. "We are simply pointing to the most obvious aspect when we say that in the justification of man we have to do with the expression of God's right as *Creator*; His right to man as His creature, a creature which does not belong to itself or to anyone else but to God, which as His exclusive handiwork is also His exclusive possession" (*CD* IV/1, 562). See "Resurrection as New Creation" above.

a higher level, God justifies himself as the gracious Lord of the *Covenant*.[190] Third, and at the highest level, God justifies himself in *Jesus Christ*: "But we must look higher still, to the fulfillment of justification in Jesus Christ. As it has taken place in Him as our justification, the justification of man, it is the work of God, the divine action in the death of Jesus Christ, the divine receiving in His resurrection from the dead."[191] Barth's development of this third and highest level is by far the longest. It is here that the full significance of Barth's Trinitarian theology of the raising of Jesus Christ emerges.

There are two sides to the justifying work of God in Jesus Christ: a divine acting and a divine receiving. The activity of the Son of God was fulfilled in his death.[192] The receptive side, however, is what interests us, for it displays the significance of Barth's Trinitarian theology of Easter for the doctrine of justification.

The receiving of the Son of God was fulfilled in his resurrection from the dead. Barth deploys the constructive conclusions of §59.3 to underscore the divine participation in this side of justification. "Again, here in Jesus Christ our justification is accomplished in the receiving of the Son of God, in that which comes to Him, crucified, dead and buried—and all in His unity with the man Jesus of Nazareth—as the act of grace and power of the Father in His resurrection from the dead."[193]

The Son's receiving reveals the fatherly right of God. God the Father is the one whose gracious action the Son receives. In this receiving, he is confirmed by God the Father "as our Representative."[194] The right of the Son executed in

---

190. "But His right goes deeper than that. It is the right of the Creator, but it is also the right of His grace extended to man. Man is not merely His handiwork and possession. Beyond that—in answer to the call of God—he is His covenant-partner, who has not merely been given existence, but who is appointed for salvation, to whose existence He has given the end of eternal life, i.e., of fellowship with Himself in the form of service under Him" (*CD* IV/1, 563, rev.).

191. *CD* IV/1, 563–64. Barth goes on to indicate that he really does mean to speak of a divine acting and receiving in Jesus Christ: "It is the work of God in its unity with what the man Jesus of Nazareth, our fellow-man and brother, has done and received. But in its unity with His human doing and receiving it is the work of God" (*CD* IV/1, 564).

192. Barth deploys the constructive conclusions of §59.1 for understanding justification as the act of God the Son. In this act of humility, he "proved Himself to be the Son of God, very God from all eternity.... The obligation of this Son, the Son of God, is not one which is originally alien to Him" (*CD* IV/1, 564). Barth also picks up the juridical framework of §59.2. "Recognizing and executing the right of the Father, He exercises His own right which is specifically that of the Son" (*CD* IV/1, 564). This divine acting is appropriate to him as the Son of God, and his righteous judgment is executed in his obedience unto death.

193. *CD* IV/1, 565.

194. *CD* IV/1, 565.

his death is confirmed in his resurrection as the right of the Father: "The one divine right is indeed the right of the Father."[195] In the Son's receiving, the right of God is shown to be fatherly: "The demand which Jesus Christ obeyed was therefore the demand of the fatherly right of God."[196] God the Father is revealed in the divine receiving that took place in the raising of Jesus Christ.

What does Barth mean by the fatherly right of God? The righteous demand of God, which Jesus Christ actively obeyed in his death, is revealed by the light of Easter to be the gracious, wise, and omnipotent right of God the *Father*.[197] "His resurrection from the dead by the glory of the Father is the demonstration of the fatherly, because gracious and wise and omnipotent, right of that demand."[198] In the divine verdict that the Son receives on Easter, God the Father is revealed.

What does the Son receive from the Father? He receives humanity's elected future of eternal fellowship with God: "He has indeed risen from the dead as the One who in His person receives this future for us."[199] In this divine receiving of our future there takes place "the self-demonstration of God as His [Jesus Christ's] and our gracious and wise and omnipotent and righteous Father."[200] So, in short, God the Son not only acted in his death but also received in his resurrection, the former executing his own right and the latter revealing the Father's right. Jesus Christ as true God and true man enacted and received this divine right *for us*, but first and foremost *for himself*. In other words, "It was the fulfillment of *our* justification as the *self-justification* of God."[201]

---

195. *CD* IV/1, 565.

196. *CD* IV/1, 565.

197. The right of God is fatherly in its *graciousness*: "And this fatherly right is the right of the grace, the mercy of God, the right of the One who has loved and elected man from all eternity, appointing him to His covenant with Him, making Himself his covenant-partner" (*CD* IV/1, 565–66). The right of God is also fatherly in its *wisdom*: "We can and must add that it is the right of God who in His wisdom sees and perceives and measures what is the dimension of the wrong of man, how deep is the plight in which he has plunged himself as a wrong-doer, how great is the damage which he has done in creation in so doing, and beyond that, who and what alone can ward off disaster, and beyond that again in what true and effective help and salvation consists" (*CD* IV/1, 566). Finally, the right of God is fatherly in its *omnipotence*: "We have to say further that it is the right of the omnipotence of God, who lets evil do its evil work, as it has done in the death of Jesus Christ, to the very limit of its capacity, in order to reduce it *ad absurdum* and bring it to shame by its own action, its attack upon Himself in the person of His Son" (*CD* IV/1, 566).

198. *CD* IV/1, 566.

199. *CD* IV/1, 567.

200. *CD* IV/1, 567.

201. *CD* IV/1, 567, original German emphasis restored (*KD* IV/1, 633).

This entire argument is unthinkable without Barth's Trinitarian theology of the raising of Jesus Christ as developed in §59.3. Barth appropriates the initiating act of Easter to God the Father. In his resurrection, Jesus Christ in the first instance only received what God the Father graciously gave to him. He received not only as human, but also as divine. Easter was an event of divine giving and receiving, grounded solely in a prior movement and action of grace in God himself. The Father gives grace to the Son that can only be received—an eternal movement and action that is fulfilled historically at Easter. Barth's explicit deployment of this line of thought as the basis of his unique understanding of the alien righteousness of Christ corroborates his thoroughgoing commitment to the Trinitarian theology of the raising of Christ developed in §59.3.

But the Trinitarian structure of Barth's doctrine of justification not only corroborates the main thesis of this chapter; it also demonstrates the practical significance of Barth's Trinitarian theology of Easter. The Trinitarian grammar and ground of Easter highlights the *graciousness* of the justification of humanity accomplished in Jesus Christ. God is not only gracious to us, but is first and foremost gracious in himself. This is an unthinkable thought for a solitary God. But it befits the living triune God to justify himself. He did not have to do this. But as triune, he is free to do it—free to involve himself in our situation, free to justify us by justifying himself. We know this because has done it in Jesus Christ.

What does this have to do with us? The free grace of God's self-justification entails that the knowledge of our justification is secure. Because our justification is an *actuality* in the Son of God's acting and receiving in his unity with Jesus of Nazareth, we can and must be *assured* of our justification in him. Barth makes this point in the final paragraph of §61.2 by returning again to the theme of God's freedom: "God is completely free. God does not owe anyone anything."[202] On the one hand, this freedom underlines the graciousness of God's free gift of justification. Grace that is not free is not grace. On the other hand, divine freedom, considered abstractly as capriciousness, would undermine our assurance. But God's freedom is the freedom of his love. The triune God is free to justify himself and us in Jesus Christ. "But as the living God—as distinct from all the godheads of philosophies and religions—is He not free and able to justify Himself?"[203] So, although we have no confidence in our own righteousness, we have an unshakable confidence in God's own righteousness

---

202. *CD* IV/1, 567.
203. *CD* IV/1, 567.

established and revealed in the death and resurrection of Jesus Christ. To know God in Jesus Christ is to know ourselves in Jesus Christ. And so the knowledge of our justification is secure:

> Supposing that in our own righteousness we have a complete and utter need to know Him and His righteousness on the basis of His self-demonstration, so that knowing Him we may participate in His own inner life? Well, the door is not in fact closed to us. In justifying us, God in the first instance shows Himself to be righteousness. He is revealed and may be known by us as such. Therefore we are well advised to let drop this anxious questioning of Him and instead to ask ourselves what use we are going to make of the freedom which He obviously willed to give to us in that He willed to make, and actually did make, use of this freedom of His; what use are we going to make of the freedom to know in our own justification the One who is eternally righteous, and in so doing to know the light and the power and the indisputable validity and irresistible efficacy of our own justification.[204]

In Jesus Christ, God himself acts and receives the right of his grace. Thereby, God has *assured* us of his eternal grace for us.

This assurance is the practical significance of Barth's Trinitarian theology of the raising of Jesus Christ. The Trinitarian grammar and ground of the initiating act of Easter developed in this chapter is therefore not merely a clever systematic experiment. It is intended to underwrite the confidence with which we may and must hear and speak the gospel of God's free grace. There is grace and receptivity in the triune God, which is freely fulfilled in the raising of Jesus Christ, and so there is grace for us in him.

However, "The Verdict of the Father" is not Barth's only Trinitarian perspective on Christ's resurrection. Its emphasis on the activity of the Father in the initiating act of Easter befits the Christology of IV/1 and, as I have just shown, serves the practical purposes of that volume well. But Barth also speaks of Easter as the ongoing activity of Jesus Christ in and with the Holy Spirit. This ongoing activity comes to the foreground in the subsequent transitional subsections, "The Direction of the Son" (§64.4) and "The Promise of the Spirit" (§69.4). To these texts, and the different but complementary Trinitarian theology of Easter operative within them, we now turn.

---

204. *CD* IV/1, 568.

3

The Direction of the Son and the Procession of the Spirit

Jesus Christ not only was raised by God the Father but also *arises in the power of the Holy Spirit*. This second aspect of Barth's Trinitarian theology of Easter made a brief appearance in the previous chapter,[1] but the question of the meaning and purpose of Christ's own activity in the Easter event remained open. Chapter three takes this second aspect as its theme. The central claim is that, according to Barth, Jesus Christ as God's new humanity arises in the power of the Holy Spirit, and that this transitional event has its basis in the eternal fellowship of the majestic Son with his merciful Father mediated by the Spirit. Once again, we see that Barth's answer to the question "Why Easter?" requires a Trinitarian explication.

I will develop and defend this claim by means of a close reading of "The Direction of the Son" (§64.4). This reading will proceed in four steps, following the pattern laid down in chapter two.[2] First, I will situate §64.4 in its structural context. Second, I will analyze the Trinitarian grammar operative in §64.4 in order to show how and why Barth identifies the Holy Spirit as the power of Christ's arising. Third, I will follow Barth in asking after the Trinitarian ground of this aspect of the Easter event. Fourth, and finally, I will indicate the significance of this Trinitarian theology of Christ's arising within the context of IV/2.

By placing this pneumatological focus alongside the patrological focus developed in the previous chapter, this chapter contributes to the overall thesis of this book that the subject and basis of Christ's resurrection is the triune God. Although in a certain sense these two foci complete Barth's Trinitarian theology of Christ's resurrection, the mere dialectical juxtaposition of the two begs for a

---

1. See ch. 2, "Jesus Christ" and "The Holy Spirit."
2. In fact, this pattern is modeled after the structure of §64.4.

unified perspective—not a synthesis per se, but a synoptic vision. Barth provides this synoptic vision in "The Promise of the Spirit" (§69.4). But in order to move the argument of the book along this trajectory, we must now bring into sharp relief the unique focus of §64.4.

The Transition of the Exalted Son of Man

"The Direction of the Son" is a transitional discussion, lying between Christology proper and the remaining topics of IV/2.[3] According to Barth, Christ's resurrection is his transition from himself in his life history to us in our sphere. Barth advances this argument by means of a Trinitarian analysis of the Easter event. In order to understand the Trinitarian form of Barth's doctrine of Christ's arising, we must first understand its transitional function. How does §64.4 function within IV/2?

In order to answer this question, we must briefly consider three features of the context of §64.4. First, we must discuss the relationship between IV/1 and IV/2 as it reflects the dialectic of humiliation and exaltation in Barth's mature Christology. Second, we must observe the special role of Christ's resurrection within §64.2 as the epistemological basis of exaltation. Third, we must show how the Christology of IV/2 uniquely frames the problem of transition in §64.4. Taken together, these considerations serve to situate §64.4 in its context, and thereby put its Trinitarian theology of Christ's arising in proper perspective.

Exaltation and Humiliation: The Relationship between IV/1 and IV/2

Parallelism runs throughout *CD* IV/1–3, from entire part-volumes down to the titles of sections and subsections. The parallelism of the christological sections (§§59, 64, 69) determines both the structure of Barth's doctrine of reconciliation and the place of his doctrine of Christ's resurrection within it. Barth develops the Christology of IV/2 in parallel to the Christology of IV/1. Jesus Christ is not only the Lord as Servant, but also the Servant as Lord. He enacts not only the obedience of the Son of God on his way into the far country, but also the exaltation of the Son of Man as he comes home. He is not only the judge judged in our place, but the royal human.

This parallelism must not be dismissed as mere window dressing, for it reflects the material claims of Barth's Christology. Of these claims, two are especially relevant for interpreting the doctrine of resurrection in IV/2. First, *Barth coordinates Christ's humiliation with his true deity and Christ's exaltation with*

---

3. Regarding transitional discussions in general, see ch. 2, "The Transitional Subsections of IV/1–3."

his true humanity. This inversion is central to Barth's doctrine of reconciliation: true deity is known in its abasement in Jesus Christ, and true humanity is known in its exaltation in Jesus Christ. This twofold movement has its basis in God's eternal self-determination, in which he chose rejection for himself and election for us. This double predestination of God was fulfilled in the one event of Christ's life of obedience unto death. Barth views this event from two different perspectives, first from above in §59 (deity humbled), then from below in §64.4 (humanity exalted).[4] Consequently, Barth's discussion of the exaltation of Jesus Christ in §64 does not focus on his deity but on his humanity.

What does this imply for Barth's doctrine of Christ's resurrection in IV/2? It means that Christ's *humanity* is in the foreground when Barth comes to discuss Christ's resurrection in §64.4. This is significant because in §64.4 the *activity* of Jesus Christ as the one who arises is developed, in dialectical juxtaposition to the receptivity of Jesus Christ as the one who was raised (§59.3). This coordination inverts the pattern of thought in traditional resurrection theology, in which Jesus Christ as God arises while Jesus Christ as human was raised. But Barth's inverted coordination of deity with receptivity and humanity with activity, counterintuitive though it may be, fits well within the structure of his mature Christology.

The consequence for the Trinitarian form of §64.4 is that, even though it is named after the Son, the Holy Spirit emerges as "the true theme of this section."[5] The centrality of the Spirit in §64.4 is a direct result of the emphasis on the true humanity of Jesus Christ in IV/1, for it is because the Son has assumed human essence that he stands in need of the Spirit's empowerment. Although Barth mentions it periodically in his discussion of the incarnation in §64.2, this pneumatological aspect comes into the foreground in his discussion of the transitional function of Christ's arising in §64.4. How else can our fellow human be for us and give us divine direction except by being alive to us in the Spirit?[6]

However, this pneumatological aspect does not displace the activity of the rising Son. As we shall see, Barth's claim is that the Holy Spirit is the

---

4. Barth's coordination of deity with humiliation and humanity with exaltation can already be found in his revised doctrine of "double predestination" in *CD* II/2, 162–75.

5. *CD* IV/2, 339.

6. The pneumatological focus of this subsection is also important to note in preparation for the discussion of §69.4 in ch. 4, for despite its title ("The Promise of the Spirit"), its central theme is the threefold parousia of the one Jesus Christ. Although it includes an important discussion of the Spirit, §69.4 is not the primary site for discerning the pneumatological aspect of Barth's Trinitarian theology of Easter.

Spirit of the living Jesus Christ. Just as the appropriation to God the Father in §59.3 did not exclude the distinctive participation of the Son in a sense befitting the Christology of IV/1, so the activity of the Holy Spirit emphasized in §64.4 does not exclude the continued activity of the Son in a sense befitting the Christology of IV/2. In fact, Barth's emphasis on the Spirit in §64.4 leads him to reflect on the Son's relation to the Father, a reflection that inverts the Trinitarian perspective of §59.3. So, the patrological perspective and the pneumatological perspective are two complementary aspects of Barth's one, christocentric, Trinitarian theology of Easter. All of this will become clear later in this chapter. At this point, it is enough to point out that the structure and substance of the Christology of IV/2 leads to an emphasis on the Holy Spirit in §64.4.

The second relevant observation about the parallel structure of Barth's Christology in IV/1–2 is that *the humiliation of deity and the exaltation of humanity in Jesus Christ occur in an ordered simultaneity*.[7] These are not sequential "states" in the history and existence of Jesus Christ.[8] Barth does not coordinate humiliation with Christ's death and exaltation with Christ's resurrection. Rather, humiliation and exaltation are two aspects of the one event of Christ's life of obedience unto death. Consequently, his exaltation is not coordinated with his resurrection and ascension, but with his incarnation. "Incarnation" here must be taken in the broad sense of Christ's entire life of obedience unto death as the fulfillment of God's eternal decision to assume human essence in order to bring it into perfect fellowship with himself. But even in this broad sense, Barth's coordination of exaltation with incarnation instead of resurrection and ascension marks a shift away from a more traditional understanding of Christ's states. The events of human exaltation and divine humiliation are two aspects of the same event, viewed from two different perspectives. They have a definite order: God humbles himself so humanity may be exalted. But within this ordered relationship, they occur simultaneously.

What then is the function of Christ's resurrection in IV/2 if it is not the occurrence of his exaltation? Christ's resurrection in IV/2 functions as the

---

7. Although this insight is rooted in Barth's revised doctrine of election, it is not yet fully developed in *CD* II/2. At that point, Barth continued to coordinate humiliation with Christ's death and exaltation with Christ's resurrection (*CD* II/2, 161–75).

8. *CD* IV/2, 110: "God humbling Himself in His grace and *at the same time* that of man exalted in the reception of God's grace" (emphasis added). See also Barth's exegetical substantiation of this claim in *CD* IV/2, 135–40. The same goes for the offices of Christ: they are not sequential but simultaneous. I will discuss the consequences of this for Barth's doctrine of Christ's resurrection in ch. 4, "He Lives: The Role of Christ's Resurrection in §69."

revelation of the exaltation of humanity that occurred in his life of obedience unto death. Jesus Christ in his resurrection does not complete an unfinished work of exaltation, but rather reveals himself as the Lord in whom humanity has been exalted once for all. He reveals himself as exalted so we may participate in his exaltation.[9] Easter is thus the outworking of exaltation, but not in itself the occurrence of exaltation.

As indicated before, Christ's resurrection has a revelatory function throughout Barth's doctrine of reconciliation.[10] Although at this point in his career Barth no longer reduces resurrection to a function of revelation, revelation remains an important function of resurrection. This revelatory function is necessary within the context of his mature Christology, for resurrection cannot be understood as a "step" in a sequence of "states" if the humiliation of deity and the exaltation of humanity in Jesus Christ are but two aspects of the one act of obedience fulfilled in his death. So the resurrection of Jesus Christ does not effect the exaltation of humanity in abstraction from his preceding life history. Rather, Jesus Christ in his resurrection reveals himself as the exalted Son of Man.[11]

In sum, what is the significance of the relationship between IV/1 and IV/2 for this study? First, Barth's doctrine of Christ's resurrection in IV/2 is developed from the perspective of Christ's exalted humanity and its concomitant pneumatological aspect. Second, Christ's resurrection functions in Barth's mature Christology as the revelation of the exaltation achieved in his life history of obedience unto death. We must keep in mind these architectonic observations and their material consequences when discussing the Trinitarian grammar and ground of Christ's arising in §64.4. But before turning directly to that discussion, there are two further considerations necessary to situate §64.4 in context.

EXALTATION REVEALED: THE ROLE OF CHRIST'S RESURRECTION IN §64.2

I concluded the discussion of the relationship between the IV/1 and IV/2 by noting Barth's coordination of exaltation with the entire life history of Jesus Christ and the consequent de-coupling of exaltation and resurrection. Barth is not unaware of the oddity of this move. Is not Christ's resurrection (along with his ascension) obviously the event of his exaltation, according to the New Testament?

---

9. In this I concur with R. Dale Dawson's interpretation of the relationship between resurrection and exaltation in *The Resurrection in Karl Barth* (Burlington, VT: Ashgate, 2007), 138–41.

10. See ch. 2, "Resurrection as Revelation."

11. In this paragraph, I am summarizing the argument of *CD* IV/2, 116–54.

In asserting the ordered simultaneity of humiliation and exaltation of humanity in Jesus Christ, Barth does not wish to obscure the positive connection between resurrection and exaltation. As stated, Barth develops this positive connection in terms of the revelatory function of Christ's resurrection. Because of this revelatory function, Barth's primary discussion of Easter falls at the end of Christology proper in a transitional subsection (§64.4). However, Barth does not completely displace Christ's resurrection from his discussion of exaltation in §64.2. In fact, Barth devotes the third and final part of §64.2 to a lengthy discussion of the resurrection and ascension of Jesus Christ as the epistemological basis of exaltation.[12] I will briefly summarize this argument as an important backdrop to Barth's lengthier discussion of Christ's resurrection in §64.4.[13]

---

12. *CD* IV/2, 118: "We come now to the ground of its [the exaltation of humanity] revelation in the resurrection and ascension of Jesus Christ." Hereafter I refer to this section as §64.2-III. My phrasing here is an adaptation of Bruce McCormack's formula, "Christology is the epistemological basis of election, and election is the ontological basis of Christology" ("Karl Barth's Version of an 'Analogy of Being': A Dialectical No and Yes to Roman Catholicism," in Thomas Joseph White, ed., *Analogia Entis: Invention of the Antichrist or the Wisdom of God?* [Grand Rapids: Eerdmans, 2011], 90). The truth of this formula is evident in §64.2, where Barth briefly discusses election as the basis of the exaltation of humanity in Jesus Christ before his lengthy treatment of the historical fulfillment of exaltation in the incarnation. My adaptation serves to signal that the risen Jesus Christ is the epistemological basis of Christology, and only from the perspective of this Easter revelation is Christology then the epistemological basis of election.

13. The role of Christ's ascension in Barth's theology has become a topic of discussion in recent literature. Unfortunately, the resurrection and ascension are too often separated from each other, which leads to distortion. Although I will not discuss the ascension at length, acknowledging its unity with Christ's resurrection is essential. Andrew Burgess has defended Barth's position as upholding traditional claims in *The Ascension in Karl Barth* (Hampshire: Ashgate, 2004). Though not false, such a conclusion can be misleading. Two things set Barth's doctrine of ascension apart from more traditional formulations: (1) it is the revelation rather than the actualization of Christ's exaltation, and (2) it is only one side of the twofold yet singular event of the risen Christ's self-revelation, rather than a separate event with its own independent meaning. Douglas Farrow has criticized Barth's position for downplaying the significance of the ascension as Christ's withdrawal to make space for the church in *Ascension and Ecclesia: On the Significance of the Doctrine of the Ascension for Ecclesiology and Christian Cosmology* (Grand Rapids: Eerdmans, 1999), 229–54. Although such a criticism is not entirely misplaced given Farrow's own commitments, it does not account for the larger context of Barth's Trinitarian theology of Christ's resurrection. The ascension is the conclusion of the forty days, and so the sign of the transition from the primal form of Christ's *parousia* to its intermediate form in the promise of the Spirit. The Spirit does not work in the church in abstraction from the incarnate Son, for the Spirit mediates the presence of Christ, who, though hidden, is not absent in the intermediate time. Finally, Katherine Sonderegger's excellent discussion of the role of Christ's resurrection in the theological method of Karl Barth and Robert Jenson notes the unity of resurrection and ascension as it comes to expression in §64.2-III, in "Et Resurrexit Tertia Die: Jenson and Barth on Christ's Resurrection," in John C. McDowell and Mike Higton, eds.,

The central question of §64.2-III is, What is the basis of our knowledge of the exaltation of humanity accomplished in Jesus Christ?[14] Barth's answer proceeds in three steps. His first is a general statement that the knowledge of the divine act of exaltation is based on nothing else but this act itself.[15] Barth's second step concretizes this statement by identifying the witness of the Holy Spirit as the subjective basis of the knowledge of human exaltation in Jesus Christ.[16] Although this pneumatological answer is "sufficient, exhaustive and all-embracing,"[17] Barth argues that, since the Holy Spirit's witness always refers to Jesus Christ, a christological answer must also be given.[18] So, Barth's third and final answer is that Jesus Christ in his resurrection and ascension reveals himself as the one he was and is.[19]

Only in his resurrection and ascension? Barth acknowledges that the whole life of Jesus Christ had this character of revelation.[20] But the resurrection and ascension are distinctively revelatory. Why? As already noted, in Barth's mature Christology the exaltation of humanity was fulfilled in Christ's death. "His death on the cross was and is the fulfillment of the incarnation."[21] Therefore, exaltation cannot be completely revealed until it is completely fulfilled.[22]

Conversing with Barth (Hampshire: Ashgate, 2004), 191–213. However, she focuses the majority of her attention on Barth's methodological reflections in *CD* I/1-2, and does not draw out the consequences of §64.2-III for Barth's mature theology of Christ's resurrection.

14. *CD* IV/2, 118: "How do we really know what we have declared and developed, and especially the decisive and central fact from which all the rest derives, that Jesus Christ was and is and will be the eternal Word of God in our flesh, the Son of God who becomes and is also the Son of Man, in whom, therefore, our human essence is exalted to fellowship with God?"

15. *CD* IV/2, 119–25.

16. *CD* IV/2, 125–31.

17. *CD* IV/2, 126.

18. *CD* IV/2, 128: "The reference to the Holy Spirit and His witness has, then, the force of a first and final word. But this is only when it is understood as a reference to the powerful and effective presence of Jesus Christ Himself—not to a second force beside Him, but to His force."

19. Although the argument of the third part of §64.2 does not contradict §64.4, the Trinitarian movement of thought runs in the opposite direction. Simply put, whereas §64.4 moves from Christ to the Spirit, §64.2-III moves from the Spirit to Christ. This different movement of thought corresponds to the architectonic context of each argument. As a transitional discussion, §64.4 focuses on our subjective participation in the risen Christ by the Spirit. As a part of Christology proper, §64.2-III focuses on the objective revelation of Jesus Christ in his resurrection and ascension. So these two sections are complementary in content, though they arrive at their conclusions by different routes.

20. *CD* IV/2, 134–40. Here Barth discusses a series of events in Christ's life that were revelatory in character (e.g., his baptism, Peter's confession, the transfiguration, etc.). The list here closely parallels the one found in *CD* III/2, §47.1.

21. *CD* IV/2, 140.

The importance of §64.2-III for this study is that Barth here argues for *the active subjectivity of Jesus Christ in his resurrection*. Christ is the one who arises to reveal the exaltation of humanity fulfilled in his life history.²³ This argument is important to keep in mind, because from this point forward Barth presupposes that Christ in his resurrection and ascension is the acting subject of his self-revelation as the exalted Son of Man. This activity of the Son is the point of entry for his later discussion of the Holy Spirit as the power of Christ's transition to us. In other words, the christocentric starting point of Barth's Trinitarian theology of Christ's arising is already established by the end of §64.2.

Exaltation Concealed: The Problem of Transition in §64.4

The contribution of §64.4 to Barth's overall Trinitarian theology of Easter is that Jesus Christ also arises in the power of the Holy Spirit, and that this movement too is grounded in the triune life of God. This Trinitarian perspective on Easter, however, does not fall from the sky. Rather, Barth begins with a problem and then introduces this rich doctrine of Christ's resurrection as the solution to that problem. And so we must begin where Barth begins: with the problem of transition.

The problem of transition in general has already been addressed.²⁴ What is of interest here is how the Christology of IV/2 uniquely frames the problem of transition in §64.4. Whereas in IV/1 the problem of transition concerns whether there is any room left for us sinners after we have been justly put to death in Jesus Christ, in IV/2 the problem of transition concerns how we come to participate in the exaltation of humanity to perfect fellowship with God actualized in the incarnation. In both cases, the solution to the problem of transition is Christ's resurrection. But the form of both the problem and the solution is framed by their different structural contexts.

The problem is simple yet profound: Jesus died. The exaltation of humanity accomplished in Jesus Christ was concealed in death. Up to this point in IV/2, Barth has been arguing that all humanity has been exalted in the life-act of Jesus Christ. He has explored the actualization of this exaltation in the incarnation (§64.2), and he has developed the concrete shape of this exaltation as narrated in the Gospels (§64.3). The troubling last word in this narration is the death of the one in whom all humanity is exalted.²⁵ The death of Jesus

---

22. *CD* IV/2, 141: "How could that which had not yet been completed be revealed as completed?"

23. Barth makes his case from a reading of the Gospel narratives concerning the risen Christ's appearances during the forty days (*CD* IV/2, 142–50).

24. See ch. 2, "The Transitional Subsections of IV/1–3."

25. *CD* IV/2, 247–64.

Christ is especially troubling because it is the very climax and *telos* of his life. It is no mere accident, but the very will of God, that true humanity is cruciform.[26] This means the "ontological connection"[27] between the man Jesus and all other human beings, which is the joyful content of "the Christmas message,"[28] and which the New Testament takes with utter realistic seriousness,[29] is concealed in contradiction. "The concealment of the being of Jesus Christ and of our being in him . . . rests on the mystery of his cross."[30]

This is good news. Our true humanity has already been graciously actualized in Jesus Christ by his obedience unto death. So the sheer fact of Jesus' death is not the problem, but *good* news. The problem is how we could even come to know such news. If the good news of our exaltation in Jesus Christ remains concealed in his death, it is not good *news*. To be news that we can hear and attest, it must come to us from beyond the frontier of death.[31] This is the problem of transition in §64.4.

As should now be evident, this problem is internal to the event of reconciliation, and so the need for a transitional subsection is not merely literary or stylistic, but structural and substantive. What is the solution to this problem? Who will save us from this concealment in death? The short answer is the risen Jesus Christ by the power of the Holy Spirit. But Barth is not known for short answers. Or, put differently, Barth is known for long, complex expositions of short, simple answers. So let us turn our attention to the answer in order to understand its unique contribution to Barth's Trinitarian theology of Easter.

---

26. *CD* IV/2, 290–96. Barth develops and substantiates this claim in part IV of §64.3 (*CD* IV/2, 247–64). This material is incorrectly marked as part "V" in the standard English translation (*CD* IV/2, 247). For the correct numbering, see Karl Barth, *Die Kirchliche Dogmatik*, Band IV, 2 (Zürich: Theologischer Verlag, 1980), 274, hereafter cited as *KD* IV/2.

27. *CD* IV/2, 275; see also 281. E. Jüngel comments on this passage, noting that this ontological connection funds the Christian community's outward orientation, including its expectation to find parables of the kingdom in the secular sphere (*God's Being Is in Becoming*, 136–37). I will return to this outward orientation and its grounding in Christ's resurrection in ch. 4, "The Significance of a Trinitarian Theology of Christ's Parousia (§71.2)."

28. *CD* IV/2, 270.

29. See *CD* IV/2, 274–280 for Barth's exegesis of numerous NT texts, especially Romans 8.

30. *CD* IV/2, 296.

31. *CD* IV/2, 296–97: "Reality which does not become truth for us obviously cannot affect us, however supreme may be its ontological dignity."

The Trinitarian Grammar of Christ's Arising (§64.4)

The central claim of this chapter is that Barth identifies the Holy Spirit as the power of Jesus Christ's arising to us, and that this transitional event has its basis in the eternal fellowship of the Son with the Father mediated by the Spirit. In this section, I will substantiate the first half of this claim by means of a close reading of §64.4. I will show how Barth attributes Christ's arising to the Spirit without leaving Christ behind, because for Barth the Spirit is none other that the power of Christ's arising. This argument is significant because (a) it displays the pneumatological aspect of Barth's Trinitarian grammar of Easter in its close connection with the active subjectivity of Christ, and (b) it sets up the argument of the next section concerning the ontological ground of Christ's arising in the triune life of God.

Before jumping into this close reading, it is necessary to reiterate and expand upon the reason for the pneumatological focus of §64.4. In light of its title ("The Direction of the Son"), this seems odd. But, as already indicated above, such a pneumatological focus fits the Christology of IV/2.[32] Just as the humiliation of the Son of God brought to the foreground the Father as the one who raised Jesus Christ, so the exaltation of the Son of Man brings to the foreground the Spirit as the power of Christ's arising:

	"Nature"	"State"	Resurrection	Trinity
IV/1:	Deity	Humiliation	Raising	Father
IV/2:	Humanity	Exaltation	Arising	Spirit

This pneumatological focus does not displace Barth's emphasis on the active subjectivity of Jesus Christ, but rather develops it in a manner befitting the Christology of IV/2.

In light of this context, it is fitting that Barth's pattern of thought in §64.4 moves *from* a discussion of Christ's activity as the one who arises *to* a discussion of the Holy Spirit as the power of Christ's arising.[33] This movement is then followed by discussions of the divine basis of this event and the manner of the Spirit's operation. The remaining sections of this chapter will address these further elements of Barth's argument in §64.4. This section will follow Barth's

---

32. See above, "Exaltation and Humiliation: The Relationship between IV/1 and IV/2."

33. This reverses the pattern of thought in §64.2-III. See above, "Exaltation Revealed: The Role of Christ's Resurrection in §64.2."

pattern of thought by moving from Jesus Christ as the subject of his arising to the Holy Spirit as the power of this event.

JESUS CHRIST

Jesus Christ arises and reveals himself, and within him is included all theological knowledge. This is Barth's constant refrain.[34] After setting up the problem of exaltation concealed,[35] Barth asserts that Jesus Christ in his resurrection reveals the exaltation of humanity, achieved in his life of obedience unto death. This self-revelation has two sides. First, he reveals himself as the true human being.[36] Second, he reveals our true humanity as actualized in him.[37] This revelation means that we are not left to our own resources in relation to Jesus Christ and our true being in him.[38] He comes to us. He is not alone, and so we are not alone as we follow his direction. Christ's resurrection is thus the outworking of the exaltation of humanity, as it is the means by which we come to participate in it. This is Barth's initial statement of the solution to the problem of transition in §64.4.

Evident in this initial statement is the predication of active verbs to Jesus Christ. Jesus Christ is the acting subject of his arising. Although such active christological grammar can be found in §59.3, it was secondary to and dependent on the patrological grammar of God the Father raising Christ.[39] But in §64.4, the activity of Christ is prominent and primary. In order to flesh out this side of Barth's Trinitarian grammar of Easter, especially in its dialectical juxtaposition with the other side, I will make three observations about Barth's initial statement of the solution to the problem of transition. These observations function to substantiate the claim that, for Barth, Jesus Christ is the acting

---

34. *CD* IV/2, 300: "All Christian knowledge and confession, all Christian knowledge of God and humanity and the world, derives from this self-declaration of Jesus Christ, from his resurrection."

35. See above, "Exaltation Concealed: The Problem of Transition in §64.4."

36. *CD* IV/2, 299: "He is risen, and reveals Himself. He Himself, Jesus Christ, declares His majesty. He declares Himself to be the royal man."

37. *CD* IV/2, 300: "as He discloses Himself to us, He also discloses us to ourselves. For He is not without us. As He is human, the first-born brother of all humans, He is the head and representative of humanity. He Himself *is* only as *we* also are elected and called in Him. . . . The revelation of His majesty discloses also the relative and subordinate but genuine majesty to which we are elected and called in Him."

38. *CD* IV/2, 300–301: "But this being the case, it means that the situation is radically challenged in which we think we are shut out in relation to the truth of Jesus Christ and left to our own very inadequate resources."

39. See ch. 2, "Jesus Christ."

subject of his arising. How this claim coheres with the pneumatological focus of §64.4 will be the burden of the next subsection.[40]

(1) The first observation is that the term for arising (*Auferstehung*) and its cognates dominate §64.4. The term for "raising" (*Erweckung*) and its cognates appear only five times in §64.4, and not once is the term used to denote Christ's resurrection.[41] Although both terms appear in §59.3, *Erweckung* was predominant, in keeping with the patrological focus operative there. The receding of *Erweckung* does not entail that Barth has dropped the substantive distinction between the raising of Jesus Christ and his own arising.[42] Rather, this recession is a consequence of the distinction. Although Barth does not absolutize the terminological distinction, the substantive distinction between the raising of Jesus Christ and his own arising as two aspects of the one event of Easter underlies its Trinitarian grammar. The receptive and active senses in which Jesus Christ is the subject of his own resurrection are Barth's point of entry for reflecting on the patrological and pneumatological aspects of Easter: Jesus Christ was raised by God the Father and arises by the Holy Spirit. *Erweckung*, its cognates, and other passive verbs have receded in §64.4 because in this context Barth focuses on Jesus Christ, the exalted Son of Man, as the acting subject of his arising to us. And so Barth uses *Auferstehung* and its cognates to describe Easter in §64.4.

(2) Although the language of Christ's arising dominates §64.4, Barth deploys a number of rich metaphors that highlight the active subjectivity of Jesus Christ. One rich metaphor worthy of discussion is that of a door that can only be opened from the inside. This language first emerges in the context of Barth's discussion of the problem of transition. After asserting the ontological connection between Christ and Christians, Barth halts at the problem of concealment. The exaltation of humanity enacted in Christ is not just partially concealed by the brokenness of creation as a witness to the love of Christ, but

---

40. See "The Holy Spirit" below.
41. The five instances appear on pages 343, 344, 349, and 372 of *KD* IV/2 (*CD* IV/2, 308, 313, 334). The usages on pages 343, 349, and 372 are used to speak of the awakening of the Christian. The usage on page 344 refers to the raising of Lazarus. *Erweckung* is used to speak of the resurrection of Jesus in §64.2 (*CD* IV/2, 152; *KD* IV/2), but it is there appropriated to God the Father in keeping with Barth's argument in IV/1. Regarding this reference to God the Father, see "God the Father" below.
42. Dawson sharply critiques Barth for this receding use, though he acknowledges that the distinction remains in force after *CD* IV/1 (*The Resurrection in Karl Barth*, 214). I concur with Klappert that the raising/arising distinction is integrated into the structure of *CD* IV/1–3, so that the raising of Jesus Christ is the theme of §59.3, Christ's own arising is the theme of §64.4, and the parousia of Christ is the theme of §69.4. B. Klappert, "Die Rechts-, Freiheits- und Befreiungsgechichte Gottes mit dem Menschen," 462.

completely concealed by its contradiction in the sinfulness of humanity.[43] But the problem is even deeper: our true humanity was fulfilled in Christ's death.[44] So, our exaltation is concealed not only because of our weakness and sinfulness, but also and primarily because it is the will of God in Jesus Christ.[45] At this crucial point in his argument, Barth introduces the metaphor of the door: "He Himself has concealed Himself in it. He Himself has closed the door."[46] Note the reflexive pronouns, used to emphasize that this concealment is Christ's own act. What is the consequence of his self-enclosure for us? "The door cannot be opened from outside, but only from inside. It cannot be opened by us, but only by the One who closed it."[47]

Having sketched the problem of transition in terms of the closed door, Barth speaks of the solution in terms of opening that door: "We are told [by the New Testament] that the One who dwells behind the closed door which He Himself has closed, far from being unable or unwilling to open it, *flings it wide open*."[48] This flinging open of the door takes place in the fact that "the crucified Jesus Christ has *risen* from the dead."[49] The same one who enclosed himself has also disclosed himself. What is the consequence of his self-disclosure for us? In a word: revelation. "He sets Himself before us. . . . He is risen and reveals Himself. He Himself, Jesus Christ, declares His majesty. He declares Himself to be the royal man."[50] Jesus Christ himself arises and reveals himself as the one in whom humanity was exalted. He himself opens the door.

---

43. CD IV/2, 285–89. "In other words, that which conceals does not correspond in the very least to that which is concealed. It contradicts it" (287).

44. CD IV/2, 290–96. "Thus the whole existence of the royal man Jesus . . . stood under this sign" of the cross (290).

45. CD IV/2, 297: "If His cross is the mystery with which we have to do, we are at once arrested, and no penetration to the truth is in fact possible from our side. For this mystery is a matter of His will and power and act. It is the free decision of the One who dwells in this mystery, of the real Jesus whom we are to see and understand and know."

46. CD IV/2, 297.

47. CD IV/2, 297.

48. CD IV/2, 298, emphasis added. Note that Barth draws this language of a locked door from John 20, though he is not (yet) speaking of Jesus Christ overcoming the "subjective" door behind which the sinful human subject is locked, but rather of the "objective" door of death behind which Jesus Christ concealed himself. This "objective" door is not identical to the stone rolled before the tomb (which is only a *sign*), though the two are inseparable on account of the revelatory function of Christ's resurrection (i.e., the empty tomb is an *indispensable* sign).

49. CD IV/2, 298, original German emphasis restored: "daß eben der gekreuzigte Jesus Christus von den Toten *auferstanden* ist" (KD IV/2, 332).

50. CD IV/2, 299.

The reflexive pronouns in these statements are striking, for they stand in stark contrast to the passive verbs predominant in §59.3. In fact, Barth carefully avoids such reflexive pronouns in §59.3. He identifies the distinctive mode in which Jesus Christ participates in his own raising precisely in order to avoid the reflexive construction so common in the tradition, that is, that Jesus Christ raised himself.

Does §64.4, with its reflexive pronouns, contradict §59.3? No. Barth has not contradicted himself by saying that Jesus Christ opened the door from within. Barth uses the metaphor of the door to speak of Easter as the ongoing act in which Christ rises and reveals himself, in distinction from the initiating act of being raised by God the Father. Barth signals this ongoing revelatory function by mixing his metaphors. As crucifixion is to *enclosure*, resurrection is to *disclosure*. "He discloses Himself to us with the same will and power and in the same act as He closes Himself off from us. We have to hear the two sides of the message in their irreversible sequence, the first as the first (which has always to be heard too), and the second as the second. He is the Crucified who as such closes Himself off from us, and He is the Resurrected who as such discloses Himself to us."[51] Barth succinctly indicates the revelatory point of his door metaphor: "As He bursts open from within the closed door of His concealment, of His death, He reveals Himself as this exalted One."[52] The self-revealing function of Christ's arising means that reflexive constructions are wholly appropriate in this context: in his arising from the dead, Jesus Christ reveals himself.

(3) The revelatory function of Christ's arising brings me to my third observation: that Christ's arising is his own act because it is his *self-revelation*. Although all three aspects of the Easter event (raising, arising, presence) have a revelatory function, Christ's arising is consistently and distinctly linked with his *self*-revelation. Barth links arising with self-revelation when he first makes the raising/arising distinction in §59.3.[53] The raising of Jesus Christ was certainly revelatory in purpose, but it was not his own act of self-revelation. Rather, God the Father raised Jesus Christ from the dead, and secondarily and on this

---

51. *CD* IV/2, 298–99. The encloses/discloses pun in the English translation adequately reflects the *verschließt/erschließt* pun in the German original: "in demselben Willen, in derselben Macht, in derselben Tat, in der er sich uns verschließt, erschließt er sich uns auch. Wir müssen *Beides* hören, u. zw. in der unumkehrbaren Reihenfolge hören, das Erste als *Erstes* (es bleibt mitzuhören!), aber sofort auch das Zweite als *Zweites*: er ist der Gekreuzigte, der sich uns als solcher verschließt, *und*: er ist der Auferstandene, der sich uns alssolcher erschließt" (*KD* IV/2, 332–33, emphasis original).

52. *CD* IV/2, 299.

53. See ch. 2, "Jesus Christ."

basis Christ arises and reveals himself. From §59.3 on, Barth continues to link arising with self-revelation. The link appears in §64.4: "He is risen, and reveals Himself."[54] And the link persists in §69.4, where Christ's arising as his self-revelation is the primal form of his presence with us.[55]

As the act of his self-revelation, Christ's arising is his own act. It is not we who discover him, but he who discloses himself. This is critical, for in this self-disclosure he also discloses our true humanity as exalted in him: "As He discloses Himself to us, He also discloses us to ourselves."[56] The point of Barth's initial statement of the solution to the problem of transition is lost if the act of his revelation is not his own act. This claim does not deny that his act of self-revelation depends on his being raised by God the Father, nor does it deny that his act of self-revelation occurs in the power of the Holy Spirit. But Christ's arising is *his* act, or it would not be the act of his *self*-revelation as the exalted Son of Man.[57]

Jesus Christ arises. In his arising, Christ reveals himself, and so is the subject of his transition to us. This is Barth's first statement of the solution to the problem of transition. But Barth pauses here. Although this first form of the answer is true and complete in itself, it runs the risk of misunderstanding. We must not make too hasty a transition, but must explore the inner logic of the event of transition.[58]

This inner logic is Trinitarian. The transition accomplished in Christ's arising is an act of the triune God, and so exposition of this event is Trinitarian in form. In §64.4, this Trinitarian form is pneumatological in focus: Jesus Christ arises to us by the power of the Holy Spirit, who is both the Spirit of Christ and the Spirit of God the Father.

THE HOLY SPIRIT

What is the power of the risen Christ's transition to us? With this question, Barth turns to his second statement of the solution to the problem of transition.

---

54. *CD* IV/2, 299.

55. See ch. 4, "The Trinitarian Grammar of Christ's Parousia (§69.4)."

56. *CD* IV/2, 300.

57. It must be acknowledged that Barth's continued emphasis on the revelatory function of Christ's resurrection leaves him open to the charge of reducing resurrection to revelation. However, despite this emphasis, revelation is not the *sole* function of Christ's resurrection for Barth. First, revelation must not be reduced to the mere transmission of information. The risen Christ's self-revelation creates a living relationship with us, in which our knowledge of him is self-involving. Furthermore, Christ in his arising renders permanent and universal the exaltation achieved in his life of obedience unto death. It is precisely this universally relevant fact that the risen Christ reveals to us.

58. Barth explicitly warns against hasty transitions (*CD* IV/2, 267 and 301).

Although it comes second in sequence, this statement is decisive for his argument.[59] As I have already claimed, Barth's answer to the problem of transition is that the Holy Spirit is the power of Jesus Christ's arising. It is now time to develop and substantiate this claim.

It is crucial at the outset to specify that Barth identifies the Holy Spirit as the power of transition without leaving Christ behind. As shown above, Barth asserts that Jesus Christ in his arising supplies his own transition to us. So no schema that divides the work of reconciliation between Christ and the Spirit will do (for example, accomplished vs. applied). But this does not mean the Spirit is eclipsed in Barth's account. In fact, the opposite is the case: Barth's radical concentration on the life history of Jesus allows him to acknowledge the freedom of the Spirit's work. Barth has particularized the content of the Spirit's work as the freeing and empowering of human beings to bear witness to the actuality of reconciliation in Jesus Christ. But this particularity of content permits a vast multiplicity of forms. The Spirit is free to free us as witnesses precisely because he binds us to the risen Christ.[60]

Therefore, Christ and the Spirit are not in competition with one another in Barth's account. Perhaps this would be the case if Jesus were dead and gone, having performed a work that is now simply in the past. Then the Spirit would have to tack on to this past work a present work of some kind. But Jesus is risen from the dead! He is living and active, revealing himself as the one who lived and died for us. Jesus Christ does this in the power of the Spirit, who empowers us to be his witnesses. Because Christ's resurrection supplies his transition to us, there is no competition but rather a living and active relation between Christ and the Spirit.

So it is fitting that Barth's reference to the ongoing activity of the risen Christ leads to a reference to the work of the Spirit. As is his custom, Barth takes his time getting there, asking after the power of Christ's transition from cross to resurrection.[61] At first, Barth answers this question without naming the Holy

---

59. "This [question] demands a further and decisive turn in our treatment" (*CD* IV/2, 302).

60. Although I will address their concerns in ch. 4, "The Holy Spirit and the Intermediate Form of Christ's Parousia," it is worth noting now the critiques of Barth's pneumatology by Jenson and Rogers: Robert W. Jenson, "You Wonder Where the Spirit Went," *Pro Ecclesia* 2:3 (1993): 296–304; Eugene F. Rogers, "Eclipse of the Spirit in Karl Barth," in John C. McDowell and Mike Higton, eds., *Conversing with Barth* (Hampshire: Ashgate, 2004), 173–90. Neither discusses §64.4, which I am arguing is the central text for understanding the pneumatological aspect of Barth's Trinitarian theology of Easter.

61. *CD* IV/2, 302: "In His death we too have attained our goal; and in His resurrection we have been set in a new beginning. . . . What is the fact and force and event indicated by these two statements concerning Him and us? We cannot be too careful in our discussion of the power of transition assumed by the New Testament when it relates these two statements in this sequence."

Spirit. Then, once he has identified the Holy Spirit as the power of transition, he specifies the Spirit's identity in relation to Jesus Christ on the one hand and to God the Father on the other.

In what follows, we will follow Barth's pattern of thought: First, I will discuss what Barth means by the "power of transition." Second, I will show that Barth does not leave Christ behind, because he identifies the Holy Spirit as the Spirit of the man Jesus. This discussion of the living relation between Christ and the Spirit will provide the point of entry to a brief discussion of God the Father, which will complete the analysis of the Trinitarian grammar of Christ's arising as well as set up the argument of the next section concerning its Trinitarian ground.

THE POWER OF TRANSITION

What is the power of the risen Christ's transition to us? Barth answers this question in four steps. First, his point of entry is a simple *exegetical observation* concerning the narratives of the forty days in the context of the New Testament as a whole. This exegetical observation leads to the second step, in which Barth highlights the astonishing *miraculous power* on which the New Testament relies. Even so, this miraculous power has a *definite character*, which Barth describes in a lengthy third step. Fourth, Barth finally names the power of transition as the *Holy Spirit*. Although his explicit reference to the Spirit is his final step, we should regard this whole discussion as implicitly developing the pneumatological aspect of the transition accomplished in Christ's arising.

What is the *exegetical observation* with which Barth begins this discussion? It is simple and straightforward: in the New Testament, Christ's resurrection appearances are never to neutral observers; rather, they are moments of calling. He comes to his own to direct them to their new life as his witnesses. Although the event of his arising is an objective event, it cannot be thought of in abstraction from his arising to particular persons.[62] The event of transition is a personal summons. Barth asserts that the same can be said of the whole tenor

---

62. CD IV/2, 303: "It tells it to us as witness: witness to a person, to Jesus Christ, to the whole nexus and history of reality and truth bound up in this name, as it is given by those who have the necessary information; but also witness addressed to persons, to us, who can also acquire this information by receiving the witness, and who are already claimed in anticipation as those whom it concerns. What we have said about the objective content of the truth of the reality of Jesus Christ, which includes our own reality, presses in upon us, from its objectivity to our subjectivity, in order that there should be in us a correspondence." The objectivist and personalist motifs are impressively intertwined in this statement. Cf. George Hunsinger, *How to Read Karl Barth: The Shape of His Theology* (New York: Oxford University Press, 1991), 35–42.

of the New Testament, which "lays claim on us" to correspond to Christ's self-witness.[63] So, according to Barth, the New Testament both at its center and in its entirety presses toward our subjective participation in the risen Christ's self-attestation. Although Barth develops this observation in his own characteristic language, it is nevertheless a straightforward exegetical observation. When the risen Christ appears, he summons persons to bear witness to him. And the New Testament witnesses speak with the same sort of personal appeal to their hearers.

The next step in Barth's argument is again a straightforward observation: in this summons, the New Testament counts on a definite *power*. Precisely in its straightforward confidence, the New Testament manifests its reliance on a power beyond itself. Barth specifies this power as that which frees us for conversion, that is, the event in which we correspond to our conversion accomplished in Christ by coming to know Christ, to love him, and to be Christians.[64] The power of Christ's transition to us is the power by which we are freed "to appropriate as our own conversion the conversion of man to God as it has taken place in Jesus Christ."[65]

The exegetical observation that the risen Christ lays a claim on us leads Barth to acknowledge the power that underlies this claim. This acknowledgment is also exegetically based: the New Testament witnesses rely explicitly on a power that is greater and other than themselves.[66] But that to which Barth refers is not just a feature of the New Testament witnesses but a powerful reality that transcends them. This power of Christ's transition and of

---

63. CD IV/2, 304.

64. CD IV/2, 305: "It is the power . . . of conversion. . . to see and understand and recognise it, making a response of love to the One who first loved us. . . . It is, therefore, the power in which we acquire and have and use the freedom to become and be Christians."

65. CD IV/2, 304. The conversion effected by the power of transition is one of knowledge: we come to know what has happened in Jesus Christ. But the account of knowledge in this context is not reductionist. To know Christ is to appropriate his reality in its character as truth. For Barth, knowledge is participatory: to know the risen Christ is to participate in his self-attestation. Because of the participatory character of the knowing to which we are summoned in Christ's arising, this summons rests on a definite power. Our exaltation is not just an abstract idea to which we assent by our own power, but a concrete reality in which we participate by a power greater than ourselves. We participate in the exaltation of humanity in Jesus Christ by bearing witness to him, and this witness relies on a power other than ourselves. In his treatment of Barth's transitional discussions, Joseph Mangina is right to assert the participatory and personal character of knowledge in Barth's theology. For the most part, however, he relegates the category of "witness" to §69.4 alone, rather than identifying witness as the consistent form of our participation in the risen Christ (*Karl Barth on the Christian Life: The Practical Knowledge of God* [New York: Peter Lang, 2001], 51–81).

66. CD IV/2, 306: "It is a power which is greater and other than what may be described as the power of the New Testament witness itself and of those who bear it."

our conversion is a *miraculous* power. That we become witnesses to Jesus Christ is no less a miracle than Christ's resurrection from the dead.[67] In fact, Barth suggests that this miracle of conversion is greater than the transition from death to life, for the problem of our sin is even deeper than the problem of death. The power of transition on which the personal summons of the New Testament counts is a miraculous power.

However, Barth's appeal to miracle is not an avoidance of explanation. The miracle of transition is not formless, but has a *definite character*. Therefore, "We have to say more than just . . . that it is a miraculous power"; we must "define this more closely."[68] There are many astonishing powers at work in the world, so this miraculous power must be distinguished from others. In fact, this power is "absolutely unique."[69] Although he is speaking here of a miraculous power that transcends even the New Testament witnesses, Barth speaks with confidence and clarity regarding the definite character of this power. He goes so far as to say that "we can read this character almost as in a book."[70] Barth proceeds to identify five marks of the power of Christ's transition: it has the character of light, liberation, knowledge, peace, and life.[71] Its character can be so defined because, although its operation is miraculous, its origin and result are a matter of human will and action. Its origin is Jesus Christ, the exalted Son of Man, and its result is the "concrete alteration of [the Christian's] existence."[72] This is not to deny the deity of its origin or operation, but simply a reminder that the "work of this power is not to destroy our earthliness, but to give to it a new determination."[73]

After his lengthy description of the character of the miraculous power upon which the personal summons of the New Testament counts, Barth finally

---

67. *CD* IV/2, 308: "What has to take place if a man is really to be a Christian? . . . By what miraculous happening do we live? Does not the raising of Lazarus pale before that of which we are ourselves the witnesses and theatre? Or the Virgin Birth of Jesus Christ? Or His empty tomb?"

68. *CD* IV/2, 309.

69. *CD* IV/2, 310.

70. *CD* IV/2, 310.

71. *CD* IV/2, 310–18. Barth's discussion of these five marks is rich and worthy of reflection. However, detailed exposition of this discussion is not necessary for this argument.

72. *CD* IV/2, 319.

73. *CD* IV/2, 318–19. Bruce McCormack highlights this pattern of thought primarily as it operates within Barth's Christology in "Participation Yes, Deification No: Two Modern Protestant Responses to an Ancient Question," in idem, *Orthodox and Modern: Studies in the Theology of Karl Barth* (Grand Rapids: Baker Academic, 2008), 235–60, esp. 236–47. As McCormack states (ibid., 247), this pattern applies not only to Christology proper but also to the present partnership between the risen Christ and Christians in the power of the Holy Spirit.

names the *Holy Spirit* as the power of the risen Christ's transition to us. "The power whose operation is presupposed in the New Testament is the outgoing and receiving presence and action of the Holy Spirit."[74] The power is a person. Everything Barth has said up to this point is attributed to the person of the Holy Spirit.

Barth briefly recapitulates his argument by transposing his descriptions of the power of transition into active verbs predicated of the Holy Spirit:

> It is He who brings it about that men like all others, existing in the same limitations, can also be, and are, witnesses of Jesus Christ. It is He who brings it about that others are awakened and moved by their witness. . . . It is He who creates the fellowship. . . . It is He who opens its mouth. . . . It is He who directs its *kerygma*. And it is He who gives to it . . . the appropriate contour and impression and form and direction. . . . It is He who calls them. . . . It is He who directs and controls their activities. It is He who gives them the power to execute them.[75]

Although Barth has been speaking of the operation of the risen Christ's transition to us as a nameless power, he now speaks clearly of the Holy Spirit as the personal agent who acts in this event. The Holy Spirit is a personal agent: he awakens and moves and creates and directs and calls and empowers the Christian community.

Although Barth ascribes such agency to the Holy Spirit in all three transitional subsections of *CD* IV/1–3, it is most prominent here in §64.4. In this discussion more than the others, the Holy Spirit is highlighted as the agent of Christ's resurrection. As already indicated, such a pneumatological focus befits the Christology of IV/2. Jesus Christ the exalted Son of Man arises to us, summoning us to a fraternal fellowship with him. He comes to us as one of us, giving concrete direction to our lives. As such, both he and we rely on the Holy Spirit to act as the mediator of this directive fellowship.

However, this is only one side of the matter. The Holy Spirit is not only the one who acts between Jesus Christ and us, but also the one in whom Christ himself acts. Christ and the Holy Spirit are not two competing agents performing independent works; rather, the risen Christ acts in the Holy Spirit, and the Holy Spirit acts in Christ's arising. This is where the Trinitarian grammar of Christ's arising gets complicated, for Barth is not content to merely

---

74. *CD* IV/2, 319.
75. *CD* IV/2, 319–20.

describe the power of transition and name it "Spirit." He wants to identify the Spirit in terms of his relation to Jesus Christ. Just as in §59.3 Barth did not speak of God the Father as the one who raised Jesus Christ in abstraction from the Father's relation to the Son in the Spirit, so also in §64.4 Barth does not speak of the Holy Spirit as the power of Christ's arising in abstraction from the Spirit's relation to the Son and the Father. So, having shown that Barth names the Spirit as the power of Christ's arising to us, it is now time to show that in so doing Christ is not left behind.

THE SPIRIT OF JESUS CHRIST

Once Barth has named the Holy Spirit as the power of transition, he asks what constitutes the holiness of the Holy Spirit. In this inquiry, Barth turns from the task of individuating the Spirit to the task of identifying the Spirit.[76] The Spirit can be individuated, or "picked out," as the power by which human beings participate in Jesus Christ's self-witness. But the Spirit can only be *identified* by his active relation to Jesus Christ and God the Father. Just as God the Father and Jesus Christ are identified by their relation to one another in the Holy Spirit, so also the Holy Spirit is identified by his relation to Jesus Christ and God the Father. In these active relations, we know who the Holy Spirit is. This move is crucial, because although the Spirit is the basis of our subjective correspondence to Christ's revelation, he cannot be reduced to our subjectivity. So we must speak of the Spirit's identity vis-à-vis Jesus Christ and God the Father in order to bear witness to his subjectivity over against us as one who comes to us.

The Holy Spirit is holy because he is the Spirit of Jesus Christ. The Spirit not only separates us, but is himself separate.[77] He not only makes us holy, but is himself holy. In what does the Spirit's sanctity consist? Why is the Spirit by definition holy? "The answer is staggering in its simplicity. He is the Holy Spirit in this supreme sense—holy with a holiness for which there are no analogies—because he is no other than the presence and action of Jesus Christ himself: his stretched out arm; he himself in the power of his resurrection, i.e., in the power of his revelation as it begins in and with the power of his resurrection and continues its work from this point."[78] The unique identity of the Holy

---

76. I am borrowing this conceptual distinction from Bruce Marshall, who in turn borrowed it from David Davidson. See Bruce Marshall, "Israel," in James J. Buckley and David S. Yeago, eds., *Knowing the Triune God: The Work of the Spirit in the Practices of the Church* (Grand Rapids: Eerdmans, 2001), 231–64.

77. *CD* IV/2, 322: "We are speaking of the Holy Spirit, and therefore, if we are to do justice to the meaning of the term, of a Spirit who is separate, and who separates, in the supreme sense."

78. *CD* IV/2, 322–23. Barth goes on to say, "He is the power in which Jesus Christ is alive among these persons and makes them His witnesses. . . . It was in the power of the Spirit that He went to His

Spirit over against both us and all other spirits consists in his being the Spirit of Jesus Christ. "He legitimates and proves himself as the Spirit of Jesus Christ, the Spirit who is 'sent' or 'poured out' by him, the Spirit who is given by him to the community, to Christians."[79]

This is a bold claim. Barth risks undermining his foregoing claim that the Holy Spirit is the one who acts in the occurrence of Christ's transition by speaking of the Spirit as the presence and action of Jesus Christ. But Barth does not make this claim without justification. First of all, Barth dedicates a seven-page excursus to an exegetical substantiation of this claim.[80] Secondly, the whole aim of Barth's argument in §64.4 is to demonstrate that Jesus Christ and the Holy Spirit do not compete with one another but in fact participate in the act of transition as distinct modes of God's triune being. Supporting this second, much larger claim is the burden of this chapter. But Barth's exegetical substantiation is immediately relevant. What is Barth's alleged exegetical basis for claiming that the Holy Spirit is holy because he is the Spirit of Jesus Christ?

Barth introduces his exegetical excursus with the following thesis: "In what the New Testament thinks and says about the Spirit there is in this respect a clear and almost direct line from Jesus Christ Himself to His community, to us Christians."[81] The excursus follows along this line. At each point, Barth argues that the New Testament thinks and speaks of the Spirit in terms of this movement from Jesus Christ to us. The New Testament always describes the Holy Spirit in the concrete context of this living relation. Therefore, Barth's identification of the Spirit as the Spirit of Christ does not reduce the Spirit to an attribute of Christ. Rather, it aims at following the New Testament witness in its strict avoidance of any independent pneumatology—independent, that is, from the living and active relation of the risen Jesus Christ with his community, upon which the New Testament counts at every point.

As Barth moves along this line from Jesus Christ to Christians, he makes four points. First, the Spirit is holy because he is the Spirit of the man Jesus. Barth supports this claim mainly from the Synoptic Gospels.[82] Second, the

---

death; and it was also in the power of the Spirit that He was raised again from the dead in order that what happened in His death should not be hidden but revealed. . . . Thus the Spirit who makes Christians Christians is the power of this revelation of Jesus Christ Himself—His Spirit. And for this reason, and in this fact, He is the Holy Spirit" (*CD* IV/2, 323).

79. *CD* IV/2, 323.

80. *CD* IV/2, 323–30.

81. *CD* IV/2, 323.

82. According to the Synoptic Gospels, the Spirit was at work in Christ's conception, at his baptism, in his conflict with Satan, in his death, and decisively in his resurrection from the dead (*CD* IV/2, 324). This

Spirit is holy because he proceeds from Jesus Christ and only from him. Barth develops this second point mainly from Acts and John, where such a "processional" logic is most evident.[83] Third, the Spirit is holy because he witnesses to Jesus Christ and only to him. For this point, Barth relies heavily on the description of the Spirit's work in the Johannine farewell discourses.[84] Fourth, and finally, the Spirit is holy because he unites Christians with Christ. Barth supports this claim with reference to the testing of spirits in 1 Corinthians 12 and 1 John 4.[85] Barth concludes this excursus by returning to the great passage concerning the ontological connection between Christ and Christians: Romans 8.[86]

In sum, Barth's exegetical argument is "that in the New Testament the Spirit is called the Spirit of Jesus Christ in the fourfold sense . . . as the Spirit who is first the Spirit of the man Jesus Himself; who proceeds from Him and

---

man Jesus traverses this way as the very Son of God: "It is in this radical sense that the Holy Spirit is the Spirit of Jesus Himself. Because and as He is the Son of God, Jesus is the spiritual man" (*CD* IV/2, 325).

83. Jesus Christ as the humiliated Son of God and the exalted Son of Man comes forth in his Spirit. "He lives in this twofold and simple majesty as the Son of God, as the Subject of this twofold and simple occurrence" (*CD* IV/2, 325). Christ himself creates in his community a correspondence to his humility and majesty. He does so by sending his Spirit. There is no other "Holy Spirit except as the One whom He sends to them as the Crucified and Risen" (*CD* IV/2, 325). Christ sends his Spirit from the "far side" of his relation to us (*CD* IV/2, 325). He sends his Spirit to us as the crucified and risen one. In this sense, the Holy Spirit proceeds from Christ. In this procession, the Holy Spirit is distinct from Christ, yet everywhere and always related to him.

84. In John 14 and 16, the Spirit is identified as the one who will come to bear witness to Jesus Christ and only to him. This promise of the Spirit's coming does not entail that Christ will be left behind: "this promise is a living promise because He Himself, raised again from the dead, lives within it, making Himself present in it. This is where the Spirit comes in as His Mediator, Advocate and Representative" (*CD* IV/2, 327). The Holy Spirit testifies to the living Christ; Christ testifies to himself in and through the Holy Spirit. These are two sides of the same coin. Viewed from either side, the Holy Spirit is the Spirit of Christ.

85. In these passages, the Christian community is instructed to test the spirits by asking to whom they testify (*CD* IV/2, 327–28). The Holy Spirit enables human beings to know themselves in Jesus Christ and therefore be with him. In other words, the Holy Spirit makes Christians. True Christians, those who are empowered by the Holy Spirit, bear witness to Christ. In this activity they are united with the living Christ. Because the Spirit so acts, he is the Holy Spirit.

86. *CD* IV/2, 328–30. Barth already discussed this passage at length when setting up the problem of transition (*CD* IV/2, 278–80; see above, "Exaltation Concealed: The Problem of Transition in §64.4"). There he observed the realism of its claims and the problem of their concealment. Here Barth observes that the Holy Spirit is the power by which we know the truth of the reality of our exaltation in Jesus Christ. The ontological connection described by Romans 8 is already real in Jesus Christ. However, its reality is known in its character as truth by the power of the Holy Spirit, who unites us with the risen Christ.

only from Him; who witnesses to Him and only to Him; and in whom we know ourselves in this man and may therefore be with Him."[87] Although it complicates his attribution of the occurrence of transition to the Holy Spirit, Barth's identification of the Holy Spirit as the Spirit of Jesus Christ is exegetically justified.

After completing this substantiation, Barth displays that this christological complication does not undermine the pneumatological focus of Christ's arising by returning to the metaphor of the door. He says that "the door which is closed from within to the being of Jesus Christ and our being in and with Him has actually been opened from within, in the power of His life as the royal man. It has been opened once and decisively in His resurrection, and it is continually opened in the presence and action of the Holy Spirit."[88] Christ opened the door objectively once for all, whereas the Holy Spirit opens the door subjectively again and again. The correlation of Christology with objectivity and pneumatology with subjectivity is a long-standing pattern in Barth's theology.[89] However, it is misunderstood when taken as a strict, reductive correlation. As evinced by Barth's exegetical excursus, *the Spirit was at work there and then in the life of Jesus Christ, and the living Jesus Christ is at work here and now in the Spirit.* This perichoretic pattern disrupts any crude chronological relation between Christ and the Spirit. The relation is temporal, because it occurs in a history; but Christ and the Spirit are not simply assigned separate points on a time line.

Although this perichoretic pattern of thought will come decisively into the foreground in §69.4, the mutual interpenetration of Christ and the Spirit in the event of transition is already operative here in §64.4. So it is fitting that Barth dialectically intertwines the christological and pneumatological aspects of Christ's transition: "Thus according to the New Testament the Holy Spirit is holy in the fact that He is the self-expression of the man Jesus, and that as such He is Himself His effective turning to us and our effective conversion to Him; His disclosure for us and our disclosure for Him; and, as this comes to us in this twofold sense, the new thing in earthly history, the alteration in human life and nature which is meant when we talk of the existence of the Christian

---

87. *CD* IV/2, 347. Note that this summary statement appears later in §64.4, specifically at the conclusion to the first half of Barth's argument concerning the Trinitarian ground of Christ's arising to us by the Spirit. Its presence at this crucial point in Barth's argument signals the importance of Barth's exegetical findings.

88. *CD* IV/2, 331.

89. All three cycles of Barth's dogmatic prolegomena deploy this basic pattern of thought: *Göttingen Dogmatics*, §6–7; *Christliche Dogmatik* §14–19; and *CD* I/2, §13–18.

community, the existence of Christians."[90] In a nutshell, this complex statement expresses the Trinitarian grammar of Christ's arising, at least in its christological and pneumatological aspects. What remains to be seen is how God the Father fits into all this.

GOD THE FATHER

In Barth's discussion of the activity of Christ and the Spirit in the ongoing history of Easter, has God the Father receded completely from view? Is God the Father relegated exclusively to the initiating act of Easter? Does God the Father only raise Jesus Christ but not participate in Christ's own act of arising? By no means! Although not the focus of §64.4, God the Father appears at the decisive turning point in Barth's transitional argument. Before he can speak of the divine basis of Christ's arising by the Spirit, he must attend to the fact that the Holy Spirit is not only the Spirit of Jesus Christ but also *the Spirit of God the Father*.[91]

The Holy Spirit as the power of transition is identified not only in relation to the man Jesus, but also in relation to God. Although this complicates the grammar even further, it is this factor that renders Barth's theology of Christ's arising fully Trinitarian in form, and in turn leads him to inquire into the basis of this transitional event in the triune God himself. So we must ask what Barth means when he says that the Holy Spirit is also the Spirit of God the Father.

At the outset, Barth insists that this claim does not correct or weaken his prior claim that the Holy Spirit is the Spirit of Jesus Christ. At the end of his prior discussion, Barth asks, "Is this the only answer that can be given?" He then replies, "It is indeed the only answer. It is complete in itself. It cannot be augmented or superseded. Jesus Christ is the Holy One beside or above whom there can be none holier. . . . We say the supreme and all-embracing thing of the holiness of the Holy Spirit when we follow this New Testament line from

---

90. *CD* IV/2, 331.

91. Because of its pivotal function, this discussion of God the Father is the most relevant one for the Trinitarian grammar of Christ's arising. But it is worth noting a previous reference in *CD* IV/2 to God the Father in connection with Christ's resurrection. In his discussion of the resurrection and ascension of Jesus Christ as the revelation of humanity's exaltation (§64.2-III, cf. above, "Exaltation and Humiliation: The Relationship between IV/1 and IV/2"), Barth specifically identifies God the Father as the one who raised Jesus Christ from the dead and as the one to whose right hand Jesus Christ ascended (*CD* IV/2, 151–54). With the exception of adding Christ's ascension into the mix, Barth simply recapitulates in a different context the central claim of §59.3: that God the Father *raised* Jesus Christ (*CD* IV/2, 152; *KD* IV/2, 169–70).

above to below and call Him the Spirit of Jesus Christ."[92] Why, then, does Barth add that the Spirit of Jesus Christ is also the Spirit of God the Father?

The New Testament drives Barth to make this claim. "The fact is that the New Testament does not describe the Holy Spirit as consistently as we might at first sight expect as the Spirit of Jesus Christ. On the contrary, in a considerable number of passages, although with no deviation in the description of His operation, it calls Him the Spirit of God, or of the Lord, or of the Father; and it often links the origin of His coming, of His being given, not only with the name of Jesus Christ, but also exclusively with these other names."[93] Barth cites and discusses a series of passages to support this claim, drawn primarily but not exclusively from Johannine and Pauline sources. So, at least at the level of New Testament exegesis, Barth has no choice but to attend to this other way of identifying the Spirit. How, then, does Barth incorporate this other way into his account without weakening his prior claim that the Holy Spirit is the Spirit of Jesus Christ?

Barth asserts that this other way of identifying the Spirit is an *elucidation* of the prior, christological mode of identifying the Spirit. "We can say at once that it does not involve any material restriction or amendment or even overthrow of our previous conclusion. It is not a superior conclusion by which we have to correct it. Nor is it a parallel conclusion that has to be placed alongside it. Its function is to elucidate."[94] This other way of identification clarifies the first by indicating that the history of the risen Christ's transition to us by the Spirit has a background in the very will of God. The history of transition is not just the peculiar history of Jesus with his own; it is the fulfillment of the plan of God for all creation.[95] The transitional work of the Spirit is the work of God in history, and as such is the temporal execution of God's eternal will to create the Christian community as the representation and foretaste of God's will for all creation.[96] Put simply, the Spirit of Christ *is* the Spirit of God.

92. CD IV/2, 331.
93. CD IV/2, 332.
94. CD IV/2, 333.
95. CD IV/2, 333–34: "When the New Testament also speaks in the same sense and context of the fact that God or the Father is and acts as Spirit, it shows us that this history which takes place on earth and in time, and the being and operation of the Spirit in it, have a background from which they come, and in the light of which they have a decisive reach and significance, not only for the being or non-being of the community and Christians, but also for the being or non-being, the life or death, of the world and all men."
96. CD IV/2, 334: "The insignificant and petty history of Christians, as capacitated and actualised by the Holy Spirit, is not merely one history among others . . . but a kind of central history among all others. It is in order that it may occur that world history and time continue."

In light of this clarifying function, the additional claim that the Holy Spirit is also the Spirit of God the Father does not weaken but rather deepens the force of the prior claim that the Holy Spirit is the Spirit of Jesus Christ. Barth does not merely set these two claims side by side.[97] Rather, Barth has developed this Trinitarian dialectic from the perspective of the particular event of Christ's arising to us. He has shown that the transitional event has a deep Trinitarian grammar: Jesus Christ arises to us in the power of the Holy Spirit by whom we bear witness to him, and this Spirit is both the Spirit of the man Jesus and the Spirit of God himself by whom all things are made new. Therefore, the history of transition from Christ to us is the work of the triune God: "God himself is at work in this occurrence."[98] The differentiated structure of this occurrence points to the differentiated subjectivity of the God at work in this occurrence.

Barth takes pains to clarify that this Trinitarian analysis of Christ's arising does not lead away from the sphere of history. "It is not a matter of bringing our discussions into the obscure sphere of a metaphysics. We must not lose sight of the history."[99] Barth does not leave behind the history of Christ's transition to us to speculate about the divine life in abstraction from this history. Nor does he simply "apply" a ready-made Trinitarian apparatus to analyze this history. Rather, Barth commends us "to learn to know God from this history."[100]

What do we learn about God from this history? Barth begins to answer this question with a "general and formal statement concerning . . . the three decisive factors in this history."[101] The existence of the man Jesus Christ is the "first and basic and controlling factor."[102] The existence of the community is "the goal of this history."[103] The power of transition that links Christ and the community is the "third factor . . . which links the first and second."[104] We could diagram these three factors as follows:

---

97. There is a sense in which Barth is dialectically juxtaposing these two New Testament claims. The Holy Spirit is both the Spirit of Christ and the Spirit of God the Father, and we must say both of these things simultaneously, seriously, and without separation or synthesis. In this regard, Barth does here for pneumatology what he did for Christology in *CD* I/2, §13.
98. *CD* IV/2, 335.
99. *CD* IV/2, 335.
100. *CD* IV/2, 336.
101. *CD* IV/2, 336.
102. *CD* IV/2, 336.
103. *CD* IV/2, 337.
104. *CD* IV/2, 337.

Origin	Means	Goal
The man Jesus	The Holy Spirit	The Christian community

In all three factors, God himself is at work, "not only in its origin, but also in its goal and in the conjunction and unity of the two."[105] In short, God is the subject of transition. And since the transition is threefold, we "have to say a threefold 'God' if we are to see and understand this history."[106] This threefold grammar is "necessary for its understanding."[107] With this threefold grammar, Barth has completed his analysis of the formal Trinitarian grammar of Christ's arising.

Even at this formal level, we can see the significance of Barth's Trinitarian theology of Christ's arising. Since the Spirit of Christ is also the Spirit of God, our participation in the risen Christ by the power of the Spirit is our participation in God himself.

> When we see clearly and forcibly that in the history as a whole, and equally in these three moments, we have to do with God, we have understood and seen and grasped it, not merely intellectually, but (to use the expression for once) existentially, as our own history. For when we find God present and active in this history, because we none of us do not first belong to God and only then to ourselves, we also find ourselves, really ourselves, not *a priori* but *a posteriori*, our own whence and whither and how as our part in the general whence and whither and how, the whence and whither and how of all things; our part, therefore, in God.[108]

The history in which we come to know Jesus Christ is the event in which we come to know both God and ourselves. Because it is truly God whom we encounter, our participation in this history is our participation in God.

How can this be? On what basis does Barth assert that that history of Christ's transition to us is a divine history? Barth's formal statement of the Trinitarian grammar of Christ's arising cannot answer these questions. This line of inquiry requires a material statement of the extent to which the triune God

---

105. *CD* IV/2, 337.
106. *CD* IV/2, 337.
107. *CD* IV/2, 336.
108. *CD* IV/2, 337–38.

corresponds to himself in this history. And so we must ask after the ontological ground of the risen Christ's transition to us.

THE TRINITARIAN GROUND OF CHRIST'S ARISING (§64.4)

According to Barth, the subject of Christ's arising is the triune God. Jesus Christ arises by the power of the Holy Spirit, who is both the Spirit of the man Jesus and the Spirit of God the Father. This has already been established. Barth goes on to assert that *in this history God is faithful to himself*. The self-differentiated God at work in this occurrence corresponds to the self-differentiated fellowship of God's own triune life. Because of his basic conviction regarding God's self-correspondence, Barth moves from his analysis of the formal Trinitarian grammar of Christ's arising to its material Trinitarian ground.

In order to show how and why Barth makes this move, I will execute a close reading of Barth's lengthy discussion in §64.4 of the theme of God's self-correspondence in the event of Christ's transition to us by the Spirit. According to Barth, the Holy Spirit can and does mediate between the risen Christ and us because he first and foremost mediates between the Father and Son. As the eternal mediator of this fellowship, the Holy Spirit truthfully attests to the divine basis of Christ's own arising, that is, the majesty of the Son in his eternal fellowship with the merciful Father. Therefore, the transitional event of Christ's resurrection, not only as God the Father's raising of Christ, but also as Christ's arising by the Holy Spirit, has its basis in the triune life of God.

THE MEDIATION OF THE SPIRIT

In the first part of his discussion of the Trinitarian basis of Christ's transition to us, Barth argues that God corresponds to himself in the history-in-partnership between Christ and us because the Holy Spirit who empowers this occurrence among us is also and primarily the Lord of the history-in-partnership within the triune God.

Barth develops this argument in two steps.[109] First, Barth justifies his move from the economic to the immanent Trinity. Second, he describes the problem and solution of transition in God's own being. In what follows, I provide a detailed exposition of both these steps in order to show the extent to which Barth grounds the pneumatological aspect of Christ's arising in the triune life of God.

---

109. This is signaled by a transitional statement regarding the move from the center to the periphery, which is followed by a space in the original German (*KD* IV/2, 382).

(1) How does Barth move from the formal Trinitarian grammar of Christ's transition to its ground in the triune God? This grammar is necessary to describe what is given in the biblical witness. Even in its formality it provides the clue to its material significance. So Barth can move beyond a merely formal similarity by identifying a material coincidence within it. Whereas the origin and goal of this history stand in a formal analogy to the Father and Son within God's triune life, the mediating factor between these two materially coincides with God the Holy Spirit. "Beyond the formal similarity between that history as a whole and the triune being of God, we can also assert a material coincidence, i.e., in respect of the Holy Spirit, who is not only the divine power mediating between Christ and Christendom but the mode of being of the one God which unites the Father and the Son."[110] This "coincidence is quite unequivocal, the third and middle factor, the divine power of the transition from Christ to Christendom, being *identical* with God in the mode of being of the Holy Spirit."[111]

The material coincidence of the Spirit, both within this transitional history and within the triune life of God, can be diagrammed as follows:

<u>Origin</u>	<u>Means</u>	<u>Goal</u>
The man Jesus	**The Holy Spirit**	The Christian Community
The Father	**The Holy Spirit**	The Son

Only on this basis can we assert that it is truly God at work in this history. In fact, the material coincidence of this one factor "is a provisional confirmation that even the formal comparison of the first and second factors of that history with the first and second modes of being in God (however formal it may be) is no mere speculative venture."[112]

Barth admits that he is in a certain sense identifying what one might call a *vestigium trinitatis*.[113] He rejects the possibility that even this very special history within the creaturely world is a proper reflection of God's triunity. However, the material coincidence of the one, mediating factor in this history with the "mediating mode of being of God"[114] justifies an inquiry into what God reveals

---

110. *CD* IV/2, 339. The German alternates between the verb *koinzidieren* and the noun *Zusammentreffen* (*KD* IV/2, 378–79).
111. *CD* IV/2, 339–40, emphasis added.
112. *CD* IV/2, 339.
113. *CD* IV/2, 338–39.

of himself in this history. Not just the "Christian thought of God" but the "light of the triune God . . . shines in and over this history."[115]

So, according to Barth, this move to the immanent Trinity is justified. But is it necessary? Why not remain content with the formal similarity to the Trinity evident in the history of Christ's transition, especially since the material coincidence of one of its factors provisionally confirms it? Will not such a move turn our attention away from this history to some other realm, and therefore not ground our claims regarding this history but weigh them down with unnecessary baggage?

Barth believes this move is necessary because a merely formal similarity is insufficient "to prove our statement that in that history God Himself, the triune God, is present and active and recognizable."[116] Only by following through on the material coincidence of the mediating factor can we be certain that God corresponds to himself in this history. To rest content with a formal similarity to the Trinity would itself be a flight from history, for to do so would imply that God in himself is so utterly different than God for us that he is not really present and active and recognizable in this history. Such a division between the immanent and economic Trinity would undermine the very confidence in the Holy Spirit's work that Barth seeks to uphold in §64.4. So, Barth does not make this move in order to turn his back on history, or, worse yet, to merely display how clever he is. Rather, Barth aims to show how far we can count on God's faithfulness to us in the work of the Holy Spirit, because in this work God is first and foremost faithful to himself.

Having justified this move by identifying a material coincidence within the formal similarity, Barth begins his inquiry into the triune ground of the risen Christ's transition by returning to "the mysterious and miraculous character of the intervention of the Holy Spirit even in His function in this history."[117] This character is indicated by the fact that we may and must *pray* for the Spirit to work among us. Barth poses the question that arises from this mystery: Why is the work of the Spirit so invisible and inconceivable, and yet the transition he effects so real?[118] What must be true of God himself to account for the mysterious presence of the Spirit among us?

---

114. *CD* IV/2, 339.
115. *CD* IV/2, 339.
116. *CD* IV/2, 339.
117. *CD* IV/2, 339–40.
118. *CD* IV/2, 340: "The Holy Spirit indicates in fact . . . a reality of which we for our part can have true knowledge only as we pray that it may take place in spite of its invisibility and inconceivability. And as we pray for this . . . we testify already that even in all His invisibility and inconceivability the Holy

Barth's answer is that "it is because in this mystery of His being and work in our earthly history there is repeated and represented and expressed what God is in Himself."[119] The activity of the Spirit is not just the solution to the problem of distance between Jesus Christ and the Christian community; rather, it is first and foremost the distance-crossing activity in God's own eternal life. "In His being and work as the mediator between Jesus and other humans, in His creating and establishing and maintaining of fellowship between Him and us, God Himself is active and revealed among us humans, i.e., the fellowship, the unity, the peace, the love, which there is in God, in which God was and is and will be from and to all eternity. We speak of the fellowship of the Father and the Son."[120] The fellowship of the Father and the Son is in "the Holy Spirit, who is Himself the Spirit of the Father and the Son."[121] And so the "divine intervention which creates fellowship reveals itself and takes place, not as something which is alien to God, but as a mediation which is most proper to Him, which takes place first in Himself, in His divine life from eternity to eternity."[122] The Spirit's mediation between the risen Christ and us in time is grounded in the Spirit's mediation between the Father and the Son in eternity.

(2) What does the mediation of the Spirit teach us about the triune God? From this pneumatological point of entry, Barth goes on to show how far God is at work not only "at the center ... [but] also ... on the periphery, in the origin and goal of this event."[123] Mediation in God implies that there is a confrontation in God to be mediated. There is no mediation where there are no parties to mediate between. But this means that not only the solution to the problem of transition is grounded in God himself, but also that the problem itself is found primarily in God. And so Barth explores the "problem" of God's own being.

Barth's argument runs as follows: since (a) the solution to the problem of the distance between Jesus and us is the Holy Spirit, and since (b) the Holy Spirit is God himself at work in this solution, then (c) the problem of distance must be in God as well. The "problem of distance, confrontation, encounter and partnership" between Jesus and us is primarily a "divine problem—the problem

---

Spirit is not for us merely the great Unknown, that it is not the case that we simply do not have Him, but that we know His power and efficacy."

119. *CD* IV/2, 341. Repetition, representation, and expression are common terms in Barth's theology for God's self-correspondence.

120. *CD* IV/2, 341.

121. *CD* IV/2, 341.

122. *CD* IV/2, 341.

123. *CD* IV/2, 342.

of God's own being."¹²⁴ Only if the problem is also grounded in God's being can we be sure that the "Holy Spirit is not a magical third between Jesus and us. God Himself acts in His own most proper cause when in the Holy Spirit He mediates between the man Jesus and other humans."¹²⁵

Barth is aware that placing the problem of distance in God's own life is shocking. Does God's being permit of problems? Is this a proper way of speaking about God?¹²⁶ Barth does not accept the premise of questions, that is, the assumption that we know in advance what constitutes divine majesty and perfection. Barth's whole theological enterprise takes aim at such presumption. Instead, the being of God must be learned from the history of God-with-us.

By taking his bearings from this history, Barth is led to a critique of received wisdom regarding God's being. "God is not the great immovable and immutable one and all which can confront us and our questions and answers only at an alien distance."¹²⁷ This picture of God is only a reflection of human limitations, that is, of our own death.¹²⁸ But "God in the Holy Spirit, as He acts and reveals Himself between the man Jesus and other men, is the living God, and as such, our God, who really turns to us and not under a mask behind which He is really another, because in the first instance distance and confrontation, encounter and partnership, are to be found in himself."¹²⁹ The reality of God as the one in whom there is partnership crowds out the received wisdom that "God" is immutable and immovable, and so relates to us in a wholly external mode of being.¹³⁰

---

124. *CD* IV/2, 342–43.

125. *CD* IV/2, 343.

126. This is not the first time we have encountered strange language attributed to God in the context of Barth's doctrine of Christ's resurrection. Barth speaks of a movement of grace and receptivity in God in §59.3 (cf. ch. 2, "The Trinitarian Ground of the Raising of Christ (§59.3)"). The same analogical rules apply in this case, though we need to attend to the specifics of the analogy at hand.

127. *CD* IV/2, 343.

128. *CD* IV/2, 343: "This is how man imagines 'God' without realising that what he is thinking or trying to think . . . is only the thought of his own limitation, or, to put it more sharply, the thought of his own death."

129. *CD* IV/2, 343.

130. Barth is not rejecting divine immutability in this passage. Rather, he is rejecting a certain interpretation of immutability on the basis of his more thoroughgoing interpretation of immutability. For Barth, God is immutable in that he is utterly faithful to himself in his external works, which entails that he is in himself as he is revealed in his external works. This requires the rejection of divine immutability in the sense of an *immovable* being, a being that cannot in any sense be affected from the outside. Instead, Barth reinterprets immutability as God's ever-renewed *constancy*. Barth's earlier discussion of immutability as constancy instead of immovability can be found in *CD* II/1, 491–522. For an analysis of divine constancy as it is developed in Barth's later doctrine of reconciliation, see Bruce L.

This critique is made possible because God reveals himself as triune. "God is in Himself—and here we have the distance and confrontation, the encounter and partnership, which are first in Him—Father and Son."[131] So the negative critique of the received wisdom is based on the positive confession that God is triune. The "antitheses in God's own being and life . . . are eternally fruitful" because they "do not involve any rigid abstract separation, but . . . stand always in a mutual relationship of self-opening and self-closure."[132] This is good news for us because it means God "knew this problem long before we did, before we ever were and before the world was. For He knew Himself from all eternity, the Father the Son, and the Son the Father."[133]

It is crucial to note that the language of "problem" is attributed *analogically* to God. The element of dissimilarity lies in the fact that there is no gap between problem and solution in God's being. Barth emphasizes that we only know of this problem of God's being in immediate conjunction with it solution: "A problem of God Himself? We can say this only if we underline at once that in God Himself, as the question of the relationship of the Father and the Son, it never could nor can be posed except in and with its answer and solution. What is primarily in God is the *transition* which takes place in that distance, the *mediation* in that confrontation, the *communication* in that encounter, the *history* in that partnership."[134] Therefore, the "Father and the Son are not merely alongside one another in a kind of neutrality or even hostility. They are with one another in love."[135] In the work of the Holy Spirit, God reveals himself as the one in whom there is *both* the problem of distance, confrontation, encounter, and partnership, *and* the solution of transition, mediation, communication, and history. While the language of problem-and-solution is admittedly odd, Barth believes it is analogically adequate to the task of bearing witness to God's faithfulness to himself in the event of Christ's arising to us by the Holy Spirit.[136]

McCormack, "Divine Impassibility or Simply Divine Constancy? Implications of Karl Barth's Later Christology for Debates over Impassibility," in James F. Keating and Thomas Joseph White, eds., *Divine Impassibility and the Mystery of Human Suffering* (Grand Rapids: Eerdmans, 2009), 150–86.

131. *CD* IV/2, 343.
132. *CD* IV/2, 343.
133. *CD* IV/2, 344.
134. *CD* IV/2, 344, emphasis added.
135. *CD* IV/2, 344.
136. John Thompson finds the analogical language of a problem in God to go to far in "On the Trinity," in *Theology Beyond Christendom: Essays on the Centenary of the Birth of Karl Barth* (Allison Park, PA: Pickwick, 1986), 13–32. He argues that one must temporarily omit the solution of the Holy Spirit to

However, Barth wants more. He aims to say something more concrete. The language of problem and solution, though appropriate, is too abstract. So he selects one of the four problem-solution pairs mentioned above in order to flesh out the triune ground of Christ's arising to us.

The pair Barth selects is history-in-partnership, "because it is particularly important for our present purpose."[137] No doubt he chooses this pair because it fits the main argument of §64.4, which aims to show how humans become partners with Jesus Christ in his living act as the exalted Son of Man. Identifying the divine basis of this all-too-human partnership is the purpose of §64.4. Barth narrates the history of this human partnership with special reference to the divine subject of this history: the Holy Spirit. And the work of the Holy Spirit reveals that this human history-in-partnership is based on the history-in-partnership of God's own life. "What was and is and will be primarily in God Himself, and not primarily in the form in which we know or think we know it, is history in partnership."[138]

Barth develops the significance of both elements in this expression. First, it is "*partnership*, and not therefore the history of an isolated individual. God was never solitary. Therefore the thought of a solitary man and his history can only be the aberration of a thinking which is either godless or occupied with that alien God which is properly death. God was always a Partner. The Father was the Partner of the Son, and the Son of the Father."[139] Partnership in God thus signifies the eternal differentiation between the Father and the Son.

---

identify the problem of the Father and the Son, though he admits that Barth says the two are only known together (ibid., 30). Thompson considers this move a case of abstraction, which Barth otherwise rails against. It seems to me that the procedure of temporarily omitting one element in order to ascertain the inner logic of the whole befits the faith-seeking-understanding methodology Barth critically appropriated from Anselm.

137. *CD* IV/2, 344. Barth indicates on page 345 that the triune life of God could be described along the same lines by selecting any of the other pairs: (1) transition-in-distance, (2) mediation-in-confrontation, and (3) communication-in-encounter. Barth does not attend much to (3) in this context, though this conceptual pair is important in Barth's anthropology (*CD* III/2, 247–74). It is interesting that Barth does not select (1) or (2), inasmuch as the terms "transition" and "mediation" are both prominent throughout §64.4. Then again, perhaps this prominence is a reason to select another pair in order to view the ontological basis from a fresh perspective. Though not in itself a sufficient reason, such a stylistic consideration is not irrelevant.

138. *CD* IV/2, 344, original German emphasis restored (*KD* IV/2, 384). Again, note the analogical similarity within dissimilarity: history in partnership is truly in God, but not in the form in which we know or think we know it.

139. *CD* IV/2, 344, original German emphasis restored (*KD* IV/2, 384).

Second, it is "*history* in this partnership: the closed circle of the knowing of the Son by the Father and the Father by the Son."[140] Barth explores this second element in two ways: biblically and dogmatically. Barth indicates that this closed circle "according to Mt. 11:27 can be penetrated only from within as the Son causes a man to participate in this knowledge by His revelation."[141] Then Barth re-describes this history "in the language of dogma" as "the Father's eternal begetting of the Son, and the Son's eternal being begotten of the Father, with the common work which confirms this relationship, in which it takes place eternally that the one God is not merely the Father and the Son but also, eternally proceeding from the Father and the Son, the Holy Ghost."[142] History in God thus signifies the unity of the Father and the Son in the Holy Spirit. So, the expression "history-in-partnership" with reference to God signifies the whole triune life of God himself.

Barth underscores that neither partnership nor history is more basic than the other. On the one hand, his epistemic point of entry in §64.4 is the history, communication, mediation, and transition enacted by the Spirit in our sphere. On the other hand, his logical presentation always begins with the partnership of the Father and the Son, and then turns to the history of this partnership in the Spirit.[143] Barth is here re-conceptualizing the classical language of begetting and proceeding. He follows the tradition in speaking first of the generation of the Son and then of the procession of the Spirit, but the language is thoroughly rethought in terms of the personalist and actualist language of partnership and history.

Since both partnership and history are in God eternally, neither precedes the other ontologically. Barth explicitly reaffirms the *filioque* clause.[144] In this

---

140. *CD* IV/2, 344, original German emphasis restored (*KD* IV/2, 384).

141. *CD* IV/2, 344. This move parallels the argument concerning primary and secondary objectivity in *CD* II/1, 16–27 and 48–50.

142. *CD* IV/2, 344.

143. In this, Barth follows the tradition in speaking of the Holy Spirit as the *third* person of the Trinity, though he does so in a manner befitting his basic christocentric orientation.

144. He even quotes the Latin version of the Nicene Creed (*CD* IV/2, 345). David Guretzki has recently discussed—and for the most part defended—Barth's reception and use of the *filioque* doctrine in *Karl Barth on the Filioque* (Hampshire: Ashgate, 2009). Guretzki discusses §64.4 as an instance of the return of *Römerbrief*-style dialectical thinking into Barth's use of the *filioque* (163–73). This is an interesting claim, especially because it highlights the difference between the pneumatologies of I/1 and IV/2. However, this mode of analysis leads him to identify an ambiguity in Barth concerning the occasion of the Spirit-mediated confrontation: is it because we are creatures or because we are sinners? If the latter, then doesn't this mean that Barth reads sin back into the inner life of the triune God? See ibid., 173, 187–92. It seems this whole problematic can be avoided by attending to the larger context of Barth's

context, the *filioque* means that the partnership between the Father and the Son *logically* precedes their history in the Spirit. But as an eternal act in God's being, the procession of the Spirit from the Father and the Son coincides with the event in which the Spirit actively unites the Father and the Son. "The presence of the partnership means also the occurrence of the history. And the occurrence of the history means the eternal rise and renewal of the partnership. There is no rigid or static being which is not also act. There is only the being of God as the Father and the Son with the Holy Spirit who is the Spirit of both and in whose eternal procession they are both actively united."[145]

This means that the history-in-partnership between the Father and the Son in the Holy Spirit is ontologically basic. Before there was any history-in-partnership between Christ and us, there was the history-in-partnership in God himself. And so God can enter into free partnership with us because God is free partnership in himself: "The Father and the Son are not two prisoners. They are not two mutually conditioning factors in reciprocal operation. As the common source of the Spirit, who Himself is also God, they are the Lord of this occurrence. God is the free Lord of His inner union. Concretely, He is Spirit."[146] So the risen Jesus Christ can enter into full and genuine partnership with us without sacrificing his freedom as Lord, because he does so in the Spirit, who is in God himself the occurrence of the history-in-partnership between the Father and the Son. In other words, *the procession of the Holy Spirit is the basis of the Easter direction of the Son.*

For us, this means that the man Jesus can become our partner in the Spirit because he was and is and will be God the Father's partner in the Spirit. "The mystery of Jesus, the Son of Man, is that He is primarily the Son of God the Father, and as such Himself God, and then, and as such, also the Son of Man. This being the case, His Spirit . . . is none other than the Spirit of God acting and revealing Himself in the created world among and to us."[147] The

---

argument. Barth is clear about what occasions the problem of transition: it is not just because we are creatures or sinners, but because true humanity is actualized in Jesus Christ as *cruciform*, i.e., obedient unto death (*CD* IV/2, 288–90; cf. Barth's discussion of death in *CD* III/2, 587–640). Jesus' human act of love for God and others is analogous to the eternal encounter between the Father and the Son, and the risen Christ's self-attestation to us in the power of the Spirit is analogous to the Spirit's eternal mediation between the Father and the Son. In this analogical scheme, positing confrontation and mediation in God does not entail positing sin in God as well.

145. *CD* IV/2, 344–45. In this quotation, partnership and history correlate with being and act, which is fitting since both pairs are conceptual redescriptions of the confession that God is the living God, i.e., Father, Son, and Holy Spirit. See *CD* II/1, §28.1.

146. *CD* IV/2, 345.

147. *CD* IV/2, 347.

eternal history-in-partnership between the Father and the Son in the Spirit is the ontological ground of Christ's arising to us by the Spirit, and so of our participation with him in his self-attestation, which is the mode of our participation in the exaltation of humanity accomplished in him. And since this history takes place first and foremost in God, our participation in this history is our participation in God himself. "Thus we for our part, as history in partnership is the portion which is allotted to us in his free grace, genuinely exist in participation in himself, in his triune life, and in the problem of this life, and its answer and solution."[148] Therefore, our partnership with the risen Christ in the Spirit *is* our participation in God.[149]

Before turning to the remainder of Barth's discussion of the Trinitarian ground of Christ's arising, it is necessary to address two pressing questions. First, to what extent is Barth simply recapitulating in this unique context a traditional "Augustinian" framework regarding the Holy Spirit? *Barth is Augustinian but also more than Augustinian.* Barth adopts the Augustinian framework of the Holy Spirit as the union of the Father and the Son, and so of the procession of the Spirit from the Father and the Son.[150] However, at a crucial point he turns this framework on its head. Seeing the Holy Spirit as God's third mode of being actively mediating between his first two modes, Barth speaks of the Spirit as the *culmination* of the divine life: "The history between the Father and the Son culminates in the fact that in it God is also *Spiritus Sanctus Dominus vivifans, qui ex Patre Filioque procedit*."[151] As the culmination of the Father and the Son, the Spirit is God in his free lordship even over his inner history. "God is the free Lord of His inner union. Concretely, He is Spirit."[152] The Spirit is not only the bond of union between the Father and the Son, but also and primarily the free Lord of this union. So, according to Barth's critical reception of Augustinian framework, the personal agency of the Spirit is expressed and emphasized.

This reference to divine freedom brings us to our second question. Does Barth's inclusion of history within God's own being go too far toward entangling God in the becoming of creation? Or, to press the question from a different direction, has Barth so enclosed the category of history within God's being that history as we know it is a mere appearance, an ephemeral reality

---

148. *CD* IV/2, 346.

149. I will address this practical significance in greater detail below, in "The Significance of a Trinitarian Theology of Christ's Arising."

150. Daniel L. Migliore, "Vinculum Pacis: Karl Barths Theologie des Heiligen Geistes," in *Evangelische Theologie* 60:2 (Jan 2000): 131–52.

151. *CD* IV/2, 345.

152. *CD* IV/2, 345.

that ceases to concern us? The answer from both directions is No.[153] The inner history-in-partnership of God's own life, his eternal being-in-act, is the *basis* of God's history-in-partnership with us. "The triune life of God, which is free life in the fact that it is Spirit, is the basis of His whole will and action even *ad extra*, as the living act which He directs to us."[154] Barth attributes self-sufficiency and perfect beatitude to this triune life.[155] So, the triunity of God is not dissolved into historical becoming or reducible to economic distinctions. Rather, God's own triune life is the basis of the Trinitarian structure of God's history with us.

Barth's talk of history in God does not mean, however, that God is separated from our history. God's external works are external only in the sense that they are directed to what is external to his self-sufficient life, for what God directs to us is his very own life. In his history with us, the triune God repeats himself: "God does not have to will and do all this. But He does will and do it. And because He is the God of triune life, He does not will and do anything strange by so doing. In it He lives in the repetition and confirmation of what He is in Himself."[156] The history-in-partnership of God's own life is not a self-enclosed abstraction. The triunity of God is never cut off from God's eternal resolve to be God-with-us. Instead, there is a strict correspondence between the immanent and economic Trinity. The history-in-partnership of God with us is the "representation, reflection and correspondence" of the history-in-partnership of God's own life.[157] This correspondence is not merely an axiom for warding off errors. Rather, the faithful correspondence of God to himself is the positive, overarching theme of Barth's Trinitarian theology of Easter and the ultimate solution to the problem of transition: "He is primarily faithful to Himself and in this way seals the reality and truth of His faithfulness to us."[158]

The Majesty of the Son

According to Barth, the triune God is faithful to himself in the event of Christ's arising by the Holy Spirit. This is the central claim of this section. We have just explored the pneumatological aspect of this Trinitarian ground, but we must remember that, since the Holy Spirit is the Spirit of the man Jesus, the Spirit's

---

153. My answer to this recurring question once again follows Eberhard Jüngel's interpretation of Barth in *God's Being Is in Becoming*.
154. *CD* IV/2, 345. Barth goes on to list all the externally directed works of God: election, creation, reconciliation, and redemption.
155. *CD* IV/2, 346: "This God is self-sufficient. This God knows perfect beatitude in Himself."
156. *CD* IV/2, 346.
157. *CD* IV/2, 346.
158. *CD* IV/2, 348.

work of mediation does not eclipse the ongoing activity of the risen Christ.[159] Therefore, a discussion of the Trinitarian ground of Christ's arising must also include its christological aspect, that is, that the exalted Son of Man who arises in the power of the Spirit is the eternal Son of the Father.[160]

Barth's development of this christological aspect of God's self-correspondence is rich and complex. Its import for this study is his identification of *the majesty of the Son* as the divine basis of the exaltation of humanity opened up by Christ's arising. Whereas the raising of Christ was grounded in the grace of the Father received by the humble Son, Christ's own arising is grounded in the Son's majestic act of free love in fellowship with his Father.

How does Barth arrive at this claim? His point of entry is the Holy Spirit's witness to the mysterious simultaneity of humiliation and exaltation in Jesus Christ.[161] Barth takes up this "paradox" in order "to seek its basis in the *doxa* of God, which means again in the trinitarian life of God."[162] He argues that the simultaneity of humiliation and exaltation is not sheer paradox, for it is an *ordered* simultaneity rooted in the singular yet differentiated will of the triune God. The self-humbling of God in Jesus Christ is ordered to the exaltation of humanity that took place simultaneously in him. He was humbled *so that* we may be exalted.

What does this have to do with the Trinitarian ground of Christ's arising? Although divine humiliation and human exaltation were both fulfilled in Christ's life of obedience unto death, the ordered relationship between these two aspects was revealed in the ordered relationship between the death and resurrection of Jesus Christ. His death and resurrection are not merely

---

159. See "The Spirit of Jesus Christ" above.

160. In turning to this christological aspect, Barth has come full circle: having developed the Trinitarian grammar of Christ's arising first from a christological and then from a pneumatological perspective, he develops the Trinitarian ground of Christ's arising first from a pneumatological and then from a christological perspective. And just as Christ and the Spirit do not compete in the ongoing history of Easter, so also Christ and the Spirit do not compete in the basis of this history in the triune God. So these two aspects are complementary, not competing, formulations of the divine basis of Christ's arising. The difference is perspectival: whereas the eternal mediation of the Spirit is the ground of the Spirit's work of mediating the risen Christ to us, the eternal majesty of the Son is the ground of Jesus Christ's own arising for us.

161. In accordance with the turn from pneumatology to Christology, Barth's language shifts from the *mediation* of the Spirit to the *witness* of the Spirit. George Hunsinger discusses the relationship between these two concepts in the constructive ecumenical proposals of *Let Us Keep the Feast: The Eucharist and Ecumenism* (Cambridge: Cambridge University Press, 2008), 184–86, 218–19, and 259–60. I will return to the Spirit's role in this portion of Barth's argument at the end of this major section.

162. *CD* IV/2, 348.

juxtaposed but united by an inner dynamic and teleology, which corresponds to the dynamic and teleology of God's own life.[163] Christ's resurrection follows his death not merely as a defiant contrast but also and primarily as a joyful Amen.[164] Jesus Christ, in the power of his arising as the exalted Son of Man, attests to the majesty of the eternal Son of God as the basis of his mysterious existence.

What does Barth mean by the majesty of the Son? In keeping with his overall pattern of thought, Barth speaks of the Son's majesty not in terms of an abstract characteristic of his being, but as a concrete description of his being-in-act. Accordingly, Barth alternates between the *majesty* of the Son and the *majestic act* of the Son.[165]

What is the content of this act? The majestic act of the Son is one eternal act with two directions. The first is toward the Father. The Son freely loves the Father in the fellowship of the Holy Spirit.[166] In this act of love, he is exalted with the Father, sharing equally in his majesty.[167] The eternal Son is not only humble before the Father but also majestic with the Father.

The second direction of the majestic act of the Son is toward us. The Son freely decides to become our brother.[168] He chooses from all eternity to exalt humanity by becoming human and living a life of obedience unto death in perfect fellowship with the Father. Although distinct, this second direction takes place within the first. The Son's own decision to exalt humanity occurs in free obedience to his Father whom he loves. The Son's majestic act toward us is the outworking of his majestic act toward the Father. These two directions of the one act coincide in God's eternity.

This one eternal act of love is the sole basis of the exaltation of humanity, both as it was fulfilled in Christ's life of obedience unto death and as it is revealed in Christ's arising from the dead. "The majesty of the Son of God is the mystery, the basis, of the exaltation of the Son of Man."[169] Because of this, "the elect man Jesus ... is the new and true and royal man, who is triumphantly alive even, and especially, in His death."[170] Christ's arising fittingly and effectively

---

163. *CD* IV/2, 357: "For what is denoted, represented and reflected in the riddle of the existence of Jesus Christ is the dynamic and teleology of the divine life, the way of the divine will and resolve and work."

164. *CD* IV/2, 355.

165. *CD* IV/2, 357–58.

166. Cf. *CD* IV/2, 359, where Barth refers explicitly to both the inward and outward direction of the free love of the triune God.

167. *CD* IV/2, 357–58.

168. *CD* IV/2, 357–58.

169. *CD* IV/2, 358.

reveals his exaltation. It neither contradicts nor supplements the exaltation of humanity fulfilled in his death, but is the outworking of the majesty of the Son. It was God's good pleasure that we would participate in our true humanity by attesting its reality in Jesus Christ. By arising from the dead, Jesus Christ himself commences this ongoing history of attestation. This human Amen to the divine Yes is secure because it is grounded in the inner dynamic and teleology of the triune God's own life.

At this point, I must note the important role of *election* in Barth's understanding of the Trinitarian ground of Christ's arising. Throughout this portion of his argument Barth makes repeated reference to God's decision, will, decree, and choice. Reference to God's self-determination emerged in the above discussion of the triune ground of the raising of Jesus Christ.[170] However, election is even more prominent here. The reason for this prominence is that in order to speak of the *divine* basis of the arising of the *human* Jesus, Barth must speak of the eternal divine *decision* to become human.

The prominence of election in this portion of §64.4 raises an important question: Does the grounding of Christ's arising in divine election constitute an *alternative* to my thesis that the Easter event is grounded in the triune God? No. Trinity and election are not competing grounds for the Easter event. First of all, I do not assert that according to Barth the *doctrine* of the Trinity is the ground of the Easter event. Rather, I have maintained that the event of Easter is grounded in the *triune God himself*. Such a claim includes rather than excludes the triune God's eternal will to be God for us. Secondly, God's self-differentiation and self-determination, though conceptually distinguishable, coincide in God's eternity.[172] From and to all eternity, the triune God is the one who elects, and the one who elects is the triune God.[173]

---

170. *CD* IV/2, 358.

171. See ch. 2, "The Grace of the Father."

172. For instance, Barth argues for the unity and differentiation of humiliation and exaltation in Jesus Christ *both* in terms of the twofold singular will of God *and* in terms of the fellowship of the Father and the Son in the Holy Spirit, without assigning priority to either one (*CD* IV/2, 350–51, 358).

173. This discussion brings us into the sphere of the current debate concerning the relationship between Trinity and election in Barth's theology and beyond. For a recent review of the literature, see Bruce L. McCormack, "Trinity and Election: A Progress Report," in *Ontmoetingen Tijdgenoten en getuigen: Studies aangeboden aan Gerrit Neven*, ed. Akke van der Kooi, Volker Küster, and Rinse Reeling Brouwer (Kampen: Uitgeverij Kok, 2009), 14–35. Although one could potentially broach this topic from the vantage point of Christ's resurrection, it is not necessary to do so in order to develop and substantiate my thesis. The triune God himself is the sole ontological basis of Christ's resurrection whether or not one assigns a logical priority to either self-differentiation or self-determination. There is textual evidence from §64.4 to support the claim that triunity is logically prior to election even in Barth's mature

What, then, does talk of election add to this discussion of the divine basis of Christ's arising? Reference to God's eternal decision underscores the *freedom* of Christ's arising to attest himself to us. The arising of the Son of Man befits him in his identity with the eternal Son of God. This antecedent fitness accounts for the inner "necessity" of Christ's transition from dying to rising.[174] Yet this triune basis does not make his arising necessary. The man Jesus arises in the freedom with which the eternal Son of God chose to become human. Christ's arising is grounded in nothing but the active majesty and majestic act of the eternal Son of God.

Now all this talk of the Son's activity appears at first glance to contradict the findings of the previous chapter. Has Barth abandoned his critique of the traditional formula, that is, that Jesus Christ according to his deity raised himself from the dead? No, for two reasons. First, the distinction between raising and arising is still operative in §64.4, and so we are speaking of Jesus Christ's active subjectivity only in terms of his arising, which is logically subsequent to his being raised by God the Father.[175] Whereas the raising of Jesus Christ is grounded in the Son's receptivity to the Father's grace, Jesus Christ's own arising is grounded in the Son's majestic activity.

Second, Barth does not speak of the majesty of the Son in abstraction from the humanity of Jesus Christ. As I have stated, the majestic act of the Son includes his eternal decision to become human. "He became and was and is man. But because He did so as the Son of God He is from the very first, from all eternity in the election and decree of God, elect man, exalted in all the lowliness of His humanity, and revealed in His resurrection and ascension as man set in eternal fellowship with God, at the right hand of the Father."[176] In his self-identification with the Son of Man, the majestic Son of God arises and reveals himself as the one true living human.[177] This concrete majesty—his majesty as the eternal Son of the Father who willed to become incarnate—is the ground of his arising. So, Jesus Christ in his divine-human unity is the subject of his

---

Christology (e.g., *CD* IV/2, 345–46; cf. "The Mediation of the Spirit" above). On the other hand, Barth's discussion of the majesty of the Son shows to what extent he locates election in the very heart of God's triune life, and so could occasion a constructive development beyond Barth that would remain faithful to his insights. But since self-differentiation and self-determination are both ontologically basic as eternally coincident events in God's life, one need not assign a *logical* priority to one or the other to maintain that the *ontological* basis of Christ's arising is the triune God.

174. *CD* IV/2, 356.
175. See the section "Jesus Christ" above. See also ch. 2, "Jesus Christ."
176. *CD* IV/2, 358.
177. *CD* IV/2, 358.

own arising. And the basis of his arising is the majesty of the eternal Son, which includes his decision to become incarnate for our sakes.

Although the grounding of Christ's arising in the majestic act of the Son does not contradict the findings of the previous chapter, the question does arise: What is the Father's mode of participation in the Trinitarian ground of Christ's arising? What is the patrological counterpart to the majesty of the Son?

The Mercy of the Father

According to Barth, the Father's mode of participating in the Trinitarian ground of Christ's arising is his merciful act of fellowship with the Son. The Father lives in so perfect a fellowship with his Son that he wills to co-suffer with him in his death for us. This act of fellow suffering is the outworking of *the mercy of the Father*. This merciful act of the Father is aimed toward the majestic act of the Son, which in turn fulfills the merciful act of the Father. These two acts, in this order, coincide exactly in the one living act of God, that is, the free love of the Father and the Son in the Holy Spirit.

The best way to understand the mercy of the Father is to attend to Barth's dialectical inversion of the Trinitarian pattern of thought. Although not contradictory, the Trinitarian ground of Jesus Christ's arising stands in stark contrast to the Trinitarian ground of the raising of Jesus Christ. There are two aspects to this dialectical inversion. First, Barth attributes divine "majesty" to the Son in §64.4. Although majesty is never strictly denied the Son in §59.1, it is consistently attributed to the Father in explicit contrast to the humility of the Son. The inverted perspective of §64.4 provides an important qualification to this contrast. Again, this qualification is not a denial, for the majesty of the Son consists in his eternal fellowship with the majestic Father. Barth clearly states that the Son is exalted *with* the Father, and the Son's eternal majesty is fulfilled precisely in his humble obedience as a human being. So the attribution of majesty to the Son does not contradict the attribution of humility. But this inversion introduces an important qualification that prevents the conclusion that Barth speaks of divine majesty as a property of the Father alone.[178]

Second, Barth inverts the coordination of Trinitarian persons and christological events. In §59.3, Barth speaks of the *death* of Jesus Christ as the goal to which the humble obedience of the *Son* is aimed, and of the *raising* of Jesus Christ as the historical fulfillment of the grace of the *Father*.[179] In §64.4,

---

178. This inversion also softens (though does not supplant) Barth's conception of the Trinitarian taxis in terms of superordination/subordination.
179. See ch. 2, "The Grace of the Father."

Barth speaks of Jesus Christ's *arising* as the outworking of the exaltation of humanity that is grounded in the majestic act of the *Son*, and the *death* of Jesus Christ as grounded in the merciful fellowship of the *Father* with the Son.[180] This inversion is dialectical: neither coordination is absolute, and so they do not strictly contradict one another. But the inverted pattern has significant consequences.

The immediate consequence is that Barth recognizes "a *particula veri* in the teaching of the early Patripassians. This is that primarily it is God the Father who suffers in the offering and sending of His Son, in His abasement."[181] Barth qualifies this claim by noting that this suffering is alien to the Father, for it is human suffering and the Son alone becomes incarnate.[182] But the Father's suffering is nonetheless real.[183] Barth does not deny that Christ's death is the fulfillment of the Son's act of obedience, for he speaks clearly of the Father suffering *with* the Son. Nor does he deny that Christ's resurrection is the fulfillment of the Father's act of grace, for he speaks of the Son being exalted *with* the Father. But the co-suffering of God the Father means that the coordination of Trinitarian persons with christological events does not set the Father and Son in opposition to each other, but rather speaks of the differentiation with which the one God acts.

This reference to the self-differentiated unity of God brings us to the most significant consequence of the dialectical inversion for Barth's Trinitarian theology of Christ's arising. Barth asserts that the merciful act of the Father *coincides exactly* with the majestic act of the Son. These two things, "for all their difference," are "true and actual as united in the one free love which is God Himself."[184] He goes on to explain, "The deepest divine mercy and the loftiest divine majesty coincide exactly at the basis of the existence of Jesus Christ. For the merciful act of the Father aims at the majestic act of the Son. And the majestic act of the Son takes place in exact fulfillment of the merciful act of the Father."[185] The mercy of the Father and the majesty of the Son are not aimed in opposing directions; rather, the former is ordered to the latter in the differentiated unity of God's own triune life. In this ordered togetherness, they

---

180. *CD* IV/2, 357: "This Fatherly fellow-suffering of God is the mystery, the basis, of the humiliation of the Son; the truth of that which takes place historically in His crucifixion."

181. *CD* IV/2, 357.

182. *CD* IV/2, 357: "The suffering is not His own, but the alien suffering of the creature, of man, which He takes to Himself in Him."

183. *CD* IV/2, 357: "But He does suffer it."

184. *CD* IV/2, 358.

185. *CD* IV/2, 358–59.

are *one*: "As God the Father and the Son is one God, the two acts are, in this sequence, the one incontestable living act of God, the act of the one free love which is His essence and work both inwards and outwards."[186] Therefore, Jesus Christ's arising as the exalted Son of Man is grounded not only in the majesty of the Son but also in the mercy of the Father.

The fellowship of the Father and the Son brings us back to the *Holy Spirit*. In mediating the risen Christ to us, the Holy Spirit truthfully attests the eternal fellowship of the Father and the Son. Barth concludes his development of the theme of God's self-correspondence with a reference to *the witness of the Holy Spirit*.[187] The ordered unity of the Father and the Son, which grounds the ordered unity of Jesus Christ's existence, occurs in the Holy Spirit. The Holy Spirit is both the Spirit of the Father and of the Son (*filioque*). As the one who actively unites the Father and the Son in God, the Spirit can and does truthfully attest to the eternal fellowship of the majestic Son with his merciful Father. The Holy Spirit as the power of Christ's arising assures us of God's eternal purpose for us to have fellowship with him. So the multiple aspects of the Trinitarian ground of Christ's arising developed throughout this section underscore this one main point: we can trust the Holy Spirit's witness to the love of God for us in Jesus Christ, because he is the Spirit of the Father and the Son, that is, God the Holy Spirit.

THE SIGNIFICANCE OF A TRINITARIAN THEOLOGY OF CHRIST'S ARISING

This talk of Christian assurance and trust leads to a reflection on the practical significance of Barth's Trinitarian theology of Christ's arising. Jesus Christ arises to us by the Holy Spirit, who is the Spirit of the man Jesus and the Spirit of God the Father. This event has its basis in the Spirit's eternal mediation of the fellowship between the majestic Son and his merciful Father. This Trinitarian theology of Christ's arising is significant because it provides a theological rationale for the *confidence* with which Christians follow the *concrete* direction given in and by the Holy Spirit.

I will substantiate this claim by drawing on two different portions of §64.4.[188] The first portion consists of the clues Barth sprinkles throughout §64.4

---

186. *CD* IV/2, 359.

187. *CD* IV/2, 359: "This witness is the Holy Spirit as the Spirit of Jesus. He is the Spirit of the Son who is also the Spirit of the Father—the Spirit of God. We can now repeat that He is the Spirit of truth because He lights up the life of the man Jesus as the life of the Son with the Father and the Father with the Son; and He lights up the antithesis which controls this life in its necessity but also in its unity, in the dynamic and teleology which are first in the living act of God Himself."

regarding the significance of his argument. These clues highlight the *confidence* with which we follow the risen Jesus Christ in the power of the Holy Spirit. This confidence is grounded in the *deity* of the Spirit. The second portion is the final twenty pages of §64.4, where Barth develops the manner of the Holy Spirit's working by means of the concept of "direction." This discussion highlights the *concreteness* of the direction given to us in and by the Holy Spirit. This concreteness is grounded in the *humanity* of the Spirit's operation, that is, the eternal Son of God became and was and is human, and so the divine direction given in and by his Spirit can be concretely described in human terms. After developing and supporting these two sides of my claim, I will identify an important consequence of Barth's Trinitarian theology of Christ's arising—its critical assimilation of "ontological" and "moral" understandings of the work of both Jesus Christ and the Holy Spirit.

Confidence

Barth's Trinitarian theology of Christ's arising accounts for the *confidence* with which Christians follow the risen Jesus in the power of his Spirit. Barth identifies this practical significance throughout §64.4. Three of these references are of special interest, because they appear at key turning points in Barth's argument.

First, at the conclusion of his development of the Trinitarian grammar of Christ's arising, Barth explains why it is necessary for him to press on to the ground of this event in God himself. It is necessary because otherwise we will likely treat this event as a myth rather than as the very pragmatics of God.

> We have now to ask concerning God in the light of this holiness and this particular history. Why is this? Because it might well be the case that, for all the pains we have taken to understand it, we are not really taking it as seriously as it has to be taken, but allowing it only to soar away from us as a kind of (logically and aesthetically, perhaps,

---

188. In contrast to chapters 2 and 4, it is not necessary here to leave the boundaries of the transitional subsection under investigation in order to develop the practical significance of the Trinitarian theology of Christ's resurrection. This is because Barth spells out this significance with such clarity and detail, especially toward the end of §64.4. However, the decision to stay within the confines of §64.4 does not imply that the significance of Barth's doctrine of Christ's resurrection is not detectable throughout the remainder of IV/2. To cite just two examples: (1) the doctrine of sin as sloth (§65) is developed in its contrast with the living Son of Man and draws explicitly on the concept of direction, and (2) the doctrine of sanctification (§66) relies heavily on the understanding of the Christian's concrete partnership with and participation in the risen Christ developed in §64.4.

very impressive) myth, if we do not realise that its pragmatics are the pragmatics of God, that in it we have to do with Him, with the First and Last in every human life, with the One who cannot be mocked because He is source and sum of all power as well as pity, with the One whom none can escape because He encloses us on all sides, and we all, unasked and whether we know and like it or not, derive from Him and return to Him.[189]

In this passage, Barth indicates that the seriousness of our practice as disciples of Jesus Christ in the power of the Holy Spirit depends on understanding that the triune God is at work in this transitional event. Therefore, Barth's Trinitarian theology of Christ's arising is intended not solely as a theoretical explanation of the ontological basis of our practice, but as a witness to *God's practice*. This divine praxis has its inward and outward aspects, but it is praxis all the way down. The precedence of the divine praxis means that we may practically participate in it with confidence.

Second, at the conclusion of his discussion of the eternal mediation of the Spirit, Barth draws the practical conclusion that, since the triune God is in himself history-in-partnership, our history-in-partnership with the risen Christ in the power of the Spirit is our participation in God himself:

> As He does not withhold Himself from us but reveals Himself as our Partner and acts as such, ... He is primarily true to Himself, revealing Himself as the One He is in Himself, as Father, Son and Spirit, in expression and application and exercise of the love in which He is God. Thus we for our part, as history in partnership is the portion which is allotted us in His free grace, genuinely exist in participation in Himself, in His triune life, and in the problem of this life, and its answer and solution.[190]

Because our partnership with him is our participation in him, we can walk with confidence: "Receiving the Holy Spirit, giving Him our trust and obedience, we are taken under His protection. We do not need to walk uncertainly. We stand and walk on a rock. Neither in heaven nor on earth can we expect any deeper comfort or higher direction. We can only cling to the fact that by the Holy Spirit we may be and live with God Himself. We may do so only of

---

189. *CD* IV/2, 335.
190. *CD* IV/2, 346.

grace. But we may do so without reserve, because in His Spirit God Himself is present."[191]

Third, at the conclusion of his discussion of the eternal majesty of the Son, Barth highlights the assurance that follows from the deity of the Holy Spirit. The Spirit's work among us is trustworthy and true because he bears witness to the truth of God himself: "He awakens true knowledge and faith and confession because, proceeding from the man Jesus exalted at the right hand of God, poured out and given, He is not merely the *gift* of the Father and the Son and therefore of God, but is *Himself God* with the Father and the Son, and therefore the Giver and source of truth, *Creator Spiritus*."[192] As such, the Spirit is "the Creator also of all knowledge of the truth, of all walking and life in it; the Paraclete who really guides the community into all truth."[193] Barth explicitly draws the practical consequence: "That is why the community, when it hears and obeys His witness, cannot go astray, or give itself too willingly or wholeheartedly to His illumination and direction. It receives in Him . . . that which *is*; which is for us because it is primarily *in God Himself*."[194] We may follow the Spirit's direction confidently because the Spirit of the man Jesus is the very Spirit of God. Barth's Trinitarian theology of Christ's arising supports this confidence.

Concreteness

In addition to these periodic comments, Barth takes up the practical significance of his argument as his theme in the final pages of §64.4. To the call for confidence Barth now adds a remarkable *concreteness*. He does so by developing the manner of the Holy Spirit's work by means of the concept of "direction" (*Weisung*). Although this concept is found in the title of §64.4, it does not play a major role prior to this final portion of the argument. The Son's direction up to this point has been developed in terms of the risen Christ's movement to us in the Spirit. Thus the concept of "transition" has been dominant.[195] For Barth, the concept of "direction" primarily denotes the commission and guidance that Jesus Christ is for us and gives to us in the Holy Spirit. The work of the Holy Spirit is not vague, indefinable, and formless. Rather, the Holy Spirit gives a concrete, definable direction to our lives.

---

191. *CD* IV/2, 346–47.
192. *CD* IV/2, 359, original German emphasis restored (*KD* IV/2, 401).
193. *CD* IV/2, 359. Barth is alluding again to John 16.
194. *CD* IV/2, 359, original German emphasis restored (*KD* IV/2, 401).
195. The multivalent term "direction" can carry this sense of movement as well. The risen Christ is on his way. In which direction is he going? To us! But this is not Barth's primary use of the concept.

On what basis does Barth claim that the work of the Holy Spirit is so concretely definable? Barth admits that the deity of the Holy Spirit might lead us to avoid any concrete definition of the Spirit's work: "Since we know that in Him we have to do directly with God Himself, there is a temptation either to avoid an answer to the question put in this way (for who can know or try to say how God works?), or to be satisfied with the veiling, and to that extent evasive, answer which merely indicates the mystery."[196]

Barth's rejoinder to this strategy of avoidance is that it does not "harmonise with the fact that in the Holy Spirit, although we have to do with God, we do not have to do with Him in His direct being in Himself, which might well reduce us to silence or allow us only to stutter and stammer, but with God (directly) in the form of the power and lordship of the man Jesus."[197] Even in his deity, the Spirit proceeds also from the Son. And so the direction he gives to us has concrete and definable features: the features of the man Jesus. "The man Jesus as the exalted and true and new man has definite features and so too have His power and lordship, so too has the transition from Him to us, so too the power of our participation in His exaltation, and therefore so too the operation of the Holy Spirit."[198]

Whereas Barth's argument for confidence appealed to the deity of the Spirit, Barth's argument for concreteness appeals to the Spirit's procession from the human Jesus. The movement from Jesus Christ to us in the Spirit "is an operation from man to man."[199] This statement is not a denial of the deity of Christ or the Spirit, for the operation of the Holy Spirit "is divine because the man from whom it proceeds is the eternal Son of God."[200] But this operation is definitely "also human, and can therefore be defined and more clearly described, because the eternal Son of God who is its origin is a man."[201]

Having justified his inquiry into the concrete definition of the Holy Spirit's operation, Barth introduces the concept of direction. The exalted human Jesus is for us and gives to us *direction*: a concrete commission and orientation for our lives. He does this as a living human being who rose from the dead. As we all know, "one man can be for, and give to, others direction."[202] A wise man can for others "be himself their exemplary wisdom."[203] The human Jesus is our

---

196. *CD* IV/2, 360.
197. *CD* IV/2, 360–61.
198. *CD* IV/2, 361.
199. *CD* IV/2, 361.
200. *CD* IV/2, 361.
201. *CD* IV/2, 361.
202. *CD* IV/2, 361.

exemplary wisdom. But he is not an exemplar merely in the way any historical figure might be. Rather, because he arose from the dead in the power of the Spirit, Jesus Christ is a living subject who is for us and gives to us a divine direction. The concept of direction displays the practical significance of Barth's Trinitarian theology of Christ's arising.

Barth develops the concept of direction under three headings. The direction of the Son given in and by the Spirit is a *placement*, a *correction*, and an *instruction*.[204] Barth develops this threefold direction by means of an exegesis of exhortation passages in the New Testament epistles. It is interesting to note this selection of texts. He has already treated many of the relevant New Testament texts on the Holy Spirit in his previous discussion of the character and identity of the Spirit.[205] So it is fitting that he turns to a fresh set of texts. Nevertheless, his selection is striking, for in these passages the Spirit appears but is certainly not the dominant theme. Instead, these texts speak of concrete ethical issues, setting a clear path for following Jesus in everyday life.[206] It is for this very concreteness that Barth selects these texts as the exegetical explanation and substantiation of the Spirit's directing work. The selection of these texts shows how far Barth emphasizes the *concreteness* of the direction given in and by the Holy Spirit, and so also how supremely practical are the consequences that follow from his Trinitarian theology of Christ's arising.

When taken together, the confidence and concreteness that comprise the practical significance of Barth's Trinitarian theology of Christ's arising show how far Barth has critically assimilated "ontological" and "moral" understandings of the work of both Jesus Christ and the Holy Spirit. Christians are confident in the work of the Spirit among us because in the partnership he creates there is genuine human participation in God. And Christians so participate by following a concrete direction, given in the divine power of the Spirit but concretely characterized by the human life of Jesus. So the present

---

203. *CD* IV/2, 361. This is a pun on *Weisung* ("direction"), which has the same root as *Weise* ("wise").

204. *CD* IV/2, 362. The close relation of these terms to the concept of direction in Barth's original German is nearly impossible to render in English. The *Weisung* of the Son is an *Einweisung*, a *Zurechtweisung*, and an *Unterweisung*. The above translations will suffice for our purposes, but it is at least worth noting the inner connection. In translating *Einweisung* with the spatial term "placement" instead of the more abstract term "indication," I am following Darrell Guder's translation in Eberhard Busch, *The Great Passion: An Introduction to Karl Barth's Theology* (Grand Rapids: Eerdmans, 2004), 232.

205. See "The Holy Spirit" above.

206. The concept of "direction" also plays an important role in Barth's ethics. See Karl Barth, *Church Dogmatics*, Vol. III, Part 4 (Edinburgh: T&T Clark, 1961), 3–31.

activity of Jesus Christ in and by the Holy Spirit is both "ontological" and "moral."

Because Barth starts with Jesus Christ in his resurrection, he is able to critically appropriate the insights of both ontological and moral-influence theories of the atonement. On the one hand, Barth makes bold claims about the Christian's participation in the triune life of God, but does so without rejecting the once-for-all forensic character of Jesus Christ's life of obedience unto death or in any way blurring the Creator-creature distinction. This critical appropriation is made possible by Barth's Trinitarian theology of Christ's arising, according to which participation in God is identical to human partnership with the risen Christ in his self-attestation by the power of the Spirit. Since this participation occurs by means of the *self-revealing* activity of the risen Christ, it acknowledges the finished work of Christ. And since this participation occurs perpetually through the *human* Jesus who rose from the dead, it respects the Creator-creature distinction.[207]

On the other hand, Barth can speak comfortably of the Christian life as following Jesus, being like him, obeying his commands, taking up our crosses, and so on, but does so without reducing Jesus Christ to a mere moral example from the past or undermining Christ's deity.[208] This critical appropriation is made possible by Barth's Trinitarian theology of Christ's arising. Since Jesus Christ directs our lives in the present as the one who is risen in the power of the Spirit, he is a living subject who acts, not a dead figure from whom we draw moral inspiration and instruction. And since the man Jesus is our divine direction only because he is identical with the Son of God, his deity is logically indispensable to his moral influence.[209]

This two-sided critical appropriation displays the assimilative power of Barth's Trinitarian theology of Christ's arising.[210] Although not a sufficient

---

207. Barth's emphasis on this distinction gets the last word in §64.4 (*CD* IV/2, 377).

208. *CD* IV/2, 375. See also Barth's doctrine of sanctification in §66, especially "The Praise of Works" (§66.5) and "The Dignity of the Cross" (§66.6), which works out in detail the basic move made at the end of §64.4. This move confirms Eberhard Busch's thesis that "affirmation and positive reception" determine the later Barth's interaction with pietism, especially in *CD* IV/2, in *Karl Barth and the Pietists: The Young Karl Barth's Critique of Pietism and Its Response* (Downers Grove, IL: InterVarsity, 2004), 298.

209. Bruce Marshall deploys the conceptual distinction between "logically indispensable" and "materially decisive" in *Christology in Conflict: The Identity of a Saviour in Rahner and Barth* (Oxford: Blackwell, 1987).

210. Assimilative power is the third of John Henry Cardinal Newman's seven notes of a true development of doctrine in his classic *An Essay on the Development of Doctrine* (South Bend, IN: University of Notre Dame Press, 1989), 183–89 and 355–82. Although I do not endorse Newman's entire project, this note points to the following truth: that a proposal's capacity to incorporate the insights

reason in itself, such assimilative power corroborates the practical possibilities of Barth's position. By developing this Trinitarian theology of Christ's arising, Barth has offered an account of the *confidence* by which Christians follow the *concrete* direction of Jesus Christ. Such an account includes both ontological and moral categories, because our *participation* in God consists in our *partnership* with the risen Jesus Christ by the power of the Holy Spirit.

In this chapter, I have shown that, for Barth, Jesus Christ not only was raised by God the Father but also arises in the power of the Holy Spirit. In §64.4, Barth identifies the Holy Spirit as the power of Jesus Christ's arising, and argues that this transitional event has its basis in the Spirit-mediated fellowship of the majestic Son with the merciful Father. This pneumatologically focused Trinitarian theology of Easter fits the Christology of IV/2 and serves the purposes of that volume well. I have now placed this pneumatological focus alongside the patrological focus developed in the previous chapter. We have seen how §64.4 complements §59.3 even as it inverts it. However, the dialectical juxtaposition of these two is not Barth's final word on the subject. He goes on in "The Promise of the Spirit" (§69.4) to develop their unity in terms of the teleology of Christ's risen presence. To this third and final transitional discussion we now turn.

---

of other proposals is a vote in its favor. Barth is a truly "catholic" thinker, inasmuch as his theology is both thoroughly committed to its central claims and able to include a vast array of alien claims. For more recent literature on assimilative power, see William A. Christian, *Doctrines of Religious Communities: A Philosophical Study* (New Haven, CT: Yale University Press, 1987), 145–218; and Bruce Marshall, "Absorbing the World: Christianity and the Universe of Truths," in idem, ed., *Theology and Dialogue: Essays in Conversation with George Lindbeck* (South Bend, IN: University of Notre Dame Press, 1990), 69–102.

4

The Promise of the Spirit and the Periochoresis of God

Jesus Christ was raised by God the Father. Jesus Christ arises in the power of the Holy Spirit. Although not mutually exclusive, these two statements stand in tension with each other. The question "Who is the subject of Christ's resurrection?" is not sufficiently answered by the mere dialectical juxtaposition of these two statements, nor do we yet have the full picture of the divine basis of the Easter event. Although Barth believes both to be correct, they are one-sided answers. A synoptic vision is needed. This vision is provided by the third part of the doctrine of reconciliation, *Church Dogmatics* IV/3.

In this chapter, I will show that Barth understands the *unity* of the Easter event in terms of its *teleology*. This teleological unity can be seen from the perspective of Jesus Christ as the one who was, is, and will be *present* with us. Christ was raised for us by God the Father and arises to us by the Holy Spirit in order to be present with us in the promise of the Spirit. The final purpose of Christ's resurrection is his ongoing prophetic mission, in which we participate as free human agents.[1] The many forms of Christ's risen presence are united as this one purposive movement, which in turn is grounded in the triune life of God. Tracing these connections is the burden of this chapter.

I will substantiate this web of claims by analyzing the Trinitarian grammar of Christ's parousia in §69.4, and then by unpacking the Trinitarian ground of this living movement as its comes to expression in §69.2. Once again, we will see that for Barth the grammar and ground of Christ's resurrection is the triune God, but in this context the emphasis will be on the teleological unity of Christ's risen presence. Specifically, Christ's parousia in its threefold structure follows a perichoretic grammar and is grounded in the very life of the triune God,

---

1. Although participation has been a recurring theme throughout this study, the mode of our participation (as missionary witness) comes to the foreground in IV/3.

the God who comes again and again in his perichoretic self-communication and self-impartation. I will set forth the practical significance of this aspect of Barth's Trinitarian theology in a final section. But first, we must understand the Christology operative in these texts, and so I will begin by situating them within the structure of *CD* IV in general and *CD* IV/3 in particular.

The Transition of the Glorious Mediator

"The Promise of the Spirit" (§69.4) is a transitional discussion. Like its parallel subsections, "The Verdict of the Father" (§59.3) in IV/1 and "The Direction of the Son" (§64.4) in IV/2, it supplies the transition from Christology proper to its anthropological/ ecclesial effects and consequences. I have already shown that this transitional function reflects Barth's understanding of Christ's resurrection as his transition from himself in his life history to us in our sphere, and that Barth advances this argument by means of a Trinitarian analysis of Easter. In short, Barth's doctrine of Christ's resurrection is transitional in function and Trinitarian in form.[2] These features apply in IV/3 as well.

However, IV/3 is a different sort of book. It stands in a unique architectonic relationship with the previous two part-volumes, and bears a unique internal structure. These peculiarities yield consequences for the christological claims advanced in IV/3, and also for the doctrine of Christ's resurrection that emerges within its pages. Thus it is necessary to attend to the structural features unique to IV/3 before delving into its contribution to a Trinitarian theology of Easter.

I will explore three such features that are relevant for this study. First is the unique relationship of IV/3 to IV/1–2, which consists in the restatement of dialectically juxtaposed perspectives in terms of their teleological unity. Second is the central role of Christ's resurrection in §69 as a whole, and the consequences of this role for the shape of this study. Third, the Christology of IV/3 uniquely frames the problem of transition in §69.4. These three considerations situate Barth's Trinitarian theology of Christ's risen presence in its proper context.

Teleological Unity: The Relationship between IV/1–2 and IV/3

In "The Promise of the Spirit" (§69.4), Barth does not add a third component of the doctrine of reconciliation alongside those found in §59.3 and §64.4. Rather, he asserts their teleological unity.[3] This approach fits the larger structural

---

2. See ch. 2, "The Transition of the Humiliated Son of God," and ch. 3, "The Transition of the Exalted Son of Man."

relation between IV/1–2 and IV/3. The first two parts describe two complementary perspectives that are the mirror image of one another, whereas the third part redescribes the first two parts from the perspective of their unity. Barth understands this unity in terms of its teleological or eschatological determination. The threefold doctrine of reconciliation is less like three columns and more like an arrow: Barth first looks at the arrow from above (IV/1), then from below (IV/2), and then traces its outward trajectory (IV/3).[4]

What is the christological basis for this unique relationship between IV/1–2 and IV/3? In the first two parts of the doctrine of reconciliation, Barth actualizes, correlates, and dialectically juxtaposes the two "natures" and two "states" of Christ. Christ is both the humiliated Son of God and the exalted Son of Man. The third part of the doctrine of reconciliation narrates the outward movement of this one mediator. Jesus Christ is not only the humiliated Son of God and the exalted Son of Man, but also the Glorious Mediator who goes out to attest his reconciling work.[5]

---

3. The notion that the *unity* of Jesus Christ is the theme of IV/3 should be uncontroversial. See *CD* IV/1, 79, and Karl Barth, *Church Dogmatics*, Vol. IV, Part 3 (Edinburgh: T&T Clark, 1961–2), 38–43, hereafter cited as *CD* IV/3. The language of *teleology* is also prominent in both the survey of the third part of the doctrine of reconciliation in *CD* IV/1 (108) and the main christological section of *CD* IV/3 (59, 168, and 281).

4. This way of describing the relation is aimed against interpretations that reduce IV/3 to a noetic counterpart of IV/1–2. Though it is certainly true that Christ's self-revealing work is on display in IV/3, this must be understood as the eschatological determination of the whole work of reconciliation. Gregory Alan Robertson has successfully argued against these interpretations in his study of IV/3, "'Vivit! Regnat! Triumphat!': The Prophetic Office of Jesus Christ, the Christian Life, and the Mission of the Church in Karl Barth's *Church Dogmatics* IV, 3" (Unpublished Th.D. Thesis, Wycliffe College and the University of Toronto, 2003), esp. 1–17 and 116–134. Although he does not discuss IV/3, my non-reductive reading of Barth's understanding of revelation coheres with Ingolf U. Dalferth's in "Karl Barth's Eschatological Realism," in S. W. Sykes, ed., *Karl Barth: Centenary Essays* (Cambridge: Cambridge University Press, 1989), 14–45.

5. *CD* IV/3, §69.1; cf. also *CD* IV/1, §58. Later in his life, Barth clearly indicated the historical character of his account of the unity of Christ's two natures in a letter to Dr. Setsuro Osaki: "When you allege specifically against me that my reflection on the two natures of Christ implies a static and to that extent ontological thinking on the relation between God and man, I may simply appeal to your reading of *C.D.* and ask whether I really regard speaking about the two *natures* of Christ as legitimate and permissible except in the context of his *history*. (If in your work you had consulted just a little more intently Vol. IV, 3 of *C.D.* with its consideration of the prophetic office of Christ, your suspicion regarding the role of the two natures of Jesus Christ in my books would have cleared up for itself.)" Karl Barth, *Letters: 1961–1968*, ed. Jürgen Fangmeier and Hinrich Stoevestandt (Grand Rapids: Eerdmans, 1981), 239–40.

The content of this outward movement is self-declaration. Therefore, Barth speaks of it in terms of Christ's *prophetic office*.[6] As we have seen, Christ's movement of self-attestation is the theme of all the transitional discussions of IV/1–3. So, in a certain sense, the relationship between IV/1–2 and IV/3 is structurally similar to the relationship between the christological subsections and their corresponding transitional discussions. Under the rubric of the prophetic office, IV/3 takes up the revelation of reconciliation and treats it as a locus of Christology proper.

What does this location of IV/3 mean for Barth's Trinitarian theology of Christ's resurrection? In the transitional subsection of IV/3 (§69.4), Barth asserts the unity of the previous two perspectives. In §59.3, Barth asserted that God the Father graciously raised Jesus Christ in the freedom of the Holy Spirit. Jesus Christ, the humiliated Son of God, participates in this act as the one who receives, and only secondarily and on this basis is he the active subject who arises to reveal himself in the authority of the Spirit. Accordingly, his resurrection is the historical fulfillment of the eternal movement of grace and receptivity in the triune God himself. In other words, the generation of the Son is the basis of the Easter verdict of the Father.

In §64.4, Barth asserted that Jesus Christ, the exalted Son of Man, himself arises to reveal his ontological connection with us. He does so by the power of the Holy Spirit, who is both the Spirit of Christ and the Spirit of God. In this directive fellowship, the Spirit corresponds to himself as the Spirit of the Father and the Son, that is, God as the mediator of the eternal fellowship of the majestic Son with his merciful Father. In other words, the procession of the Spirit is the basis of the Easter direction of the Son.

In §69.4, Barth asserts the teleological unity of these two aspects of Easter. The glorious mediator Jesus Christ reveals himself in his presence as the living reconciler between God and humanity. This revelatory mediation is initiated by the new act of God the Father at Easter: the raising of Jesus Christ. But the effective presence, or parousia, of the risen Christ is not a moment but a

---

6. There is a tradition that interprets Barth's doctrine of Christ's prophetic office as determined and/or over-determined by Barth's engagement with the epistemological problematic of modern theology, e.g., Karin Bornkamm, "Die reformatorische Lehre vom Amt Christ und ihre Umformung durch Karl Barth," in *Zur Theologie Karl Barths*, ed. Eberhard Jüngel; *Zeitschrift für Theologie und Kirche*, Beiheft 6 (1986), 1–32. Gregory Robertson has argued successfully against Bornkamm's criticisms in "Vivit! Regnat! Triumphat!" 120–34. However, Robertson tends to underemphasize the extent to which Barth thoroughly revises the doctrine of Christ's prophetic office to address the problem of Christian mission under the conditions of modernity. For a recent positive assessment of IV/3 read along these lines, see Annelore Siller, *Kirche für die Welt: Karl Barths Lehre vom prophetischen Amt Jesu Christi in ihrer Bedeutung für das Verhältnis von Kirche und Welt unter den Bedingungen der Moderne* (Zürich: TVZ, 2009).

movement. The risen Christ is on his way *from* his being raised by God the Father *to* his final coming again in glory *through* his intermediary presence with us in the promise of the Spirit. These three forms of the parousia of Jesus Christ are one as the Father, Son, and Spirit are one, that is, perichoretically. Each form retains its particularity as it fully indwells the other two. This Trinitarian grammar of Christ's risen presence points to its Trinitarian ground: God is in himself a living, self-declarative movement. In other words, the purposive perichoresis of God is the basis of the Easter promise of the Spirit.

Observing the structural relationship between IV/1–2 and IV/3 helps to set aright one's expectations concerning the Trinitarian grammar of §69.4. If one took the Trinitarian titles of the transitional subsections as the sole clue to their content, then one would expect the Holy Spirit to come to the foreground in §69.4 as the subject of Christ's resurrection.[7] Now the Holy Spirit does move to the foreground at the end of this subsection, though primarily as the mode of Jesus Christ's act and only within this horizon as an agent of his own activity. Throughout §69.4, Jesus Christ stands at the center as the acting subject of his risen presence. If this were the only place Barth spoke of the Spirit, this would be devastating for constructing a fully Trinitarian theology of Christ's resurrection. But, as we have already seen, the Holy Spirit appears in all three discussions. The pneumatological dimension of Christ's resurrection is developed in each according to the Christology governing the part-volume in which it appears.[8]

More importantly, we saw that the Holy Spirit emerged as the "true theme" of §64.4.[9] This was surprising in light of its title: "The Direction of the Son." But in light of the Christology of IV/2, that is, the exaltation of the Son of Man, an emphasis on the Spirit fits. Just as the humiliated Son of God stands in need of the gracious verdict of the Father to raise him from the dead, so the exalted Son of Man relies on the power of the Spirit to arise to his fellow human beings. So, despite its title, the unique contribution of "The Promise of the Spirit" is not the inclusion of the Spirit. Rather, §69.4 develops the teleological unity of

---

7. Both Robert Jenson and Eugene Rogers seem to assume as much in their critiques of §69.4. Rogers identifies this subsection as an example of the eclipse of the Spirit in Barth, "Eclipse of the Spirit in Karl Barth," in *Conversing with Barth*, ed. John C. McDowell and Mike Higton (Hampshire: Ashgate, 2004), 174. Jenson also identifies this subsection as an instance of Barth's binitarianism, "You Wonder Where the Spirit Went," *Pro Ecclesia* 2:3 (1993): 298. Both consider it a problem that Barth begins by speaking of Christ's resurrection and then takes so long to get to the Spirit. Although their criticisms of Barth's pneumatology in general are not to be ignored, this particular criticism misses the mark inasmuch as it does not attend to the context of §69.4.

8. See ch. 2, "The Holy Spirit"; ch. 3, "The Holy Spirit."

9. *CD* IV/2, 339.

the manifold forms of Christ's risen presence. It contributes to the Trinitarian grammar of Christ's resurrection by asserting that the one who was raised by the Father and the one who arises to us in the Spirit are one and the same: Jesus Christ, the one mediator between God and humanity, who was and is and will be present with us.

HE LIVES: THE ROLE OF CHRIST'S RESURRECTION IN §69

The unique relationship between IV/1–2 and IV/3 affects the internal structure of IV/3 itself, especially the main christological section (§69). As we have seen, IV/3 relates to IV/1–2 in much the same way as the transitional discussions relate to their preceding christological subsections. Therefore, the whole of §69 is, in a certain sense, a transitional discussion. It is fitting, then, that Barth refers to Christ's resurrection throughout §69, and especially in §69.2, which opens "with the statement that He, Jesus Christ, lives."[10] This statement is simply another way of saying that "He, this One, has risen from the dead, and in so doing shown Himself to be who He is."[11] Whereas in §59 and §64 the primary discussions of Christ's resurrection appear at the end, in §69 Christ's resurrection appears at the beginning and permeates the whole.

The prominence of Christ's resurrection throughout §69 is a result of Barth's correlation of the prophetic office of Christ with his resurrection.[12] This correlation marks a significant break from the traditional doctrine of the prophetic office, which is typically correlated with the teaching ministry of Jesus.[13] Barth's revision of Christ's prophetic office in terms of his resurrection

---

10. *CD* IV/3, 39.

11. *CD* IV/3, 44. Christ's resurrection proceeds to permeate the rest of §69.2, so that, for instance, the existence of secular parables "derives from His resurrection" (*CD* IV/3, 116). Christ's resurrection is presupposed and periodically referenced throughout §69.3 (See *CD* IV/3, 169, 184, 186, 233, 249).

12. *CD* IV/3, 48ff.

13. I consider this break an advance. The typical correlation of Christ's prophetic office with his teaching ministry functions either to close off prophecy for the present or to construct the relation between Christ and Christians along the lines of moral influence. For an instance of the former, see John Calvin, *Institutes*, II.XV.1–2. For an instance of the latter, see Albrecht Ritschl, *The Christian Doctrine of Justification and Reconciliation*, Vol. III (Edinburgh: T&T Clark, 1900), 417–452; and "Instruction in the Christian Religion," in idem, *Three Essays* (Philadelphia: Fortress Press, 1972), 232–40. In fact, Barth thinks the weaknesses of the former led to the ascendancy of the latter. According to Barth's reading of the history, the lack of a coherent account of the relationship of the prophetic office to the priestly and royal offices opened the door to a reactionary emphasis on the prophetic office and the consequent reduction of Christ's work to his function as moral teacher. Barth's revised doctrine of the prophetic office of Christ is aimed at overcoming this modern reduction without reverting to the problems of earlier formulations. See *CD* IV/1, 108–9; *CD* IV/3, 14–18. Barth overcomes the weakness of both older

must be kept in mind when addressing the Trinitarian grammar and ground of Christ's resurrection as it comes to expression in §69.

The most significant consequence of this revision for this study concerns the selection of materials for examination in this chapter. Materials relevant to the development of a Trinitarian doctrine of Christ's resurrection appear outside the boundaries of the final transitional subsection (§69.4). This subsection will provide ample material for a third perspective on the Trinitarian grammar of Christ's resurrection.[14] But to plumb the depths of the Trinitarian ground of Easter, we must turn to the main christological argument of §69.2.[15] Although this bursting of the boundaries disrupts the parallelism of this study, it is necessary in view of the unique place of IV/3.

The role of Christ's resurrection throughout §69 has one further consequence: it seems to render superfluous a concluding transitional subsection. Why is a discussion of the transitional function of Christ's resurrection necessary when the self-revealing life of the risen Jesus Christ has already been narrated? To answer this question, I will discuss how the Christology of IV/3 uniquely frames the problem of transition in §69.4.

THE PROPHET'S REACH: THE PROBLEM OF TRANSITION IN §69.4

In general, the transitional discussions of IV/1–3 deal with the problem of how and why Jesus Christ moves to us. This is Barth's way of addressing the modern problem of faith and history, his appropriation of Lessing's problem of the "ugly ditch."[16] The problem of transition is especially acute in IV/1–2, where the main christological sections culminate in Christ's death. But the main christological section of IV/3 begins with and is permeated by the resurrection of Jesus Christ. So the problem of transition must be reframed in this light.

Put briefly, the problem of transition in §69.4 is the reach and relevance of the prophecy of Jesus Christ.[17] How do we get from Jesus Christ in his

---

and more recent formulations by correlating the prophetic history of Jesus Christ with his living, risen presence. The result of this correlation is that the primary mode of Christian participation in Christ's work is prophetic, i.e., free active sharing in Christ's self-proclamation of the reconciliation accomplished in him. This correlation does not rule out the prophetic character of Christ's life and death, as Barth takes pains to show in §69.2–3. Nor does it suppress the teaching ministry of Jesus, which Barth has already discussed under the rubric of Christ's royal office (§64.3). Understood within the context of the structure of IV/1–3 as a whole, this revision is one of the major dogmatic contributions of Barth's doctrine of reconciliation.

14. See " The Trinitarian Grammar of Christ's Parousia (§69.4)" below.
15. See " The Trinitarian Ground of Christ's Parousia (§64.2)" below.
16. *CD* IV/3, 286. Although he mentions him by name only once, Lessing's language permeates Barth's discussion of the problem, e.g., "there yawns a deep cleft" (277) and an "unbridgeable gulf" (283).

objective self-revelation to our participation in the living history of his self-witness? Throughout §69.2–3, Barth attributes a revelatory character to Christ's objective history. Jesus Christ lives, and so reveals himself and his reconciling work. In the first instance, revelation is the radiance of his own history before any mention of human reception. Yet Barth repeatedly insists that human participation is not excluded but included in this history. Prior to §69.4, however, he has only indicated this inclusion. In this transitional subsection, Barth explores *how* and *why* this inclusion takes place.[18]

Our inclusion in Jesus Christ's living self-attestation takes place by means of the temporal extension of his parousia. He does not attest himself without us, but is present with us as he is on his way toward his end. Jesus Christ thus wills that his parousia (his new coming in effective presence) take on three distinct but inseparable forms. The primal and basic form of his presence is the Easter event itself. The final and definitive form is his return as the goal of history. The form between these two is the outpouring of the Holy Spirit on the community for the sake of its mission.[19] The parousia of Jesus Christ is thus "one continuous event" that "takes place in different forms."[20]

As the answer to the problem of transition, Barth's doctrine of the threefold parousia supplies the governing structure of §69.4. Yet he does not discuss the three forms sequentially. Since the problem of transition in §69.4 is our participation in the living Christ's self-witness, Barth focuses on the intermediate form of the parousia. Per his common pattern of thought, he treats his focal point last, moving around it like a spiral to place it in context. Barth first discusses Easter in its relation to the final consummation in order to carve

---

17. *CD* IV/3, 323: "our concern is with the basic problem of the reach or relevance of His prophecy for the world reconciled to God in Him."

18. Interestingly, Barth explores the possibility that the question of transition has already been answered. Barth's "basic answer" is that "Jesus Christ is not without His own" (*CD* IV/3, 278). His personal being-in-act is inclusive (279). Barth adds the specific answer concerning the prophetic determination of reconciliation: the work of Christ has the dynamic and teleological character of movement beyond itself into our sphere (280–81). His work is determined intrinsically, to be known extrinsically. But Barth concludes that these twin answers are insufficient on their own. Without reference to the living Jesus Christ risen from the dead, they are bare assertions about his inclusive and teleological character. As Barth puts it, "His work . . . without . . . this event [of resurrection] would have remained shut up in Him" (283). One cannot merely say that the history of Jesus includes us without exploring *how* and *on what basis* it is inclusive. This basis is the Easter event in all its multiform perfection. The transition is not based on a bare assertion of an immediate connection between Jesus and our human sphere, but on the event, the happening, of the living Christ's own transition to us.

19. *CD* IV/3, 293.

20. *CD* IV/3, 293.

out the time in which the intermediate form takes place. Thus the impartation of the Spirit can only be understood in its proper place as the form of Christ's parousia *between* his first and final forms.[21]

What is of particular interest for this study is the Trinitarian grammar of Barth's doctrine of the threefold parousia. The threefold parousia is the answer to the problem of transition in §69.4, and the Trinitarian form of this doctrine serves its transitional function. Now that I have summarized the basic content of this transitional argument, it is now time to attend to the details of its Trinitarian form.

21. The structure of Barth's argument in this subsection parallels the development of the threefold parousia in the *Church Dogmatics*. IV/3 is the first place where Barth makes explicit use of this conceptual framework. Yet the preceding steps toward its deployment can be detected earlier. First, Barth outlines a radically eschatological understanding of Easter in I/2. There, Barth makes the bold claim that "the Easter story . . . actually speaks of a present without any future, of an eternal presence of God in time" (*CD* I/2, 144). Although this appears to disallow any further forms, Barth does not recant this bold statement. Rather, he consistently develops the notion of the threefold parousia as three *forms* of this one event, not as additional future events. Furthermore, at this early stage Barth already notes the connection between Easter and Pentecost, referring to the latter as "the sequel to Easter" (*CD* I/2, 114). The threefold parousia is certainly a new framework for Barth in IV/3, bringing a greater teleological emphasis that befits his mature theology, but it is developed along lines previously laid out. The next step in Barth's development is the twofold parousia found in IV/1. Here he speaks of "the message of [Jesus Christ's] first parousia which, as such, is aimed and pointed at His second, His relation to all those whom it concerns, to all those whom He judged in His death" (*CD* IV/1, 726). Here, Easter remains the definitive first form of the parousia, yet the final judgment is added as "the second and final parousia of Jesus Christ" (*CD* IV/1, 727). Does Barth's discussion of the twofold parousia contradict his earlier statement that Easter is an event without any future? Although it is certainly a significant development, the main line of emphasis remains intact, for he still speaks of Easter as the definitive event: "The first parousia of Jesus Christ might immediately have been His last" (*CD* IV/1, 734). Barth goes on to say that although it could have happened this way, it actually did not, and that the one Easter event opens up into "an Easter history in an Easter time" (*CD* IV/1, 734). Thus Easter remains an event without any *external* future, though it contains within itself an unfolding eschatological history. But how does Barth go from a twofold parousia in IV/1 to a threefold parousia in IV/3? Is this not a contradictory development? It would be if Barth's presentation were linear in structure. If Barth had simply shifted from speaking of the first and second forms of the parousia to the first, second, and third, the conceptual framework would have undergone a massive change. But Barth does not make this shift. Rather, he speaks of the first, last, and *middle* form. Thus the two poles of the parousia established in IV/1 stand firm in IV/3. Strictly speaking, Barth is not adding another form so much as exploring the middle time between the first and last forms. So there is significant development in Barth's doctrine of Christ's parousia, but it moves along a consistent trajectory. This foray into Barth's development illumines the counterintuitive structure of his argument in IV/3. Barth does not set out the three forms of the parousia as some kind of eschatological roadmap. On the contrary, his eye is focused on the outpouring of the Spirit as the transition from Jesus' sphere to ours. But in order to get there, he must clarify the temporal field in which this outpouring takes place. Hence Barth starts with the first form, moves to the final form, and then concludes with the middle form.

The Trinitarian Grammar of Christ's Parousia (§69.4)

My central claim in this section is that, for Barth, the three forms of Christ's risen presence are united in a manner analogous to the perichoretic unity of the triune God. Once again, the doctrine of the Trinity supplies the grammar for the doctrine of Christ's resurrection. Barth asserts this early in §69.4:

> If we allow the New Testament to say what it has to say, we shall be led in this matter to a thinking which is differentiated even in its incontestable unity, formally corresponding to that which is required for an understanding of the three modes of being of God in relation to His one essence in triunity.[22]
>
> When we treat the unity of the three forms or stages of the one event of the return of Jesus Christ, it is perhaps worth considering and exegetically helpful, again in analogy to the doctrine of the Trinity, to think of their mutual relationship as a kind of perichoresis. . . . It is not merely that these three forms are interconnected in the totality of the action presented in them all, or in each of them in its unity and totality, but that they are mutually related as the forms of this one action by the fact that each of them also contains the other two by way of anticipation and recapitulation, so that, without losing their individuality or destroying that of the others, they participate and are active and revealed in them.[23]

Although it appears early in his argument, this Trinitarian grammar is not a preconceived superstructure into which Barth presses the presence of Christ. Rather, it is controlled by the subject matter of the risen Christ himself. Therefore, I will structure this discussion according to Barth's appropriation of the various forms of Christ's presence to particular persons of the Trinity. Barth begins with Jesus Christ, who as true God and true human is the subject of all three forms of his risen presence. In order to underscore the radical character of Easter as the first form of the parousia, Barth then also speaks of God (the Father) as the one who raised Jesus Christ. Barth concludes with a lengthy discussion of the Holy Spirit as the mode of Christ's intermediate form of presence. Although this pattern of appropriating past event to God (the Father) and present event to the Holy Spirit is familiar from previous transitional discussions, the unique

---

22. *CD* IV/3, 294.
23. *CD* IV/3, 296.

contribution of this material is Barth's assertion of the mutual interpenetration of these forms of the one event of Jesus Christ's coming again.

Once we have this concrete Trinitarian grammar before us, we will be in a position to understand the purposive character of Barth's perichoretic analogy. The perichoretic unity of the forms of Christ's parousia is a unity of *purpose*. Christ's purpose in extending his presence along this temporal trajectory is to gather to himself fellow witnesses along his way. The perichoretic analogy is not just a clever comparison but bears witness to the living Jesus Christ in his unity as the one who is on his way. This conclusion will set the stage for an investigation of the Trinitarian ground of Christ's resurrection in the following section.

THE THREEFOLD PAROUSIA OF JESUS CHRIST

Jesus Christ is the active subject of his risen presence in all its forms. That is the central assertion of §69.4. If the basic problem of §69.4 is the reach and relevance of the prophecy of Jesus Christ, its basic theme is the parousia of Christ. Throughout this study I have followed Bertrold Klappert in maintaining that the respective themes of Barth's three transitional discussions are the *Auferweckung* (§59.3), the *Auferstehung* (§64.4), and the *Parusie* (§69.4) of Jesus Christ.[24] Although only the first two terms can be properly translated "resurrection," Barth defines the third in terms of the resurrection of Christ. In fact, the starting point of §69.4 is the simple yet profound insight that Easter is the first "coming again" of Jesus Christ.

According to Barth, strictly speaking there is no "delay" of the parousia, for Jesus Christ has come again in his resurrection from the dead. Of course, there is a delay in a certain sense, but Barth treats it as internal to the logic of Christ's risen presence. The perfection of his presence is manifest in its pluriformity. The temporal extension of Jesus Christ's parousia into its first, final, and intermediate forms is not an accidental delay in its completion, but an ordained outworking of the teleology of his presence. The purpose of his presence is the inclusion of free human subjects as coworkers in the harvest of witnesses to the reconciliation fulfilled in him. So the "delay" of the parousia is not a problem, but befits the very purpose of his coming again.

---

24. Berthold Klappert, "Die Rechts-, Freiheits- und Befreiungsgechichte Gottes mit dem Menschen: Karl Barths Versöhnungslehre (KD IV/1–3)," *Evangelische Theologie* 49:5 (1989): 460–78. Barth continues to use both *raising* and *arising* in §69.4, but now alternates between them in keeping with the Christology of IV/3. See, e.g., Karl Barth, *Die Kirchliche Dogmatik*, Band IV, 3 (Zürich: Theologischer Verlag Zürich, 1980), 324, hereafter cited as *KD* IV/3.

The relevant observation for this study is that Barth appropriates this entire threefold purposive movement to Jesus Christ. The risen Christ is the active subject of his presence in its first, final, and intermediate forms. This fits Barth's definition of parousia: "His new coming and therefore His manifestation in effective presence to the world."[25] This new coming is "His arising from the hosts of the dead."[26] It is "his act."[27] Christ is the subject of his parousia. *He* is present. He is the subject of the act of his presence. This subjectivity of Christ applies equally to all three forms of his parousia: "It is the one thing taking place in different ways, in a difference of form corresponding to the willing and fulfillment of the action of its one Subject, the living Jesus Christ. Always and in all three forms it is a matter of the fresh coming of the One who came before. Always and in different ways it is a matter of the coming again of Jesus Christ."[28]

Barth's identification of Jesus Christ as the acting subject of his parousia serves his transitional argument in §69.4. If Jesus Christ is not the active subject of his parousia, then it would not be *his* parousia, and so the problem of transition would remain unanswered. The scope of Christ's prophecy would not be adequately developed by an appeal to something or someone other than Jesus Christ in his own movement. Of course, Barth asserts the subjectivity of the risen Jesus Christ in the previous transitional discussions as well. But in those contexts it is developed primarily in relationship to either God the Father (§59.3) or the Holy Spirit (§64.4). In §69.4, the subjectivity of Jesus Christ is especially emphasized, because Barth is intent on this transition not being effected by the church or the individual Christian, but by Christ himself.[29]

These alternative bases of transition are especially tempting in this context, because Barth is equally intent that the church and Christians are included in this missionary movement as Christ's fellow witnesses. What makes this partnership genuine is that Christ himself is the firstborn from the dead, his brothers and sisters following after him in a differentiated fellowship of missionary action.[30] The power of this partnership is the Holy Spirit, who

---

25. *CD* IV/3, 293.
26. *CD* IV/3, 297.
27. *CD* IV/3, 303.
28. *CD* IV/3, 293.
29. *CD* IV/3, 349: "There can be no question of Jesus Christ being even temporarily directed in his absence to let Himself be represented by an honoured Christianity and the holy Church. . . . He cannot be replaced by Christianity."
30. Adam Neder rightly highlights the phrase "differentiated fellowship of action" as a description of human participation in the living Jesus Christ in *Participation in Christ: An Entry into Karl Barth's Church*

promises and is promised. This intermediate form of Christ's presence is not inferior to his first or final forms. Ours is not a time of Christ's absence during which the Spirit "fills in." It is Jesus Christ himself, true God and true man, who was present during the forty days and will be present as judge and redeemer at the end, who is present now by his Spirit.

Confidence in this presence is the import of the transitional discussion in §69.4. The Trinitarian grammar operative in this context serves to support this argument. Consequently, the perichoretic analogy is in the first instance a strictly formal grammar used to describe the mutual interrelation of the three forms of Christ's active presence. Barth speaks of an "analogy to the doctrine of the Trinity" and of a "kind of perichoresis."[31] This Trinitarian grammar helps to understand how the three forms of Christ's presence are "mutually related as the forms of this one action by the fact that each of them also contains the other two by way of anticipation and recapitulation, so that, without losing their individuality or destroying that of the others, they participate and are active and revealed in them."[32] The perichoresis of the forms of Christ's parousia is, in the first instance, simply a way of underscoring that the one and the same Jesus Christ is the acting subject of the many forms of his presence.

However, the initial formality of this analogy does not rule out a material development of the Trinitarian structure of Christ's risen presence. The subjectivity of Jesus Christ in his parousia includes the participation of God the Father and the Holy Spirit. Just as the appropriation to God the Father of the raising of Jesus Christ does not exclude the participation of the Son and the Spirit (§59.3), and just as the appropriation to the Holy Spirit of Jesus Christ's arising to us does not point away from, but rather to, the fellowship of the Son with the Father (§64.4), so also the appropriation of the threefold parousia to the risen Jesus Christ does not exclude but includes the act of God the Father and the Holy Spirit (§64.4). I will address each in turn, making sure to show where and why they appear in the context of Barth's transitional argument.

GOD THE FATHER AND THE PRIMAL FORM OF CHRIST'S PAROUSIA

The identification of Jesus Christ, true God and true human, as the acting subject of his presence does not exclude the role of God the Father. In §69.4, Barth attributes Christ's resurrection to God the Father in two crucial contexts. In both contexts, the attribution is implicit. God the Father as the subject of

---

Dogmatics (Louisville, KY: Westminster John Knox, 2009), 79. This phrase comes from §71.3 (*CD* IV/3, 598). I have added the adjective "missionary" to more emphatically identify the content of this action.

31. *CD* IV/3, 296.
32. *CD* IV/3, 296.

Christ's resurrection never becomes a major theme in this material. Instead, the appropriation to God the Father performs a primarily critical function, advancing Barth's transitional argument by disrupting easy answers to, and accentuating the difficulties of, the problem of transition. These implicit appropriations are important for this study insofar as they highlight the material Trinitarian structure of Barth's doctrine of Christ's parousia.

It must be emphasized that these appropriations are *implicit*. Barth speaks generically of "God" in these portions of his argument. In many cases, the term "God" in Barth's theology refers to the triune God: Father, Son, and Holy Spirit. However, sometimes "God" stands in implicitly for the Father. Context is determinative to know which is being used. There are two contextual clues for Barth's implicit reference to the Father in §69.4. The first is the terminological switch from arising (*Auferstehen*) to raising (*Erweckung*). As we saw in chapter two, Barth identifies God the Father as the acting subject of the raising of Jesus Christ, and there is no evidence to suggest that Barth has abandoned this claim. The second contextual clue is the recapitulation of arguments and themes from "The Verdict of the Father" (§59.3). For instance, Barth speaks of the raising of Christ as an exclusively divine act, a claim that in §59.3 is advanced by means of the appropriation to God the Father. So there is sufficient evidence in these passages that Barth is referencing the activity of God the Father in his relation to the Son, Jesus Christ.

(1) The first implicit reference to God the Father appears in the context of Barth's initial christological answers to the question of transition. In this context, the appropriation of Christ's resurrection to God the Father functions to disrupt an "easy" answer to the problem of transition. In order to see how it does so, I will first summarize Barth's initial christological answers.

Barth asserts two christological answers to the question of transition: one general, one specific. Generally, "Jesus Christ is not without his own."[33] As such, he is on the move from himself to the world with us. Specifically, the prophetic determination of his reconciling being and act includes his "moving out"[34] so that we may share in his self-declaration. This moving out is the purpose and result of Christ's resurrection: "it is the reference to the living Jesus Christ risen from the dead which makes it possible and necessary for us to give this particular answer to our question. The particular event of His resurrection is thus the primal and basic form of His glory, of the outgoing and shining of His light, of

---

33. *CD* IV/3, 278.
34. *CD* IV/3, 280.

His expression ... of His prophetic work."[35] This line of thought is essentially a recapitulation of §69.2.

After making these two christological assertions as his initial answer to the problem of transition, Barth reflects on their Easter basis. "They are statements of Easter knowledge on the basis of His Easter revelation."[36] Barth identifies three implications of the Easter basis of these christological assertions. First, "while the two christological assertions with which we started ... are correct in themselves, they are not adequate as a positive answer ... to our question."[37] He goes on to put the point even more strongly: "No Christology can reproduce either the Easter event ... nor [Jesus Christ] Himself as the living One who attests Himself."[38] Restating christological truths will not in itself cross the ugly ditch between history and faith.

This limiting implication leads into Barth's second point, that "we can never cease to be astonished" by the event of Easter and its transitional function, because "it was the event of a new and special act of God."[39] Barth here reiterates the argument of §59.3: Easter was not one more act in a series of acts performed by Jesus Christ, but first and foremost an act performed on Christ by God (the Father). Barth switches to the term *Erweckung* to describe this act.[40] His verbs are rendered past and passive, reminiscent of the grammar of §59.3. The passive voice implies that another raised him: namely, God the Father. "We count upon this special act of God ... when we answer positively the question of this transition."[41] Barth goes on in his third point to highlight the confidence in Christ's transition that follows from it being based on "God's own act."[42]

Although Barth is recapitulating an argument from §59.3, it performs a function unique to this context. Because explicit reference to the risen Christ already looms large in the preceding christological subsections,[43] Barth must overcome the temptation to take for granted Christ's transition and so move too easily to the remaining topics of IV/3. Reference to the new and special act of God (the Father) in the Easter event disrupts any such "easy" answer. "Unless we hear the Halt which is here required of us, there can be no Forward."[44] So,

---

35. *CD* IV/3, 281.
36. *CD* IV/3, 284.
37. *CD* IV/3, 285.
38. *CD* IV/3, 286.
39. *CD* IV/3, 287.
40. *KD* IV/3, 331 and 333.
41. *CD* IV/3, 287.
42. *CD* IV/3, 288.
43. See above, "He Lives: The Role of Christ's Resurrection in §69."

the appropriation to God (the Father) of the raising of Jesus Christ, though brief and implicit, performs a critical function in setting up the transitional argument of §69.4.

(2) The second implicit reference to God the Father appears in the context of Barth's discussion of the distinctive features of the "resurrection of Jesus Christ as the commencement of His new coming as the one who came before."[45] This discussion of the primal form of the risen Christ's presence serves Barth's overall argument by setting up the question to which the intermediate form (that is, the promise of the Spirit) is the answer. In the context of this discussion, the appropriation to God the Father functions to underscore the radicality of the primal form of Christ's presence, and thus the seriousness of the problem it poses for us.

What does it mean that Easter is the primal form of the risen Christ's presence? Barth identifies three features of Easter as the primal form of the parousia, each of which points to an aspect of the problem of our present existence. The three features are (1) its *once-for-all*, irrevocable actuality as the self-declaration of Jesus Christ; (2) the *unrestricted* determination of the world and humanity that takes place in it; and (3) its absolute *newness*, that is, its eschatological character. The three aspects of the problem of transition raised by these features are (1´) the *distance* between the "once" of Jesus Christ and the "for all" of our sphere; (2´) the *invisibility* of the Easter determination; and (3´) the *delay* of the final consummation of the new creation present in the risen Christ.[46]

In his discussion of the first and third features, Barth implicitly refers to the act of God the Father in raising Jesus Christ. Again, Barth picks up language from §59.3 to advance an argument unique to the context of §69.4. In both instances, the reference to God the Father functions to underscore the radicality of the Easter event.

With regard to the first feature, Barth substantiates the irrevocability of Christ's Easter self-declaration by appealing to the act of God the Father. Barth does not attribute Christ's resurrection exclusively to God the Father. Instead, Barth alternates between the raising and the arising of Jesus Christ, which befits the Christology of IV/3.[47] Barth introduces the irrevocability of Christ's Easter self-declaration in terms of his arising: "In His new coming, in His arising from the hosts of the dead, it took place that the alteration of the situation between

---

44. *CD* IV/3, 287.
45. *CD* IV/3, 296.
46. *CD* IV/3, 296–317.
47. See above, "Teleological Unity: The Relationship between IV/1–2 and IV/3."

God and man accomplished by Him was actualized by taking place immediately and completely in noetic form also as the prophecy of Jesus Christ, by being brought out of concealment and revealed and made known to the world."[48]

After this reference to Christ's arising, Barth immediately switches to speak of God raising Christ. Per his usual grammar, this divine raising is in the perfect tense: God "*has* acted," "*has* acknowledged," "*has* publicly bound," "*has* said in raising (*auferweckte*) Jesus Christ," and "*has* spoken."[49] These implicit references to God the Father's act of raising Jesus Christ underscore the irrevocability of the Easter declaration by describing Easter as a divine "acknowledgement" and "decision" concerning Christ.[50] "In Jesus Christ God has not merely acted as man's Judge and Liberator, restoring and renewing him. In so doing, He has acknowledged this action in the resurrection of Jesus Christ. And this means supremely that He has publicly bound and committed Himself to man."[51] This divine declaration casts out fear: "The resurrection of Jesus Christ is the pronunciation of the great divine Yea and Amen to which God will be as faithful as He is to Himself and after which everything which can and may be expected to follow from Him can consist only in repetitions, developments and confirmations. Hence we need not fear the being and rule of a *Deus absconditus* limiting and even questioning the being and act of God in Jesus Christ."[52] The perfect tense of this divine pronouncement, which fits the grammar of appropriation to God the Father, functions to highlight its irrevocability: "He has spoken in acting. Hence He has spoken unequivocally, once for all and irrevocably."[53] God not only speaks now but also and primarily *has* spoken in his act of raising Jesus Christ from the dead. "As God's particular act the resurrection is the particular Word of the faithfulness of God."[54]

Now it must be acknowledged that Barth quickly switches back to the present and active grammar of Christ's resurrection, and so to the Son's arising.[55] This switching back and forth befits the context of §69.4, in which Barth asserts the unity of Jesus Christ both as the one who was raised and the one who arises. But Barth's brief reference to God (the Father) and the divine acknowledgment and decision made in his raising of Jesus Christ serves

---

48. *CD* IV/3, 297.
49. *CD* IV/3, 297, emphasis added.
50. *CD* IV/3, 297. This language is reminiscent of §59.3 (see ch. 2, "Resurrection as Revelation").
51. *CD* IV/3, 297.
52. *CD* IV/3, 297.
53. *CD* IV/3, 297.
54. *CD* IV/3, 297.
55. Cf. *CD* IV/3, 298–99.

to underscore the radicality of Easter as the primal form of the parousia. Barth concludes that "the new creation has taken place in the resurrection of Jesus Christ."[56] In light of this radical presence of the future in the Easter event, we must take with utter seriousness the problem of the distance between this perfect-tense reality and our present existence.[57] Barth's appropriation to God the Father thus performs a critical function, moving the argument along by accentuating the problem of Christ's intermediate presence. So, although the promise of the Holy Spirit emerges as the final answer to the question of §69.4, Barth does not arrive at this answer without first considering how radical is the Easter event, in which God the Father raised his Son Jesus Christ and thereby irrevocably bound himself to humanity. It is because this first form of Christ's presence is so radical that we must ask after the purpose a further, intermediate form of Christ's presence with us.

Barth identifies two further features of Easter as the primal form of Christ's parousia. Barth presupposes the appropriation to God the Father in his discussion of the second feature: its unrestricted determination of the world and humanity.[58] However, this appropriation does not perform any discernible function. The same cannot be said of the third feature: the strictly eschatological content and character of Easter. In the context of his discussion of this feature, Barth's identification of God the Father as the one who raised Jesus Christ continues to underscore the radicality of Easter and the seriousness of the problem it poses for us.

Barth's basic argument concerning the eschatological character of Easter is that Easter was an eschatological event in the strictest sense of that term, that is, it was an act beyond the capacity of humanity. The new coming of the one who came before was not produced by his first coming, for it followed his death. It was his new coming in the eternal life that comes from God alone. As such, the new coming of the forty days of Easter was an eschatological event: an event in humanity's future made possible by God alone.

Befitting the Christology of IV/3, Barth's discussion of the eschatological character focuses primarily on the active subjectivity of Christ as both true God and true human. He came again and appeared to his disciples as the true human being he was before, but he came also in the mode and manner of God.[59] His

---

56. *CD* IV/3, 300.

57. *CD* IV/3, 300: "The fact that it has done so is to be taken rather more seriously than is often the case in our thinking about Easter or Sunday, or in the normal Christian celebration of Easter or Sunday."

58. The universal calling effected in Christ's resurrection is foundational for Barth's doctrine of vocation, to which I will turn in the fourth section of this chapter ("The Significance of a Trinitarian Theology of Christ's Parousia").

new coming as the one who came before was a divine happening. Therefore, it was an eschatological event: the coming of God as the future of humanity.

To underscore the eschatological content and character of this new coming, Barth speaks not only in terms of the deity of Jesus Christ himself but also of Christ's relationship to God (the Father). The particularity of Christ in his new coming points back to his death: "To say death is to deny any future to the one who existed."[60] This negative, anthropological point can be restated as a positive, theological point: "God alone can be its future."[61] Therefore, "The life of a creature after death cannot in any sense or circumstances be anything other than its life from God and for God, i.e., the life which is not its own but is given to it by God. God alone is above death and after it."[62] The immortal life that comes to Jesus Christ after his death "can be only . . . new life from God and with God."[63] The new coming of Christ in this new life therefore depends on a new act of God performed on Christ. So it should come as no surprise that Barth, alongside his talk of Christ's active subjectivity, speaks of Christ as the passive subject of past-tense verbs, the implicit subject of which is God the Father. He was "made eternal by the omnipotence of the grace of God."[64] He has "been delivered from death, invested with divine glory, caused to shine in this glory, in virtue of [his] participation in the life of God."[65] All this took place "by the initiative, movement and act of God Himself."[66]

All this talk of God's act of giving eternal life to Jesus Christ is not meant to imply that Christ is in some sense made divine by this act. God is triune, not only *to* all eternity, but also *from* all eternity. I will return to this in a further section that concerns the Trinitarian ground of Christ's risen presence. At this point, I only observe that Barth underscores the radically eschatological character of Easter by implicating God the Father as the one who gives eternal life to Jesus Christ. And so the new coming of Jesus Christ in its primal form

---

59. *CD* IV/3, 312. For similar language, cf. *CD* III/2, §47.1.

60. *CD* IV/3, 310.

61. *CD* IV/3, 310.

62. *CD* IV/3, 310. Barth identifies God as the One with whom we must deal in our death. This theme was especially prominent in Barth's *Römerbrief* period and remained so during the production of his dogmatic prolegomena in connection with the doctrine of God the Father (see *CD* I/1, §10.1). As I have shown, in Barth's mature theology God the Father is more consistently spoken of in the context of the resurrection. But the identification of God as the One with whom we must deal in our death remains as the presupposition of the appropriation to God the Father of the raising of Jesus Christ from the dead.

63. *CD* IV/3, 311–12.

64. *CD* IV/3, 312.

65. *CD* IV/3, 312.

66. *CD* IV/3, 316.

was an eschatological event. It "was and is his radically and totally and absolutely new coming."[67] The "absolute newness"[68] of this first form consists in its being an act of God (the Father) beyond all human capacity. As we know from §59.3, this appropriation to God the Father does not rule out the Son's participation. What it does rule out is docetism. Jesus Christ was truly dead, and so his new coming was in the first instance an act of God alone. In other words, it was an eschatological event, the making present of the future.[69]

Barth's purpose in underscoring the radically eschatological character of Easter by appropriating it to God the Father is to highlight the seriousness of the problem it raises. How could the future appear in Jesus Christ without the world coming to its end? How can there be such a "delay" in the completion of Christ's parousia? Why was the primal form of his new coming only its commencement and not also its consummation?[70] This line of questioning sets up precisely the problem addressed by the promise of the Spirit. The temporal extension between the first and final form of Christ's parousia takes place in order to give time to free human beings to participate in Jesus Christ's missionary movement.

These implicit references to God the Father advance Barth's argument by increasing the tension internal to the threefold parousia of Jesus Christ. In other words, the Trinitarian form of Barth's doctrine of Christ's resurrection serves its transitional function. In the context of §69.4, the differentiated unity of the three forms of Christ's risen presence is explicated according to a Trinitarian grammar. God the Father's act of making Christ present on Easter is both differentiated from and points to Christ's intermediate presence in the promise of the Spirit.

The Holy Spirit and the Intermediate Form of Christ's Parousia

My claim in this final portion of this section is that, in the context of his doctrine of the parousia of Jesus Christ, Barth uses both agential and instrumental language to describe the work of the Holy Spirit, and that this grammar befits the structural context of this material. As true God and true human, Jesus Christ

---

67. *CD* IV/3, 309.
68. *CD* IV/3, 308.
69. *CD* IV/3, 316: "The news of the presence of this future, of this to-day of the last and first hour, of the dawn of the redemption and consummation, is the Easter message. And the presence of the future in this event is the new seed of life planted in world-occurrence on Easter Day."
70. *CD* IV/3, 316: "How was it possible that the world's future already made present there in that event should not at once engulf the whole world like a tidal wave, engulfing with its presence all the men of all times and places whose future had become present there in the appearance of the risen Jesus?"

is both the one who promises the Spirit to us and the one who bears the Spirit's promise along with us. I will substantiate this claim by (1) reviewing the spiral-like shape of Barth's argument leading up to his discussion of the Spirit, (2) analyzing the explicitly grammatical moves Barth makes in his discussion of the Spirit, and (3) explaining how this Trinitarian grammar fits the context of Barth's argument.

The immediate upshot of this argument is that Barth's critics are mistaken when they cite §69.4 as an instance of the eclipse of the Spirit in his theology.[71] Perhaps if §69.4 were an independent treatise on the Holy Spirit, such a criticism would be appropriate. But in the context of the Trinitarian grammar of Barth's doctrine of Christ's resurrection, such a criticism is wide of the mark. Beyond this immediate upshot, the claim of this final portion of "The Trinitarian Grammar of Christ's Parousia (§69.4)" advances the argument of this chapter by (a) completing the analysis of the Trinitarian grammar of Christ's resurrection operative in §69.4, (b) establishing the compatibility of Barth's appropriation of Christ's risen presence to both Christ himself on the one hand and the Holy Spirit on the other, and (c) indicating the eternal purpose of the temporal extension of Christ's parousia, which sets up the argument of the next section concerning its Trinitarian ground.

(1) As shown in the above discussion of God the Father, Barth sets up the problem of the possibility of further forms of Christ's parousia by underscoring the radicality of Easter as the once-for-all, unrestricted, and absolutely new form of Christ's risen presence. In light of these features, it is a genuinely open question whether any further forms of Christ's presence are necessary or even appropriate after that great Easter day. Barth addresses this question by means of an argument that spirals through three movements before reaching the final answer in the promise of the Spirit.

In the first movement, Barth identifies three *correct but inadequate answers*: that the reality of Easter day is hidden, that it is only a commencement, and that it is actualized in its effects, that is, the church. These answers are inadequate because each one just leads back to the question, Why is it hidden? In what sense is it only a commencement? How can it be said to be actualized in a church that is itself so imperfect?[72]

Next, after entertaining these correct but inadequate answers, Barth commends us to embrace the contradiction between Easter time and our time as the way forward.[73] In so doing, he asks after the meaning and purpose of

---

71. E.g., Robert W. Jenson, "You Wonder Where the Spirit Went" and Eugene F. Rogers, "Eclipse of the Spirit in Karl Barth."

72. *CD* IV/3, 317–25.

this intermediate time.[74] He answers by describing the *external form* of the relationship between the prophetic history of Jesus Christ and our sphere. This external form consists in Christ's will to give time and space for free human participants in his missionary movement.[75]

Third, Barth moves even closer to his final answer by identifying the *external conditions* of this relationship. These conditions consist in the distinction and solidarity between Christians and non-Christians.[76] The purpose of the intermediate form of Christ's risen presence is the proclamation of the gospel *by* Jesus Christ, *with* his own, *to* those who do not yet know him. Having identified its external conditions, Barth finally describes this relationship between Christ and our sphere in terms of its proper name: the promise of the Spirit.

Why does Barth develop his argument concerning the intermediate form of Christ's parousia in this spiral-like movement?[77] There are at least two reasons. First, Barth is intentionally avoiding an all-too-easy appeal to the Spirit's work as filling a gap between Christ and us. Though an appeal to the Spirit is not wrong in itself, it can be made in such a way that the living Christ is left behind, in which case the time between the times would be one of the absence rather than the presence of Christ.[78]

Second, the spiral shape of his argument gives Barth time to develop his understanding of the *purpose* of the intermediate form of Christ's parousia. He is concerned not only with how Christ is present in an intermediate form (that is, by the Spirit), but also *why* Christ has chosen to temporally extend his presence in this way. Discussing the external form and conditions of the relationship between Christ and our sphere serves to indicate the *missionary* purpose of this time between the times, and so sets the terms for understanding the *promissory* character of the Spirit's work.

---

73. *CD* IV/3, 325.

74. For a similar pattern of thought, see "The Time of the Community," *CD* IV/1, §62.3.

75. *CD* IV/3, 325–35.

76. *CD* IV/3, 335–50.

77. This is a common pattern in Barth's writings. But since it is certainly not his only pattern of thought, it is appropriate to ask why he uses it in a particular context.

78. Many of Barth's critics want to see the time of the church as a time of absence, which is exactly what he is trying to avoid. Such a move is often rooted in an understanding of the ascension as the removal of Jesus Christ from our sphere, rather than as the conclusion of the first form of his presence for the sake of the transition to his intermediate form. See Douglas Farrow, *Ascension and Ecclesia: On the Significance of the Doctrine of the Ascension for Ecclesiology and Christian Cosmology* (Grand Rapids: Eerdmans, 1999). A more dialectical account of presence and absence drawing on recent Roman Catholic theology can be found in Brian D. Robinette, *Grammars of Resurrection: A Christian Theology of Presence and Absence* (New York: Crossroad, 2009).

In light of these two reasons, I do not regard the late appearance of the Spirit in §69.4 as evidence of an eclipse of the Spirit in Barth's theology. Jenson and Rogers are correct when they say that Barth first speaks of Jesus Christ's own revealing activity in his resurrection before eventually getting around to the Holy Spirit, thereby revealing his unwillingness to appeal directly to the Spirit as the agent of transition from Christ to us. But this late appearance is a feature of the spiral shape of Barth's argument, which is not arbitrary but intentional. In §69.4, the Holy Spirit is not an afterthought but the climax of the argument. The structure of Barth's argument prevents an all-too-easy appeal to the Holy Spirit. He is intent on getting to pneumatology and ecclesiology, but he wants to do so within a christocentric and Trinitarian horizon.

(2) Once he has reached the final answer to the question of the intermediate form of Christ's parousia, Barth describes the work of the Spirit by means of a grammatical analysis of the biblical phrase "the promise of the Spirit."[79] Barth observes that the "of" in this phrase can be taken as a subjective or an objective genitive. Taken as a subjective genitive, the Spirit is the subject of the act of promising: "The Spirit promises."[80] Taken as an objective genitive, the Spirit is the object that is being promised: "The Spirit is promised."[81] The Spirit is both the one who promises and the one who is promised; he is both giver and gift.[82]

---

79. Barth cites the following New Testament texts: Gal. 3:14; Acts 2:33; and Eph. 1:13 (*CD* IV/3, 350). He does not engage in a detailed exegesis of these passages, so his grammatical analysis of the phrase is not strictly exegetical in character. Rather, "the promise of the Spirit" is a biblical handle for getting a grip on a conceptual distinction between two aspects of the Spirit's work. This distinction is warranted by his interpretation of a wider pattern of thought in the New Testament, not by the mere citation of proof texts. On the interplay between patterns and proof texts in Barth, see Kathryn Greene-McCreight, *Ad Litteram: How Augustine, Calvin, and Barth Read the "Plain Sense" of Genesis 1–3* (New York: Peter Lang, 1999), 190–200 and 210–13.

80. *CD* IV/3, 351.

81. *CD* IV/3, 353.

82. In this sense, Barth reconceptualizes a traditional pattern of thought; cf. Thomas Aquinas, *Summa Theologica* Ia, q. 38. The grammatical pattern is the same, though Barth renders the content eschatological by substituting "promise" for "gift." On the significance of the identification of Spirit with gift/grace in Aquinas, see Eugene F. Rogers, "The Eclipse of the Spirit in Thomas Aquinas," in *Grammar and Grace: Reformulations of Aquinas and Wittgenstein*, ed. Jeffrey Stout and Robert MacSwain (London: SCM, 2004), 136–53. Although he does not reject the attribution of gift-language to the Spirit, Barth's eschatological pneumatology does move away from the traditional identification of the Spirit as the applicator of grace. For Barth, grace is actualized in the life history of Jesus Christ. The parousia of Jesus Christ in all its forms is the eschatological event in which grace is revealed. The Holy Spirit promises and is promised to us as the means by which we participate in Jesus Christ's glorious self-attestation to the grace actualized in his life of obedience unto death. On the eschatological form of the Spirit's work, see

Barth selects this phrase because its twofold sense fits the conditions of the intermediate form of Christ's parousia. In this form, Jesus Christ comes to certain persons as the hope of all, so that these persons will bear with him the promise of the Spirit to all. The twofold grammar of the promise of the Spirit corresponds to the differentiation and solidarity between Christians and non-Christians. Just as Christ is the hope of all, so the Spirit is the promise to all. To Christians, "the Spirit promises" (subjective genitive), assuring them of the presence of Christ with them as they share in his harvest.[83] To non-Christians, "the Spirit is promised" (objective genitive), pledged to them as their not-yet-fulfilled future.[84]

This promissory work of the Spirit in its twofold sense constitutes the intermediate form of Christ's parousia. In both senses, the Spirit's promise occurs in the present but with an eye to the future. Christians are directed by the promise of the Spirit to those who do not yet know Christ as their hope. Non-Christians are directed by the promise of the Spirit to their future realization as witnesses to Christ. So, the intermediate form of the parousia is determined by the teleological character of the living Christ's self-revelation. Presence is not an end in itself. Presence is for a purpose: fellowship with Jesus Christ in the service of witness.

(3) Within the context of this twofold teleological structure, Barth's pneumatological language fits like a glove. He speaks of the Holy Spirit both as the subject of verbs and as the object or instrument of verbs predicated of Jesus Christ. The prevalence of the latter has occasioned criticisms of Barth's pneumatology. Although one may wish for greater balance, such a criticism rips §69.4 out of its context. The alternating grammar works within Barth's argument. The central claim of §69.4 is that Jesus Christ is present. It is a mark of its perfection that his presence serves his purpose by being extended temporally. The three forms that result are all forms of *his* presence. Easter as the primal form was based on an act of God the Father, but it was nevertheless Jesus Christ who was present and active during the forty days. The promise of the Spirit as the intermediate form is an act of the Spirit, but it is nevertheless Jesus Christ who is present and active today. Accordingly, Barth speaks not only of the Spirit's act of promising, but also of Christ's act of promising the Spirit.[85]

George Hunsinger, "The Mediator of Communion: Karl Barth's Doctrine of the Holy Spirit," in *Disruptive Grace: Studies in the Theology of Karl Barth* (Grand Rapids: Eerdmans, 2000), 173–79.

83. *CD* IV/3, 351.

84. *CD* IV/3, 353.

85. Another option would be for Barth to divide the intermediary work between the living Jesus Christ and the Holy Spirit, so that each would remain exclusively the subject of certain verbs. However,

The twofold grammar of the promise of the Spirit thus serves the transitional function of Barth's doctrine of Christ's parousia.

This twofold grammar also fits the larger structural context of §69.4. As discussed above ("Teleological Unity: The Relationship between IV/1–2 and IV/3"), the Christology of IV/3 focuses on the unity of God and humanity in Jesus Christ. Barth does not directly correlate the twofold pneumatological grammar with the two "natures" of Jesus Christ, but he does assert that in the promise of the Spirit, Christ is present as both God and man: "In this form of His coming He is no other, but the Son of God and Man, the Mediator between God and the world, in the totality and not merely a part of His being and existence."[86] The intermediate form of Christ's parousia is not a lesser presence, but the full presence of the God-human by means of the divine Spirit.[87] So the twofold pneumatological grammar of §69.4, though not explicitly correlated with the two "natures" of Jesus Christ, operates within the Christology of IV/3.

Finally, this twofold grammar fits the teleological aspect of reconciliation developed in IV/3. Barth understands the unity of God and humanity in Jesus Christ in the light of his glorious movement through history. The trajectory of this movement is from the particular to the universal. Accordingly, the central concern of this discussion is the non-Christian.[88] The movement of Christ to his own is the theme of all three transitional discussions, but §69.4 focuses especially on the *missionary* character of this movement. Christ is on his way to the nations—a missionary movement in which Christians cooperate with him. Thus it fits the teleological orientation of IV/3 that Barth distinguishes

---

two considerations count against this option and in favor of Barth's dialectical approach: (1) this alternative grammar requires a kind of three-subject doctrine of the Trinity that Barth has good reasons for avoiding, and (2) the Holy Spirit appears in the New Testament as both an acting subject and as the object or instrument of verbs predicated of Jesus Christ. What could be added is greater attention to the extent to which Jesus Christ bears the Spirit along with us, but this development can be executed from *within* Barth's Trinitarian theology of Christ's resurrection rather than by rejecting his basic commitments.

86. *CD* IV/3, 357. Although he does not deal with the Lord's Supper here, Barth does explicitly address traditional Lutheran and Reformed approaches to the presence of Jesus Christ. On the one hand, he maintains a genuinely human presence against the Lutheran idea of ubiquity. On the other hand, he maintains that the total God-human in both deity and humanity is present, against the Reformed tendency to lock Christ's humanity in heaven. In both cases, Barth wishes to uphold the freedom of God: Jesus is free from us and free for us. Within this critique, both of their prime concerns are affirmed: the Lutherans get a form of real presence with us while the Reformed get a form of local presence in heaven.

87. *CD* IV/3, 358: "His working in this form of His coming . . . is qualitatively no less than it was in the first form and will be in the last."

88. *CD* IV/3, 364: "The main concern of the ongoing of the history of the prophecy of Jesus Christ which fills our time is with non-Christians."

between the Spirit promising to Christians and the Spirit being promised to non-Christians. This twofold grammar befits the missionary character of the living Christ's movement.[89]

CONCLUSION: PERICHORESIS WITH A PURPOSE

Now that I have set forth the full Trinitarian grammar of §69.4, we can revisit Barth's perichoretic analogy. The mutual relation of the three forms of Jesus Christ's parousia is "a kind of perichoresis."[90] In each form, the other forms are contained by anticipation or recapitulation. This much we have already seen. The foregoing analysis of the Trinitarian grammar of Christ's parousia shows that this is not a merely formal similarity. The perichoretic relationship between the three forms of Christ's parousia corresponds to the perichoretic relationship between the concrete activity of the triune persons in this threefold event.

This correspondence is not a flat correlation of each form with each person. The thrust of Barth's doctrine of the threefold parousia presses against this, for it is Jesus Christ himself who is present in all three forms. The correspondence is subtler than that. Easter as the primal form of the parousia is based on God the Father's act of raising Christ from the dead. But the purpose of this act is the reconstitution of Christ as a living subject, who acts in his own arising. And the outpouring of the Holy Spirit as the intermediate form of the parousia is enacted by the Spirit's act of promising. But the content of the Spirit's promise to us is the presence of Christ with us. So, in each form, the persons of the Trinity mutually indwell one another in acting to and with us.[91]

This correspondence is not just a matter of applying perichoretic logic to the parousia of Jesus Christ. Instead, Barth has described the perichoretic relation of the triune persons from within the concrete history of Christ's parousia. The temporal extension of the parousia is teleological in character. The three forms of Christ's parousia are identical in content *because* the one who

---

89. Thus Barth has folded Lessing's problem of history into the problem of mission. Although Barth's solution would not satisfy Lessing on his own terms, this relocation has dogmatic significance. The problem of faith and history has been reframed missionally. Instead of the relation between the contingent facts of history and the necessary truths of reason, he speaks of the relation between one "contingent" historical fact and the universal history for which it is the one "necessary" factor with which we must contend.

90. *CD* IV/3, 296.

91. It must be acknowledged that Barth does not develop the Trinitarian grammar of the final form of Christ's parousia in this context. That would have been the subject matter of the unwritten fifth volume of *Church Dogmatics*. Although he does not explicitly anticipate its content, the threefold parousia of Jesus Christ does supply a bridge between the doctrines of reconciliation and redemption. See *CD* IV/3, 316.

is present in each is *on his way*.⁹² Jesus Christ is present with a purpose, and so the triune God manifest in Christ's presence has a purpose.⁹³ Barth's perichoretic analogy is not, therefore, just a clever analytical tool, nor does it speak of a presence that is only an end in itself.⁹⁴ Rather, it bears witness to the purposive movement of the triune God through history.

The Trinitarian Ground of Christ's Parousia (§64.2)

What is the basis of Christ's parousia? On what is the teleological character of his existence grounded? In this section I will argue that, for Barth, the living movement of Jesus Christ—his past, present, and future self-attestation—is grounded in the triune God himself. Christ's presence with others is the outworking of God's own fellowship. The triune God is not alone, for from and to all eternity he is in fellowship with himself and wills to be in fellowship with us:

> Even in the eternal divine decree of election [Jesus Christ] was not alone, but the One in whom as their Firstborn and Representative God also elected the many as His brethren because He also loved them in Him before the world was created and established. Hence He did not will to be the eternal Son of the eternal Father for Himself, but for us men. Nor did He become man for Himself, as though to be of divine essence as this one man, but in order to confirm His election as our eldest Brother, and therefore our election to divine sonship.⁹⁵

The ever-new coming of Jesus Christ is grounded in God's ever-new coming. In other words, the three-in-oneness of Christ's parousia is grounded in the three-in-oneness of God himself.

---

92. *CD* IV/3, 327: "He is on the way, moving and marching, from the commencement to the completion. . . . His intrinsically perfect work is still moving towards its consummation."

93. Its teleological character rules out thinking of the unity of the forms of Christ's presence as a sort of "eternal now" that undermines the sequence and directionality of his time.

94. This does not mean community has no intrinsic worth. Some recent trends in systematic theology treat perichoresis as an end in itself, both for God and for us; see Miroslav Volf, *After Our Likeness: The Church as an Image of the Trinity* (Grand Rapids: Eerdmans, 1997). The emphasis on community in such trends is welcome, but the tendency to abstract community from its outgoing purpose is problematic. As we have seen, Barth does speak of the church in relation to the mutual indwelling of the triune persons. But this relation is mediated through the living Jesus Christ who is on his way toward his universal self-declaration. Perichoretic logic operates within this missionary horizon.

95. *CD* IV/3, 278.

Barth argues for this divine basis from three equally basic starting points: in the life of Jesus Christ we have to do with (1) the life of God, (2) the life of grace, and (3) the eternal life of a human being.[96] From each of these starting points, Barth argues that it is fitting that the life of Jesus Christ is as such also light, that is, that he lives as the risen one who declares himself unto the end of the age. In this section I will reconstruct each of these three arguments in order to ascertain the Trinitarian ground of the risen presence of Jesus Christ.

Now it must be admitted that Barth does not discuss the Trinitarian ground of Christ's parousia within §69.4.[97] Unlike the previous transitional subsections, Barth does not turn to this question either periodically (as in §59.3) or at great length (as in §64.4). However, he does ask the question of the divine basis of Jesus Christ's living self-declaration earlier in IV/3, in §69.2. Whereas in treatments of IV/1-2 it would have been inappropriate to jump back to material prior to the transitional discussions in order to ascertain the Trinitarian ground of Christ's resurrection, in this treatment of IV/3 it is wholly appropriate to do so. As I have already shown, Christ's resurrection permeates §69.[98] In contrast to §59 and §64, the whole of §69 is controlled by the doctrine of Christ's resurrection, according to which Barth develops the meaning of Christ's prophetic office. And so it is fitting that Barth asks after the innermost basis of Christ's resurrection in the context of §69.2.[99]

Barth takes up this question right in the middle of §69.2.[100] This subsection consists of four parts. The first part lays down the "main christological thesis

---

96. These three starting points are equally basic because they are all complementary statements regarding the one living Jesus Christ. In each case, Barth speaks of the one living God who is at work in Jesus Christ. So, although the doctrine of the Trinity is the focus of the first, the doctrine of election the focus of the second, and the eternal life of the man Jesus the focus of the third, these are not three competing bases. Rather, they are three ways of speaking of the one basis of the self-declarative character of the living Jesus Christ in the living God—Father, Son, and Holy Spirit.

97. This accounts for R. Dale Dawson's inattention to this material, insofar as the focus of his study of Christ's resurrection centers on the transitional subsections (*The Resurrection in Karl Barth* [Burlington, VT: Ashgate, 2007], 175–209). I too have focused on the transitional discussions, but the nature of this study requires that I transgress those boundaries in the case of IV/3.

98. See "He Lives: The Role of Christ's Resurrection in §69."

99. Thus the argument of §69.2 parallels that of §59.1 and §64.2. Just as §59.1 asked after the basis of the Son of God's humiliation, and just as §64.2 asked after the basis of the Son of Man's exaltation, so §69.2 asks after the basis of the Mediator's glory.

100. This middle position stands in contrast to the location of the question in the parallel subsections. In §59.1, the argument moves toward the basis of divine humiliation in God's triunity as its conclusion. In §64.2, the basis of human exaltation is asserted at the very beginning of the argument by a brief reference to the doctrine of election. The discussion then reemerges at greater length near the end of §64.4 (see ch. 3, "The Trinitarian Ground of Christ's Arising (§64.4)"). In contrast to the prominent

that the life of Jesus Christ is as such light and His reconciling work a prophetic word."[101] The second part compares this prophetic word of Christ "with that of the Old Testament prophets and related it to the prophecy of the history of Israel as recounted in the Old Testament."[102] The third part halts "for a moment to discover what is the necessary and only possible demonstration of this thesis."[103] The fourth and final part makes "a conscious because necessary application of the definite article," that is, that "Jesus Christ is *the* light of life."[104] This final part, which is by far the longest of the four, contains Barth's well-known discussion of other lights.[105] What is of interest for this study is the third part concerning the demonstration of the thesis that the life of Jesus Christ is as such light.[106] This part identifies the sole basis of the inherently revelatory character of Jesus Christ's existence, and so the ground of all that follows in terms of the historicity of this revelation (§69.3) and the inclusion of free human agents in this history (§69.4). This third part demonstrates the validity of the Christology that controls the whole of IV/3.

However, this is not a typical sort of demonstration. In fact, Barth explicitly rejects any demonstration of the christological thesis that does not circle back as an affirmation and explication of this thesis. The circular nature of Barth's argument is important to note, for it shows that Barth does not depart from

---

placing of these parallel discussions, the almost parenthetical position within §69.2 of the discussion of the divine basis of the mediator's glory has perhaps contributed to its neglect in the secondary literature.

101. *CD* IV/3, 86.

102. *CD* IV/3, 86.

103. *CD* IV/3, 86.

104. *CD* IV/3, 86, emphasis original.

105. This famous passage has been the focus of much of the secondary literature on §69.2. See Hendrik Berkhof and Hans-Joachim Kraus, *Karl Barths Lichterlehre*, Theologische Studien 123 (Zürich: Theologischer Verlag, 1978); George Hunsinger, *How to Read Karl Barth: The Shape of His Theology* (New York: Oxford University Press, 1991), 234–80; Gregory Alan Robertson, "Vivit! Regnat! Triumphat!" 140–70.

106. It is striking how little attention this part of Barth's argument receives in the secondary literature concerning *CD* IV/3. Gregory Alan Robertson skips over this part in his otherwise close and careful reading of §69 ("Vivit! Regnat! Triumphat!" 134–235). John Webster's fine essay on the prophetic office briefly discusses this portion of Barth's argument, "'Eloquent and Radiant': The Prophetic Office of Christ and the Mission of the Church," in John Webster, *Barth's Moral Theology: Human Action in Barth's Thought* (Grand Rapids: Eerdmans, 1998), 125–50. However, his claim that "the fundamental principle of theological epistemology is divine aseity" (ibid., 136) conceals more than it reveals. It is true that Barth appeals in this context to a sort of divine aseity, inasmuch as the knowledge of Jesus Christ in his prophetic office is self-grounded. However, Barth's understanding of the triune God's self-sufficiency is intimately tied up with God's self-giving, not only in himself but toward us. So we are dealing with a unique conception of aseity.

the concrete history of the living Christ when he speaks of its ground in God. Therefore, it is necessary to describe briefly Barth's methodological reflections that appear in this context. Unsurprisingly, he refers to Anselm: "Methodologically our line or argument is informed by the true spirit and import of the 'ontological proof' of Anselm of Canterbury."[107] He argues at length that such a method is the only possible alternative in the face of Feuerbach, to whom Barth refers numerous times in this discussion.[108] The Feuerbachian objection—that we have merely ascribed to Jesus Christ his revelatory character—cannot be answered on its own terms. To accept these terms is to deny the very point of the thesis: that the life of Jesus Christ is light, not by our ascription but in itself and as such. Accordingly, the only demonstration of this thesis is one that thinks through its own inner rationality, not one that grounds it on some other premise.

Given this confessional stance, why does Barth bother to make any demonstration at all? Because, according to Barth, it is not we who ask the question. Rather, "The point is that the question is put to us."[109] Jesus Christ asks us "whether and to what extent His life, not in others but in ourselves, justifies, confirms and demonstrates itself as light, revelation, truth, word and prophecy."[110] He asks us whether we walk as children of the light. We can only answer this question holistically, by an entire life of obedient witness. It is primarily a practical question. However, this broader practical question of obedient action includes the small but not insignificant theoretical question of obedient thinking.[111] So, in this short but decisive part of §69.2, Barth halts to ask: What is the basis of our confession that the life of Jesus Christ is as such light, if there is no other basis to which we can appeal but Christ himself? As indicated above, Barth answers this question from three different but equally basic starting points.

The Trinitarian Being of God

Barth's first argument goes something like this: since (a) in the life of Jesus Christ God himself is present and active, and since (b) God as triune eternally speaks and shines, therefore (c) it is fitting that the life of Jesus Christ is as such

---

107. *CD* IV/3, 85.

108. *CD* IV/3, 72, 78, 80, 82, 85.

109. *CD* IV/3, 76.

110. *CD* IV/3, 76.

111. *CD* IV/3, 78–79: "It is obvious that it must be in the whole life of a man that the correctness of our presupposition and assertion must be seen. . . . We shall attempt to answer the question in the modest field of dogmatic and to that extent theoretical deliberation."

light. As Barth admits, this is a circular argument. We know God is present and active in Jesus Christ because Jesus Christ attests this. But Barth contends that this is not a vicious but a virtuous circle, for there is no other ground on which this confession can be based without denying its content. Whatever one thinks of its formal validity, what is of interest for this study is the material content of this argument. Barth explicitly grounds the revelatory livingness of Jesus Christ in the triunity of God. I will walk through each element of Barth's argument in order to display his understanding of the correspondence between the triune God and the living Jesus Christ.

(a) Barth selects as his first starting point the assertion that "in the life of Jesus Christ we deal, not with an indeterminate happening, but with the happening of the presence and action of *God*."[112] Befitting the nature of his argument, Barth indicates that this claim is contained within the main christological thesis: "Our presupposition and assertion in respect of this life includes within itself, and has as its basis and authority, the statement concerning God in Himself: that He is in Jesus Christ."[113] It is because this claim is included within the christological thesis that we cannot interrogate the prophecy of Jesus Christ, but rather he interrogates us regarding our obedience. "If it were not a matter of God, everything would be different. But it is a matter of God. Hence we can only see ourselves as those who are asked concerning our acknowledgement and respect, concerning our praise of God."[114] So, in short, the major premise of Barth's first argument is the deity of Jesus Christ.

(b) But with what kind of deity do we have to do in the life of Jesus Christ? This question brings us to Barth's minor premise: God intrinsically speaks and is bright. "Where God Himself is present as active subject, where He lives—and this occurs in the life of Jesus Christ—life is not only possibly but really, not only accidentally but determinately, not only secondarily but primarily, also declaration and therefore also light, truth, word and glory."[115] Again, we know this is true because God is revealed as such in Jesus Christ. But within this virtuous circle God is the ground of the intrinsic glory of Christ. Barth goes on to explicate this claim: "A mute and obscure God would be an idol. The true and living God speaks and is bright. If He is in large measure mute and obscure to us, this is another matter. He is in Himself, whether we perceive and accept it or not, the speaking and luminous God."[116] This speaking and shining

---

112. *CD* IV/3, 79, original German emphasis restored (*KD* IV/3, 87).
113. *CD* IV/3, 79, translation revised (*KD* IV/3, 87).
114. *CD* IV/3, 79.
115. *CD* IV/3, 79, translation revised (*KD* IV/3, 87).
116. *CD* IV/3, 79, translation revised (*KD* IV/3, 87).

of God is intrinsic: "He does not merely become it in His act in creation, time and history."[117]

This intrinsic speaking and shining is not just an abstract quality of the divine being. Concretely, God's intrinsic speaking and shining consists in his triunity: "He speaks and shines in creation and history as a result of and in precise correspondence to the fact that that He is from all eternity in Himself not only the Father but also as the Son of the Father the eternal Word, and that in the Son He has the reflection of His own glory."[118] God's triunity is the basis of his intrinsic speaking and shining: "Hence it is not accidental or external to Him, but *essential* and proper, to declare Himself."[119] The triune God is essentially one who speaks and shines.

(c) Because the triune God is present and active in the life of Jesus Christ, and because this God in himself speaks and shines, it is fitting that the life of Jesus Christ is intrinsically self-declarative. "It is in this glory that Jesus Christ lives."[120] This is why there is no appeal behind the God who is present and active in him. The triune God is the basis of Christ's intrinsic glory. But to indicate this basis is not to depart from the content of the confession that the life of Christ is light. "Even the reference which we have ventured to the Trinitarian being of God cannot be deduced from any principle, but can only describe and explain the fact that God Himself and He alone is the principle and source from which all that He is, and therefore the fact that He is self-disclosing life, does not 'derive' as in the case of a logical deduction, but is eternally repeated and confirmed in the act of His existence as the living God."[121] This God lives and so also shines in Jesus Christ: "But it is this life which discloses itself in the act of His existence that is lived by Jesus Christ as the Son of God. This is what is meant when we call His life light. This is the content of our assumption and assertion."[122] In short, because the triune God's life is as such light, so Jesus Christ's life is as such light.

What is the significance of Barth's first argument for this study? It shows that Jesus Christ's intrinsically self-declarative existence is grounded in the triune God who is intrinsically self-declarative. Since the self-declaration of Jesus Christ takes place definitively in his resurrection,[123] we can streamline

---

117. *CD* IV/3, 79.
118. *KD* IV/3, 87.
119. *CD* IV/3, 80, original German emphasis restored (*KD* IV/3, 87).
120. *CD* IV/3, 80.
121. *CD* IV/3, 80.
122. *CD* IV/3, 80.
123. *CD* IV/3, 44. Cf. "He Lives: The Role of Christ's Resurrection in §69" above.

Barth's argument and say that *Christ's resurrection is grounded in the radiance of God's triunity*. This Trinitarian ground shows that the living movement of Jesus Christ, including its threefold temporal structure, issues forth from God's own being.

Now this might sound like an argument for the necessity of Christ's resurrection. Has Barth surrendered his commitment to the freedom of God in the Easter event, asserted so strenuously in §59.3?[124] In a certain sense, Barth is risking the specter of necessity. He repeatedly asserts that "in the life of Jesus Christ we do not have an indeterminate happening."[125] The intrinsically revelatory character of Jesus Christ, and its basis in the intrinsically self-declaratory being of the triune God, is the point of this discussion. However, Barth explicitly rejects an absolute, logical necessity. Rather, he speaks of the inner rationality of the free love of God, repeated in human history. This outworking is not an absolute necessity but a *self-chosen* necessity. But the nature of divine freedom is not developed until Barth's second argument.

The Covenant of Grace

Barth's second argument goes something like this: since (a) the life of Jesus Christ fulfills God's covenant of grace, and since (b) the triune God in his grace eternally discloses and imparts himself, therefore (c) it is fitting that the life of Jesus Christ is as such self-disclosing and self-imparting. Again, this is a circular argument. The fulfillment of the covenant of grace in the life of Jesus Christ is declared by none other than the living Jesus Christ himself. Within this purportedly virtuous circle emerges another important aspect of Barth's Trinitarian theology of Christ's resurrection: a restatement of the Trinitarian ground of Christ's intrinsic glory in terms of the covenant of grace.[126] In order to see how Barth executes this restatement, I will once again walk through each element of his argument.

(a) Barth selects as his second "starting point the fact that the life of Jesus Christ is that of the *covenant of grace* willed and determined by God and addressed and given by Him to the man for whom and to whom it is active."[127]

---

124. See ch. 2, "The Trinitarian Ground of the Raising of Christ (§59.3)."

125. *CD* IV/3, 80.

126. It is important to note that this is a restatement of the first argument, not a competing argument. It is not that the self-declaratory livingness of Jesus Christ is grounded in either triunity or election, or first in triunity and only secondarily in election. Rather, the Trinitarian being of God and the gracious covenant of God are two ways of arriving at the same basic point: that the living God is at work in the life of Jesus Christ, and so his life is also light.

127. *CD* IV/3, 81, translation revised and original German emphasis restored (*KD* IV/3, 89).

What does Barth mean by grace? "Grace, willed and practised by God as His action to man, is as such God's self-disclosure and self-impartation as it takes place towards man but is grounded in His own divine being."[128] This divine grace is utterly free: "It is the choice and act of His own incomprehensible freedom to be the Almighty and Holy One, not only in and for Himself, not only in His own transcendence and self-originating life, but also beyond this in the depths."[129] The free grace of God is at work in the life of Jesus Christ. In short, the major premise of Barth's second argument is the freely willed covenant of grace fulfilled in Jesus Christ.

(b) With what kind of freedom do we have to deal in God's covenant of grace? Because it is freely willed, God's covenant of grace is self-grounded. But this does not mean it is capricious; rather, it is securely grounded in God himself: "In this freedom He is God. He is not untrue to Himself but supremely true, the living, almighty and holy God, in the fact that He is gracious."[130] In this free act of grace to us, the triune God corresponds to himself: "He is [gracious] to man, in His eternal choice to disclose and impart Himself to him, and in the historical event in which He does this, on the basis of the fact that to be gracious, to disclose and impart Himself, is already His own freedom, the freedom of the Father to be in and for Himself, yet not to be only in and for Himself, but eternally to disclose and impart Himself in the Son, and with the Son in the Holy Ghost."[131] Because the triune God is gracious in himself, his self-disclosure and self-impartation to us is not foreign to his life or unbecoming of his being. This true, living God unmasks our idols for what they are. "No idea of God, no god invented by man and exalted to divinity, is gracious in himself or to man. The true and living God is gracious. He transcends Himself. He discloses and imparts Himself."[132] Grace is free, or it would not be grace. But the grace of the triune God does not establish a merely external relation, because it is the very self-disclosure and self-impartation of God: "Grace would not be grace if it were to remain mute or obscure, or could try to be in and for itself alone. It would be a contradiction in terms if it did not mean self-disclosure and self-impartation, or were not eloquent and radiant."[133] Grace is by definition self-disclosure and self-impartation.

---

128. *CD* IV/3, 81.
129. *CD* IV/3, 81.
130. *CD* IV/3, 81.
131. *CD* IV/3, 81.
132. *CD* IV/3, 81.
133. *CD* IV/3, 81.

Barth is walking a fine line here. On the one hand, the graciousness of divine election would be undermined if it were not free. On the other hand, grace is by definition self-communicative. That God is essentially gracious means that God is truly himself when he freely imparts himself to another. Barth thinks this through in terms of the intra-Trinitarian relations. But he does not abstract these relations from God's eternal election: "In the life of Jesus Christ we are not dealing with God and His presence and action generally or abstractly, but specifically and concretely with His election and act of grace, with the election and act of His characteristically and exclusively divine freedom to disclose and impart Himself."[134] So, according to Barth, God's freedom consists in his freedom to impart himself.

(c) Because the life of Jesus Christ is the life of divine grace, and this grace is by definition self-disclosing and self-imparting, it is fitting that the life of Jesus Christ is self-disclosing and self-imparting. "Because it is the life of grace, it is this speaking and shining life."[135] This is why we cannot discover him but he discovers us, disclosing us as his witnesses.[136] In his risen life, Jesus Christ discloses and imparts himself as our gracious reconciler. "This is what is meant when we speak of the prophecy of the life of Jesus Christ."[137] The prophecy of Jesus Christ is thus grounded in the triune God's gracious decision to communicate himself to us.

But, again, in so grounding the intrinsic light of Christ's life, Barth is not departing from the inner rationality of Christian confession. To speak of the revelation of Jesus Christ is to speak of the revelation of God. "What Jesus Christ lives is God's self-disclosure and self-impartation as inscrutably grounded in His divine sovereignty. . . . Grace itself, and the light of grace, are the election and work of the divine freedom whose action is established and justified in itself alone, but in itself unshakably."[138] In this free self-impartation, God is true to himself. In other words, in the resurrection of Jesus Christ the gracious God corresponds to himself.

What is the significance of Barth's second argument for this study? It shows that Jesus Christ's intrinsic glory is grounded in the triune God not abstractly but concretely, that is, in terms of God's eternal covenant of grace. Barth's first argument, though correct in itself, might give the impression that God's Easter self-correspondence is either a logical necessity or a lucky

---

134. *CD* IV/3, 81, translation revised (*KD* IV/3, 89).
135. *CD* IV/3, 81, translation revised (*KD* IV/3, 90).
136. *CD* IV/3, 82.
137. *CD* IV/3, 81.
138. *CD* IV/3, 82.

coincidence. Both errors spring from a misunderstanding of God's free grace. God corresponds to himself in Christ's living self-declaration because God freely wills from all eternity to disclose and impart himself to us. In other words, God is gracious. This second argument concretizes the Trinitarian ground of Christ's resurrection in terms of the covenant of grace. It therefore indicates the dynamic teleology within God's own being that grounds the dynamic teleology of Jesus Christ's self-revealing movement through history in all its forms. In short, the purposive perichoresis of the three forms of Christ's parousia is grounded in God's own eternal purposive movement of self-disclosure and self-impartation.

Now these first two arguments together might appear to lose sight of the humanity of Jesus Christ. Barth's appeals to the Trinitarian being of God and the covenant of grace are meant to show that God is in himself fit for an eternal fellowship with the man Jesus and his many brothers and sisters. But the extent to which God's deity encloses his humanity does not come to the foreground in these first two arguments. For that, we must turn to Barth's third and final argument.

The Eternal Life of Jesus Christ

Barth's third argument goes something like this: since (a) the life of Jesus Christ is the life of a human being, and since (b) this human being lives an eternal life, therefore (c) it is fitting that the life of Jesus Christ speaks and shines beyond itself, encountering us in our sphere. Again, this is a circular argument. The eternal life of Christ is revealed in his resurrection from the dead and the living history that flows from it. But within this circle emerges a third crucial element in Barth's Trinitarian theology of Christ's resurrection: the eternal one who bursts forth on Easter is not only God but also a human being like us. The promise and hope of eternal life for all rests on the eternal life of this one man. As we shall see, this third argument foreshadows the transitional discussion of §69.4. It thus provides the most explicit link between the discussion of the Trinitarian ground of Christ's resurrection in §69.2 and the Trinitarian grammar of Christ's risen presence in §69.4. In order to see these connections, I will again walk through each element of Barth's argument.

(a) Barth selects as his third starting point the fact that "the life of Jesus Christ, even as the life of God and the life of His grace, is the life of a man."[139] As a human being, Jesus Christ is "one of us" and "our Fellow, Associate, and Neighbor."[140] The humanity of Christ underscores that "the life of God and His

---

139. *CD* IV/3, 83.

grace ... is not lived in a distant height and therefore in mute obscurity, but it is a concrete event in the very sphere of the event of our own lives."[141] This concrete event thus has "a voice," a "human form," and "specific contours."[142] As the one who lives the life of God and the life of grace, Christ is "placed alongside [us] as One of us."[143] So, the major premise of Barth's third and final argument is the genuine humanity of Christ.[144]

(b) But what manner of man is this? As our neighbor, Jesus Christ is also a stranger among us. Unlike us, Jesus Christ lives an eternal life. This "particular man ... even in our human situation and within our human history, has lived and lives and will live this eternal life."[145] As such, Jesus Christ is a "Stranger" and "Alien" among us.[146] "There comes to us this other man whose reality is removed, by the fact that He speaks, from the sphere in which its possibility might be contested or attempts might be made to establish and justify it; whose reality is truth as such."[147] This removal is what takes place in his resurrection: without ceasing to be human, Christ transcends the temporal limits of human possibility and comes to us of his own initiative, thereby removing all our attempts to prove ourselves concerning him. This negation is the consequence of the blinding light of contrast between his eternal life and our lives. "This is inevitable, for as the life of this Stranger the fulness of His life is set in contrast with our emptiness, its light with our darkness."[148]

But the negation is not the point. The point is that Jesus Christ lives this eternal life as a human being. "There encounters us at this very point that Fellow, Associate and Neighbor, a man like ourselves, whose human life as distinct from ours is eternal life, the life of God and His grace."[149] The point is not just that he is a stranger, but that as this stranger "He is at home among us and like us and with us, belonging as we do to our human situation and

---

140. *CD* IV/3, 83.

141. *CD* IV/3, 83, translation revised (*KD* IV/3, 92).

142. *CD* IV/3, 83.

143. *CD* IV/3, 85.

144. Working out this argument both from the perspective of his deity and from the perspective of his humanity befits the Christology of IV/3 (see above, "Teleological Unity: The Relationship between IV/1–2 and IV/3").

145. *CD* IV/3, 83. One of the strengths of George Hunsinger's analysis of Barth's doctrine of lights is that he shows the extent to which that whole discussion is grounded in the eternal life of Jesus Christ (*How to Read Karl Barth*, 240–41).

146. *CD* IV/3, 83.

147. *CD* IV/3, 84.

148. *CD* IV/3, 84.

149. *CD* IV/3, 84.

history."¹⁵⁰ The fullness of eternal life encounters us "in the human life of this human person."¹⁵¹ The abyss of our emptiness is revealed precisely in our being "prevented and delivered from plunging into the abyss. For as the Stranger who lives this other life He is at home among us. He is not merely set in contrast with us, but placed alongside as One of us."¹⁵²

Because Jesus Christ lives his eternal life as a human being like us, the eternal life of God and his grace is shown to be oriented toward humanity. And so Barth restates his first two arguments in light of his third: "He reveals the life of God which He lives to be the life of *our* God, the life of grace to be that of the grace which is directed to *us* and all men, the eternal life that of the real life ordained and promised to us."¹⁵³ As Barth puts it in a contemporaneous essay: God's "deity encloses humanity in itself."¹⁵⁴

(c) Because the life of Jesus Christ is the life of a human being, and this human being lives an eternal life, it is fitting that the life of Christ as such speaks and shines beyond itself, encountering us in our sphere. "It is because it is the life of this Alien who is so utterly at home among us and so fully belongs to us, of the near Neighbor even in all His otherness, that this life is called light, revelation and Word."¹⁵⁵ Because the event of reconciliation takes place in the life of a human being, it is also revelation. "This happening has as such a voice. It is a declaration. And as it comes to us, it is an address, promise and demand, a question and answer. This is what is meant by our presupposition and assertion that in the life of Jesus Christ we have to do with a Word and prophecy."¹⁵⁶

Both premises are necessary for this conclusion. It is because it is *human* that this alien eternal life is communicable to us. And it is because it is *eternal* that this particular human life transcends its narrow sphere. To put it differently,

---

150. *CD* IV/3, 83.

151. *CD* IV/3, 84.

152. *CD* IV/3, 85.

153. *CD* IV/3, 85, original German emphasis restored (*KD* IV/3, 94). Again, this does not mean that this third argument has added something that was missing in the previous arguments. The meaning of the doctrine of the Trinity is precisely that our God is *God* and that God is *our* God (*CD* I/1, 383). So Barth is not abandoning the Trinitarian basis of Christ's resurrection for some competing basis, but rather explicating this basis in terms of the triune God's enclosure of the man Jesus in his eternal life.

154. Karl Barth, "The Humanity of God," in *The Humanity of God* (Richmond, VA: John Knox, 1964), 50. This lecture was delivered in Aarau on September 25, 1956, and therefore immediately prior to the winter semester of 1956–57 at Basel, during which Barth began lecturing through the material later published as *KD* IV/3. Eberhard Busch, *Karl Barth: His Life from Letters and Autobiographical Texts* (Philadelphia: Fortress Press, 1976), 423–25.

155. *CD* IV/3, 83.

156. *CD* IV/3, 83.

in the resurrection of Jesus Christ the incarnation is rendered permanent. Consequently, God continues to reveal himself in this human form, and this human form continues to reveal God.

Because the event of reconciliation speaks for itself, we are both freed from having to justify our confession of it and freed for a life of living witness to it. Our obedient thinking takes place not in a vacuum, but in the fullness of the living transition from darkness to light. "And from this standpoint, too, the authentication and obedience consist in the fact that we resolutely think and speak as those who have the vacuum and darkness of their own lives directly and unforgettably behind them and the fulness and light of His life directly, dominatingly and convincingly before them."[157] Barth reiterates this point by explicitly foreshadowing the argument of §69.4: "In this transition from direct past to direct future, in this Now or present, or, as we might say already, in this presence of the Spirit, we are 'of the truth' and hear the voice of the living Jesus."[158] As we walk in the light of his intermediate presence, we are not ashamed to venture the confession that the life of Jesus Christ is light.

What is the significance of Barth's third and final argument for this study? It shows that the basis of Christ's living self-declaration in the triune God and his covenant of grace must not be understood in abstraction from the particular human life of Jesus Christ.[159] This should come as no surprise, as Barth explicitly and repeatedly claims throughout this material that he is only thinking through the inner rationality of the confession that Jesus Christ is the glorious mediator between God and humanity. But by taking the humanity of Christ as his third starting point, Barth places God's human orientation in the foreground. The triune God is the basis of Christ's resurrection, but not in abstraction from the fulfillment of his eternal decision to be God-with-us in the eternal life of Jesus Christ, who was and is and is to come.

The eternality of Jesus Christ even in his humanity is a difficult thought.[160] However, Barth understands eternity from the perspective of Christ, rather than the other way around. This does not make the thought less difficult, but it does relocate the difficulty. According to this mode of thought, eternity is not the negation of time but its enclosure. The particularities of temporal life are

---

157. *CD* IV/3, 85.

158. *CD* IV/3, 85.

159. As previously noted, Barth restates his first two arguments in light of the third (*CD* IV/3, 85).

160. Barth's earlier discussions of the meaning of eternity can be found in *CD* II/1, §31.3 and *CD* III/2, §47.1. Despite some marked differences in structure and emphasis, the basic orientation of these earlier accounts of eternal life are compatible both with each other and with the material under investigation from *CD* IV/3, §69.

affirmed even as its limitations are transcended.[161] Thus Barth speaks of the eternal life of Christ not as a singular timeless state, but as a manifold temporal movement. Christ "has lived and lives and will live this eternal life."[162] This life "has come and comes and will come to us, bearing quite unmistakably our human form."[163] This threefold temporal pattern foreshadows the threefold parousia of §69.4.

As I have already shown in my analysis of §69.4, this manifold temporal movement gives space and time for the inclusion of free human agents within Jesus Christ's living self-attestation. What comes to expression in §69.2 is the basis of this movement in the life of God himself, which includes the human life of Christ. On this basis, Barth asserts that the teleological determination of Christ is not a secondary addition to, but a primary aspect of his being and act as reconciler. The threefold parousia of Christ, which is the temporal outworking of his teleological determination, is thus securely grounded in the triune God—the self-giving God who wills not to be alone but to be with us, promising to share his eternal life.

Conclusion: The Perichoresis of God

From these three equally basic starting points, Barth has asked after the basis of Jesus Christ's living self-attestation. The life of Christ is the life of God, the life of grace, and the eternal life of a human being, and so is as such also light. The revelation of Christ in his resurrection from the dead is not foreign to his work of reconciliation. Reconciliation has this teleological determination because God himself is teleologically determined.[164] This is the contribution of §69.2 to Barth's Trinitarian grounding of Christ's resurrection. Just as the *raising* of Jesus Christ by God the Father is grounded in the movement of free grace in the Father's relationship to the Son, and just as the *arising* of Jesus Christ in the

---

161. George Hunsinger discusses this mode of thought and defends Barth against his earlier critics in "*Mysterium Trinitatis*: Karl Barth's Conception of Eternity," in idem, *Disruptive Grace*, 186–209. For an influential example of the earlier criticism of Barth on this topic, see Richard H. Roberts, "Karl Barth's Doctrine of Time: Its Nature and Implications," in S. W. Sykes, ed., *Karl Barth: Studies of His Theological Method* (Oxford: Clarendon, 1979), 88–146.

162. *CD* IV/3, 83.

163. *CD* IV/3, 83.

164. In the context of his survey of the third form of the doctrine of reconciliation, Barth anticipates this claim: "According to the witness of Holy Scripture—in correspondence with His triune being, and as indicated by the biblical concept of eternity—God is historical even in Himself, and much more so in His relationship to the reality which is distinct from Himself" (*CD* IV/1, 112). Furthermore, Barth has criticized his earlier account of eternity during the *Römerbrief* period for its lack of teleology (*CD* II/1, 635).

power of the Holy Spirit is grounded in the Spirit-mediated fellowship of the Son with the Father, so the *presence* of Jesus Christ is grounded in the purposive perichoresis of the triune God.

According to Barth, the Father, Son, and Holy Spirit mutually indwell one another as God eternally repeats himself. In this, Barth affirms the traditional doctrine of perichoresis by means of his own conceptualities. However, for Barth, divine perichoresis is not an aimless movement. God's own fellowship is *directed* to that which is not God; it is "for us." This divine self-determination is *freely* willed, and so it must not be thought of as a necessary self-expression or self-actualization. However, this divine self-determination is *eternally* willed, and so teleology is not foreign to God. The fellowship of the triune persons is meant to be shared. God is in himself for us.

> Even in the eternal divine decree of election [Jesus Christ] was not alone, but the One in whom as their Firstborn and Representative God also elected the many as His brethren because He also loved them in Him before the world was created and established. Hence He did not will to be the eternal Son of the eternal Father for Himself, but for us men. Nor did He become man for Himself, as though to be of divine essence as this one man, but in order to confirm His election as our eldest Brother, and therefore our election to divine sonship.[165]

The perichoresis of the triune God is thus not only the grammatical framework for understanding the temporal outworking of the teleological determination of Jesus Christ. The perichoresis of the triune God is also the ground of this movement. The ever-new coming of Christ is the outworking of God's ever-new coming. God is and has in himself a teleological fellowship. God is and has a purposive perichoresis that grounds the temporal outworking into which we are included. Therefore, we cannot detach the Trinitarian ground of Christ's resurrection from the living movement in which God is in fellowship with us. The protological basis of Easter points forward to the eschatological goal of Easter, that is, eternal life in a fellowship of service to God. Protology and eschatology are united in God's teleology. The Trinitarian ground of Christ's resurrection always circles back to the living Christ himself, who is on his way, bearing with us the promise of the Spirit to the ends of the earth and the end of the age.[166]

---

165. *CD* IV/3, 278.

The Significance of a Trinitarian Theology of Christ's Parousia (§71.2)

What is the practical significance of Barth's Trinitarian theology of Christ's parousia? What difference does the Trinitarian grammar and ground sketched above make for Barth's understanding of human action? The practical significance is that the subject of the event of vocation is the living Jesus Christ. Barth's understanding of the Christian life as fellowship with Christ in the service of witness hangs on this claim, and this claim rests explicitly on Barth's Trinitarian theology of Christ's resurrection. Drawing these connections and consequences is the burden of this final section.

For Barth, the Easter event is not divided up among the triune persons. Rather, Easter is one event in the history of Jesus Christ. It is a complex event, and so can be viewed from different perspectives, thereby highlighting its Trinitarian grammar and ground. Thus Barth distinguishes between the raising and arising of Christ, which brings to light the gracious activity and merciful co-suffering of God the Father, the pure receptivity and majestic activity of God the Son, and the unifying and mediating activity of God the Holy Spirit. But, as we have seen in this chapter, Easter is not two or three things, but one thing. Easter means the *one* teleologically determined movement of the living Jesus Christ, which is the outworking of the eternal teleology of the triune God. Therefore, even in this time between the times, the same Christ is present today in the promise of the Spirit as was present on Easter day and will be present on the last day. This present presence is the payoff of Barth's unique Trinitarian theology of Christ's resurrection.

What does Jesus Christ's living movement of self-attestation mean for us? Barth identifies its general significance throughout §69. First of all, the grounding of Christ's livingness in the triune life of God underscores the *confidence* with which we confess that his life is light. We need not be ashamed to join him in his self-declaration, even in the face of modern demands to justify ourselves.[167]

---

166. Although the phrase "to the ends of the earth and the end of the age" comes from the work of Lesslie Newbigin, it succinctly captures the interconnection between missiology and eschatology in Barth's theology. Lesslie Newbigin, *The Household of God* (London: SCM, 1953), 111–52; *The Open Secret* (Grand Rapids: Eerdmans, 1978), 1.

167. "The good confession of the prophecy of Jesus Christ is both legitimate and obligatory for us. We can venture it without embarrassment, and need be afraid of no Feuerbach. The only thing is that we must not be ashamed to be like children" (*CD* IV/3, 85). This childlike epistemic confidence is crucial for Barth's engagement with modernity. I concur with Annelore Siller's thesis in *Kirche für die Welt*: theological engagement with modernity, and the proper stance of the church under its conditions, is the

Secondly, we can engage in the missionary task of the church with *bold humility*, for we know that the church's mission is not grounded in itself but in the very living movement of the triune God revealed in Jesus Christ.[168] The church does not act alone in its missionary endeavor, but participates in the self-attestation of the living Christ. As living, Jesus Christ is free. He is not controlled by or limited to the church. In his resurrection, all are called to join him in his self-witness. Christians are those who recognize this and so speak and act in free correspondence to Christ in his self-witness. Since the mission is grounded in the living Christ, Christians cannot claim an exclusive property for themselves and so cannot deny the existence of unwitting witnesses to Christ outside the church.[169] Within the freedom of the living Christ, Christians are freed to boldly proclaim the truth of Christ. The Spirit frees them for this fellowship with the risen Christ in the service of witness.[170]

This general sketch of the practical significance of Barth's Trinitarian theology of Christ's parousia comes to expression within §69. It provides the context for a very specific implication that emerges within Barth's doctrine of vocation (§71). In his description of the event of vocation (§71.2), Barth explicitly recapitulates the whole of his Trinitarian theology of Easter in support of the claim that the subject of vocation is the living Jesus Christ. The synoptic vision in IV/3 of that which was dialectically juxtaposed in IV/1–2 serves in this context to identify the acting subject of the event of vocation, which in turn determines its content, form, and goal.

The problem Barth faces in this subsection is the vague and generic understanding of vocation that typifies much of the history of theology. According to Barth, the more recent history of theology was plagued by the isolation of the individual experience of the Christian, abstracted from the larger

---

central issue of IV/3. Cf. also Michael Weinrich, "Das prophetische Amt Jesu Christi und der Dienst der Gemeinde in der Welt: Skizzen zu Karl Barths Theologie der Geistesgegenwart," in *Auferweckung Jesu, Auferweckung der Toten, Auferweckung der Welt: Karl Barths Theologie aufnehmen und weiterdenken*, ed. Berthold Klappert and Michael Weinrich (Herrenalb: Evangelische Akademie Baden, 1989), 61–88.

168. Few have so clearly traced the basis of the church's mission in the triunity of God in Barth's theology as John G. Flett in *The Witness of God: The Trinity, Missio Dei, Karl Barth, and the Nature of Christian Community* (Grand Rapids: Eerdmans, 2010).

169. *CD* IV/3, 87–135.

170. Michael Trowitzsch highlights the theme of bold humility in IV/3 ("Yes and No. The 'Strange Battle' of Jesus Christ according to Karl Barth," Public Lecture at Princeton Theological Seminary, April 7, 2009). The bold humility of the church in the context of its missionary existence is a recurring theme in Barth's discussion of Christ's resurrection. For instance, Barth's final point in his discussion of the future of Jesus Christ in "Jesus, Lord of Time" (§47.1) concerns the twin dangers of underestimating and overestimating the Christian community (*CD* III/2, 509–11).

temporal-historical context of the event of vocation. Instead, he asserts that the calling of the Christian is an event that *comes* to her from beyond herself. However, Barth also warns against an overreaction in favor of the objective pole of vocation. The calling that comes to us really does come to *us*, so Barth does not wish to deny the subjective aspect of vocation.[171] His concern is rather with a problematically vague or generic doctrine of vocation, which can take either subjectivist or objectivist forms.[172]

What can render vocation concrete? Barth's answer is that the subject of the event of vocation is the living Christ. *He* renders vocation concrete. How does Barth arrive at this claim? In contrast to both subjectivist and objectivist abstractions, Barth asserts that the event of vocation is "itself a temporal event."[173] The time in which this event takes place is fulfilled time.[174] "It will thus be a history which itself makes history."[175] Yet even as a temporal-historical event, vocation is "decisively and predominantly a *spiritual* process."[176] It is not spiritual in a generic sense, but spiritual in the specific sense of being enacted by the Holy Spirit: "The Holy Ghost who does this in time and history is not an anonymous magnitude and force using the Gospel to accomplish it. As the Spirit of the Father and the Son He is the power of the Gospel itself to call and enlighten and sanctify and preserve man in the true faith."[177] This Spirit is the power of Christ's self-witness. The Spirit's work is to make him present. So, as the work of the Spirit in our time and history, vocation has as its acting subject the living Jesus Christ himself. The living Christ as both God and human embraces both the temporal-historical and the spiritual aspects of vocation. He thus renders vocation concrete. "The historical process of vocation is thus highly extraordinary and yet also supremely simple. It is a temporal and historical event among others, and yet it is distinguished by this manner and content."[178]

---

171. This dialectical assessment emerges within the context of Barth's excursus on the history of the doctrine of vocation (*CD* IV/3, 497–99). Barth cites a number of biblical and historical examples of deeply personal experiences of vocation, indicating that the primacy of the larger context of God's activity in Jesus Christ is not incompatible with the personal side of vocation.

172. *CD* IV/3, 498: "The object and theme of theology and the content of the Christian message is neither a subjective nor an objective element in isolation."

173. *CD* IV/3, 497.

174. *CD* IV/3, 500: "Time does not remain empty but is filled, nor does history break off but new history begins, where and when and whenever vocation takes place."

175. *CD* IV/3, 500.

176. *CD* IV/3, 501, original German emphasis restored (*KD* IV/3, 576).

177. *CD* IV/3, 501.

178. *CD* IV/3, 502.

This much can be drawn directly from Barth's doctrine of the threefold parousia. But, as I have indicated, the Trinitarian theology of Christ's resurrection operative in IV/3 is not just a third thing alongside the twofold dialectic of IV/1–2. The one who is present is the one who was raised and arose. The unity of the raising and the arising of Jesus Christ in his risen presence is the unique contribution of IV/3. Therefore, it is fitting that Barth, in the context of his exegetical substantiation of the claim that the living Jesus Christ is the subject of vocation, calls on the full resources of his complex Trinitarian theology of Easter.

Barth begins by observing that there is no direct New Testament evidence for the traditional attribution of the work of calling to the Holy Spirit. This does not mean the attribution is false. "The presence and action of the Holy Spirit are the *parousia* of Jesus Christ in the time between Easter and His final revelation."[179] Since the event of vocation takes place in this time between the times, it is wholly appropriate to attribute it to the Holy Spirit. But this lack of direct New Testament evidence serves as a reminder "that in this context the Holy Spirit is not spoken of in such a way that Jesus Christ is obscured or even completely concealed as the Subject who acts in Him and through Him and therefore truly calls."[180]

Barth goes on to assert that the same rule applies to our talk of "God." In this case, there is direct New Testament evidence: "Where the New Testament speaks generally of κλῆσις as the historical beginning of the Christian state, in obvious agreement with the Old it calls God Himself the great καλῶν. It does this explicitly in 1 Thess. 2:12 and 4:7, 1 Cor 1:9 and 7:15 and Heb. 5:4, and implicitly in a much larger group of sayings."[181] "Yet," Barth observes, "this does not prevent Christians from being described as the called of the *Kyrios* or of Jesus Christ, as in 1 Cor. 7:17 and Rom. 1:6."[182] In addition to these particular texts, Barth identifies a narrative pattern in the New Testament:

> And it is significant for our present purpose that whenever the process of vocation is described as such, especially in the stories of the calling of the disciples in the Gospels and of Paul in Acts, there is no question of an action of God the Father in which He in some sense by-passes or overlooks Jesus and deals with the person called simply as God. Nor is there any question of a corresponding action of the

---

179. *CD* IV/3, 503.
180. *CD* IV/3, 503.
181. *CD* IV/3, 503.
182. *CD* IV/3, 503.

Holy Spirit, just as for good reasons there is no question of a vocation of Jesus Himself, since the Word obviously does not stand in any need of a prior Word of calling. On the contrary, when vocation is recounted as a history, Jesus Christ is quite plainly the One who calls.[183]

In light of this pattern, Barth lays down the following negative rule: "If, in those passages which speak more generally of calling, God as well as Jesus Christ is described as the One who calls, this is not, of course, an indication that the New Testament knows two kinds of vocation, the one effected by God the Father, the other by Jesus Christ, and possibly a third by the Holy Spirit."[184]

Having ruled out any division or competition between God, Jesus Christ, and the Holy Spirit in the event of vocation, Barth develops the positive side of his argument by means of a direct reference to his Trinitarian theology of Easter. The alternating attribution of vocation in the New Testament "corresponds to, and is even interconnected with, the fact that in the New Testament there are also two ways of speaking of the Easter event."[185]

The correspondence consists in the pattern of multiple ways of speaking about one and the same event. In the case of Easter: "On the one side, it is Christ's raising up (*Auferweckung*) by God the Father, and on the other it is His own resurrection (*Auferstehen*), and a third possibility may perhaps be seen in Rom. 1:4 with its reference to the power (*Macht*) of the Holy Spirit operative in this event."[186] In the case of the event of vocation: "To the question of the concrete *form* in which *God* calls, the only answer is obviously that it is *Jesus* who does it in all the concreteness of His humanity. And to the question of how *Jesus comes* to do it, the only answer is obviously that in what this man does *God* is at work in His eternal mercy and omnipotence."[187] Barth concludes, "In both cases the statements are complementary."[188] His point is that in the event

---

183. CD IV/3, 503.
184. CD IV/3, 503.
185. CD IV/3, 503.
186. CD IV/3, 503.
187. CD IV/3, 503, translation revised and original German emphasis restored (KD IV/3, 579). Befitting the Christology of IV/3, Barth here maps the Trinitarian theology of Easter onto the two "natures" of Christ. Thus the Spirit appears only as a "third possibility." See ch. 5 for my constructive suggestions on how to develop the pneumatological aspect of Easter without undermining Barth's christocentrism.
188. CD IV/3, 503.

of vocation, just as in the event of Easter, "the New Testament does not see two or three different things here, but only one thing."[189]

After so describing the correspondence between Easter and vocation, Barth then indicates their interconnection. "And if by calling we do not wish to understand anything different from what the New Testament describes as such, our only option is also to see one thing, or rather one person, i.e., Jesus Christ, the true Son of God and of Man, living (*lebendig*) because risen (*auferstanden*) from the dead in the power (*Macht*) of the One who raised (*erweckte*) Him from the dead, needing no calling but Himself issuing His incomparable call."[190]

As this quote evinces, Barth's entire Trinitarian theology of Easter underwrites his claim that the living Christ is the acting subject of the event of vocation. The living Christ who is present and active in this event is the one who was raised by God the Father and who arose in the power of the Spirit. The unity of these multiple aspects is found in his livingness, that is, Jesus Christ's purposive movement of self-attestation. He lives, declaring himself as he strides through history, and calling others to join him in his self-declaration. Barth's claim that the living Christ is the subject of vocation is thus not the mere application of his Trinitarian theology of Easter to a different subject matter, but the location of that subject matter within the living history of the risen Christ.

The identification of Christ as the subject of vocation is a supremely practical matter because Barth's whole understanding of the Christian life as fellowship with Jesus Christ in the service of witness hangs on this claim. First of all, the content and form of vocation as the historical beginning of the Christian state is "established and determined by the subject who acts in it."[191] *Because* Jesus Christ is its subject, vocation is both a temporal-historical process and a predominantly spiritual process. *Because* the one Jesus Christ is its subject, vocation is a singular event,[192] and thus must be described in its unity and totality.[193] *Because* Jesus Christ is its subject, vocation is immediate, and as such both external and internal, both once-for-all and continuous.[194] Barth explicitly

---

189. *CD* IV/3, 503.

190. *CD* IV/3, 503, translation revised.

191. *CD* IV/3, 519.

192. *CD* IV/3, 505: "As surely as the one Jesus Christ is the active and effective Subject in this event, so the vocation of man is a single and total occurrence in relation to him." Barth sets this point in contrast to the notion of an *ordo salutis*, which he criticizes in this context (*CD* IV/3, 505–7).

193. Barth applies this rule to the concepts with which he describes the content of vocation: "illumination" and "awakening." Given the interconnection just sketched between the events of Easter and vocation, it is fitting that both concepts are developed with explicit reference to the resurrection of Jesus Christ (*CD* IV/3, 509 and 511–12). The living Christ himself illumines and awakens us.

grounds all these claims concerning the content and form of vocation on the thesis that the living Jesus Christ is its acting subject.

Barth's discussion of vocation in §71.2 serves to secure the meaning of the doctrine of vocation christologically. This has significant consequences for subsequent subsections. For instance, in §71.3 Barth identifies the goal of vocation as becoming a Christian, that is, sonship, fellowship, and union with the living Christ. In this context, Barth develops the meaning of union with Christ in terms of participation in Christ's prophetic office. Then in §71.4, Barth argues at great length that the essence of the Christian life is the service of witness. To be united with the living Christ is to participate in his self-witness for the sake of the world. Being a Christian is thus not about me and my salvation from the world but about Jesus Christ and his service to the world. These contributions of Barth's doctrine of vocation flow from his claim that Christ is the subject of the event of vocation. As I have shown, this claim rests on Barth's Trinitarian theology of Easter. Thus, the practical significance of Barth's Trinitarian theology of Christ's parousia, and in fact of his entire Trinitarian theology of Christ's resurrection, is that the living Jesus Christ is *with us*. He is present and active, calling free human subjects to fellowship with him in the service of witness.

By highlighting this significance, we have come to the end of this study of the Trinitarian theology of Christ's resurrection as it comes to expression in IV/3. I have once again asked how and why Christ is risen, and found that Barth's answer follows a Trinitarian logic. Christ's resurrection is his ever-new coming again, his *parousia*. This purposive movement through time follows a Trinitarian grammar and is grounded in the very life of the triune God, the God who comes again and again in his perichoretic self-communication and self-impartation. This Trinitarian theology of Christ's parousia underwrites a christocentric account of vocation, and all that such an account entails for the Christian life.

This third perspective found in IV/3 establishes the teleological unity of the perspectives dialectically juxtaposed in IV/1 and IV/2. The *raising* of Jesus Christ by God the Father and Jesus Christ's own *arising* in the power of the Spirit are *two* aspects of the *one* Easter event in which Christ *lives* and so is *present* for, to, and with us, incorporating us into his self-attestation as true God and true human. By asserting this unity, we come to the end of this analysis of Barth's Trinitarian theology of Christ's resurrection in the context of his threefold

---

194. *CD* IV/3, 514–18 and 520.

doctrine of reconciliation. The task that remains is to draw together Barth's presentation in order to assess its retrospective and prospective possibilities.

5

The Resurrected God

This study began in search of the living God. Its point of entry has been the resurrection of Jesus Christ. The good news of Easter is that God is the God not of the dead, but of the living. Barth has taught us to see how the truth of God's own livingness is embedded within this good news, that is, that the triune life of God is made manifest in the Easter event. Because God is a living fellowship, he can be both the God who resurrects and the God who is resurrected, all the while remaining one and the same God. The doctrine of the Trinity attempts to make sense of the God manifest in this event. In other words, the doctrine of the Trinity attempts to make sense of *the resurrected God*.

In this final chapter, I take up the resurrected God as my theme. This is the explicitly constructive portion of my study. Admittedly, the interpretation of Barth's theology set forth in the previous chapters is already constructive, as all acts of interpretation are. But now the constructive question takes center stage: In what does God's readiness for resurrection consist? What does it mean to say that God is eternally fit for resurrection? Although the beginnings of an answer can be found in his texts, Barth does not pose this question directly. Picking up where he left off is the task of this concluding chapter. My main constructive thesis is that God's readiness for resurrection consists in his triune life.

Retrospective

The point of entry for developing this constructive thesis involves a retrospective glance at Barth's earlier doctrine of the Trinity. In *Church Dogmatics* I/1, Barth argues that the doctrine of the Trinity is a legitimate interpretation of the concept of revelation. God reveals himself as Lord. As such, God is the subject of revelation in all its aspects. The one God is revealer, revelation, and being-revealed. God is the source, the act, and the effect of revelation. This threefold grammar of revelation is the one true vestige of the Trinity. In his threefold revelation, God corresponds to his own threefold being as Father, Son, and Holy Spirit. Because God reveals himself as triune, we know that he is triune antecedently in himself.[1] So, God's readiness for revelation consists in his triune life.[2]

The key move I wish to make is to set "resurrection" within this Trinitarian grammar. Just as God's readiness for *revelation* consists in his triune life, so also God's readiness for *resurrection* consists in his triune life. As I have already pointed out, revelation remains an important function of Christ's resurrection throughout Barth's career. So it is not a stretch to substitute resurrection for revelation in Barth's Trinity doctrine. However, Barth's mature theology of Easter overcomes his earlier tendency to reduce Christ's resurrection to its revelatory function. Therefore, bringing Barth's later Trinitarian theology of Easter to bear on his earlier doctrine of the Trinity entails revision, not merely repetition.

Making such a move suggests a subtle shift in the place of the doctrine of the Trinity in dogmatic theology. In §8.1, Barth makes a strong case for placing the doctrine of the Trinity at the head of dogmatics, within its prolegomena. Barth has Schleiermacher in his sights here, who famously placed his doctrine of the Trinity at the end of his *Christian Faith*.[3] I wholly endorse Barth's decision to treat the doctrine of the Trinity first, so that the identity of God is clear from the beginning.

However, this placement of the doctrine of the Trinity does not imply that the material exposition of the doctrine somehow precedes a priori the narration of God's works and ways with us in history. Barth is clear that this is not his intention. The *doctrine* of the Trinity arises from the *event* of revelation, not the other way around. Therefore, Barth's material exposition of the doctrine of the Trinity does not cease at the end of *CD* I/1, but continues throughout his dogmatics. So, despite their stark opposition on the place of the doctrine of the Trinity in the structure of dogmatics, Schleiermacher and Barth agree that the material exposition of the doctrine of the Trinity arises from the knowledge of God-with-us. This means that by revisiting Barth's doctrine of the Trinity in light of his later theology of Easter, I am working with the grain of Barth's intentions even as I develop his insights beyond him.

The constructive move I am making also requires a subtle shift in what Barth calls the "root" of the doctrine of the Trinity. Barth identifies this root in §8.2 as the threefold event of revelation. Stated conceptually, the one God is

---

1. I am here summarizing the argument of *CD* I/1, §8–12.
2. For use of the idiom of divine readiness, see *CD* II/1, 63–128.
3. Friedrich Schleiermacher, *The Christian Faith*, ed. H. R. Mackintosh and J. S. Stewart (Edinburgh: T&T Clark, 1999), 738–51.

revealer, revelation, and revealedness. "Revelation in the Bible means the self-unveiling, imparted to men, of the God who by nature cannot be unveiled to men."[4] The self-unveiling takes place in Jesus Christ, who is God's revelation, that is, God the Son. In this revelation, God remains the God who by nature cannot be unveiled to us, that is, God the Father. Even still, the revelation is effective, a genuine impartation of God, that is, God the Holy Spirit. Now this is all very conceptual. But Barth's threefold concept of revelation is explicitly tied to a rather straightforward threefold narrative: Good Friday, Easter, and Pentecost. The one God is veiled in the death of Jesus Christ, unveiled in the resurrection of Jesus Christ, and imparted in the outpouring of the Holy Spirit on the community of Jesus Christ.[5]

The move I am proposing is to single out the central element of this triad for further Trinitarian development. As I have shown, in Barth's later work the resurrection of Jesus Christ is itself a multifaceted event with its own Trinitarian structure. Therefore, we can say that *the event of Christ's resurrection is the root of the doctrine of the Trinity*. This is not a contradiction of Barth's claim that revelation is the root of the doctrine of the Trinity. Rather, it is a compression of that claim in terms of its center in Easter.[6] Nevertheless, this compression does yield new insights.

Stated conceptually, the one God is resurrector, resurrected, and resurrecting. Just as there is a source, act, and effect in revelation, so also there is a source, act, and effect in resurrection. God is the *resurrector*: the source, author, and initiator of the resurrection of Jesus from the dead. God is also, in his self-identification with Jesus, the *resurrected*: the one who was raised, arises, and is perpetually present. And God is the *resurrecting* power and purpose of Easter: the being-resurrected of Jesus with us, his "resurrectedness," eternal life in the Spirit. This threefold God manifest in the one event of Easter corresponds to the eternal three-in-one God.

As can already be seen in this schematic presentation, the grammar of Barth's earlier doctrine of the Trinity has shifted slightly. A more precise parallel would speak of the second person of the Trinity as the "resurrection." That would be fine, especially given the Johannine dictum, "I am the resurrection and the life" (John 11:25). However, this slight shift brings to light the Trinitarian difference Barth's mature theology of Easter makes, for Jesus Christ

---

4. *CD* I/1, 315.

5. *CD* I/1, 332.

6. Barth even highlights the centrality of Easter by disrupting the chronological sequence in keeping with his christological concentration: "Easter, Good Friday and Pentecost, or Son, Father and Spirit" (*CD* I/1, 332).

is the subject of his own resurrection precisely as the one who was raised by God the Father. The Son is the *resurrected* one. The meaning and implications of this shift cannot be explored by a mere schematic presentation. Furthermore, the formal parallel to Barth's earlier doctrine of the Trinity is not the point. It is only the point of entry to develop my constructive claim that God's eternal readiness for resurrection consists in his triune life.

Prospective

I will develop this main thesis by advancing three exploratory subtheses. God's antecedent fitness for resurrection consists in (1) the unconquerable unity of God, (2) the distinctive genetic relations within God, and (3) the livingness of God's triunity. Taken together, these three subtheses explain and substantiate the claim that God's readiness for resurrection consists in his triune life. Their purpose is to explore the theological prospects opened up by Barth's Trinitarian theology of Easter.

(1) My first exploratory thesis is that **God's readiness for resurrection consists in the *unconquerable unity* of God.** Following the order of *CD* I/1, we begin with the *oneness* of the resurrected God.[7] At first glance, it might appear that God in his eternal oneness is unfit to become the resurrected God. God as a single subject may be ready to raise another, but how can God himself undergo resurrection? If we take seriously that Jesus Christ in his divine-human unity died and was raised, then we might be tempted to soften or even reject the singularity of God's essence.

Here is where Barth's earlier Trinitarian model bears its fruit. God as one subject in three modes of being is ready for resurrection. Because God's essence is numerically one,[8] the triune God is the subject of Christ's resurrection in all its aspects. God is the source, event, and result of Christ's resurrection. God is the one who resurrects, the one who is resurrected, and the one who empowers

---

7. Barth does not begin with an *independent* doctrine of the one God and then append to it or derive from it God's triunity. He explicitly rejects such a move (*CD* I/1, 300–304). Rather, Barth begins with the oneness of God in order to accentuate the *intention* of the doctrine of the Trinity, i.e., that God is who he is in his revelation to us. Wolfhart Pannenberg, while affirming Barth's procedure, argues that Barth failed to bring the doctrine of the one God under the control of God's acts in history "because Barth subordinated his doctrine of the Trinity to a pre-trinitarian concept of the unity of God and his subjectivity in revelation" in *Systematic Theology*, Vol. 1 (Grand Rapids: Eerdmans, 1991), 299. Although such a criticism might be leveled against *CD* I/1, it does not apply to the Trinitarian moves in *CD* IV/1–3 as I have interpreted them in the preceding chapters. My constructive combination of Barth's earlier and later works ought to address Pannenberg's systematic concern.

8. *CD* I/1, 350.

and sustains resurrected life. In this threefold way, God is the *one* subject of Easter. The threeness of God manifest in the Easter event does not contradict the eternal oneness of God. God in his oneness is ready for resurrection.[9]

This claim requires us to rethink the meaning of divine unity for Christ's resurrection. God's readiness for resurrection does not consist in an abstract oneness. This negation is important, because it is tempting to appeal to the perfections of God's one essence as constituting God's readiness for resurrection. For instance, omnipotence seems a likely candidate for the divine basis of Christ's resurrection. But to think this way is to abstract the divine essence from God's actuality. The unity of God is the unity of the Father, Son, and Holy Spirit. The point of the doctrine of divine unity is that there is no partition between God as Creator, God as Reconciler, and God as Redeemer.[10] So there should be no talk of God as omnipotent Creator who can raise the dead in abstraction from God the Reconciler who tasted death for us or God the Redeemer who empowers eternal life. The one God—Father, Son, and Holy Spirit—is the subject of resurrection.

Furthermore, God's readiness for resurrection consists in his *unconquerable* unity. One of Barth's early Trinitarian moves was to identify God's essence with his lordship.[11] Although Barth has been criticized for this move,[12] it has great potential when combined with his mature Trinitarian theology of Easter in *CD* IV/1–3. Because God's unitary essence is his lordship, he is eternally fit to overcome death's threat to his unity. In the Easter event, God asserts his lordship over death by reasserting his own unique unity. God's unity does not hover over Easter. God reenacts his unity in the resurrection of Jesus Christ. When God the Father raised his Son Jesus Christ from the dead in the power of the Holy Spirit, the triune God reasserted his unity over against the separating power of death. As such, the triune God is the Lord in and over death.[13]

(2) **God's readiness for resurrection also consists in the** *distinctive genetic relations* **within God.** This second exploratory thesis turns to the *threeness* of

---

9. *Pace* the "social Trinitarian" line of criticism that the singular subjectivity of God cannot account for the differentiation manifest in the Easter event. Although my constructive reflections are not directed toward a refutation of social Trinitarianism, they do offer a defense of an alternative account of divine unity that is fit for resurrection.

10. *CD* I/1, §10–12; Cf. also *CD* II/1, 80.

11. *CD* I/1, 349.

12. E.g., Jürgen Moltmann, *The Trinity and the Kingdom* (Minneapolis: Fortress Press, 1993), 139–44.

13. Eberhard Jüngel suggests a similar line of thought in his claim that "the being of God is a unity of life and death, for the benefit of life," in "The Relationship between 'Economic' and 'Immanent' Trinity," *Theology Digest* 24 (1976): 179.

the resurrected God. Whereas my first thesis showed how far Barth's mature theology of Easter confirms his earlier Trinitarian model, this step shows to what extent Barth's mature Trinitarian theology of Easter fleshes out and so advances beyond the formality of his earlier doctrine of the Trinity. Drawing inspiration from Barth's mature theology, we can assert that God's internal relations are *repeated* externally in the Easter event. Since the triune persons are identical with their distinctive genetic relations, we can account for how one triune person can act upon another without denying the singular subjectivity of God.[14] What does this divine self-repetition teach us about the triune God's readiness for resurrection?

First, the Father's readiness for resurrection consists in his relation to the Son in the Spirit. God is the *resurrector* of Jesus Christ, that is, God the Father. As the initiator and source of the Easter event, God the Father repeats in time his eternal relation to the Son. The Father eternally begets the Son. God is not the Father in abstraction, but the Father *of the Son*. As the eternal Father of the Son, God the Father is antecedently fit to resurrect the Son in time. But we can even go a step further: God the Father raised Jesus Christ in the power of the Holy Spirit. Easter gives us grounds for saying that the Father relates to the Son *in the Spirit*. Although the Spirit proceeds from the Father and the Son, he proceeds precisely as the mediator of the relation between the Father and the Son. And so we can assert that the Father's readiness for resurrection consists in his relation to the Son in the Spirit.

Second, the Son's readiness for resurrection consists in his relation to the Father in the Spirit. God is also *resurrected* in Jesus Christ, that is, God the Son. As the one in whom the event of Easter takes place, God the Son repeats in time his eternal relation to the Father. The Son is eternally begotten *of the Father*. The Son suffers no diminution of deity in being the object and recipient of the Father's eternal act of generating him. Analogously, Jesus Christ was raised by God the Father without ceasing to be God.[15] However, the Son not only receives the Father's generating act, but also in turn loves, obeys, and glorifies the Father in the Spirit. The Son repeats this active side of his relation to the

---

14. On distinctive genetic relations identical with triune persons, see *CD* I/1, 362–68. In *CD* IV/1–3, Barth asserts the repetition of these relations in the Easter event, and therefore allows for a more clearly differentiated interaction between and among the triune persons in time.

15. Barth's earlier doctrine of the Trinity treats the Son primarily as the Father's act/means/agent in history, which is not wrong, but one-sided. Barth's mature Trinitarian theology of Easter helps us to capture how the Son can be the object and recipient of the Father's act not only in eternity but also in time. Jesus Christ is the *resurrection* for us (John 11:35), but he is so always as the *resurrected* one (Rom. 8:34).

Father in Christ's own arising in the power of the Spirit. And so, as the eternal Son of the Father, God the Son is antecedently fit to be resurrected. The Son's readiness for resurrection consists in his relation to the Father in the Spirit.

Third, the Spirit's readiness for resurrection consists in his relation to the Father and the Son. God is finally the *resurrecting* power of Jesus Christ, that is, God the Holy Spirit. The eschatological power and presence of the risen Christ is God himself in his third mode of being.[16] As the goal and effectiveness of the Easter event, God the Holy Spirit repeats in time his relation to the Father and the Son.[17] The Spirit proceeds from the Father and the Son, and unites the Father and the Son. As the mediator between the Father and the Son, the Holy Spirit is the culmination of the divine life. As was the case with the Son, both directions of this relation are repeated in the Easter event. The Holy Spirit is the power of God the Father's raising of Jesus Christ, and so mediates the risen Christ's eternal fellowship with his Father. And the Holy Spirit is the power of the resurrection as it culminates in our eternal fellowship with the risen Christ in the service of witness.[18] As the eternal Spirit of the Father and the Son, God the Holy Spirit is antecedently fit for this work. The Spirit's readiness for resurrection consists in his relation to the Father and the Son.

---

16. As I have tried to show throughout this book, Barth's mature Trinitarian theology of Easter helps him to bring into view the distinct activity of the Holy Spirit without sacrificing his christological concentration. However, its enclosure within the structure of *CD* IV/1-3 can easily obscure this view. The raising/arising dialectic correlates nicely with the deity and humanity of Jesus Christ, and so also with the Father-Son relation. The Holy Spirit is a "third possibility" from which one could speak of Easter, rather than a distinct theme (*CD* IV/3, 503; cf. ch. 4, "The Significance of a Trinitarian Theology of Christ's Parousia (§71.2)"). My systematic presentation in this final chapter develops beyond Barth the constructive prospects of the pneumatology operative in his Trinitarian theology of Easter. Although we will never know, a strong case can be made that in the projected fifth volume of the *Church Dogmatics* Barth would have begun with Jesus Christ in his resurrection from the dead in order to explicate the work of redemption appropriated to God the Holy Spirit.

17. Hans Urs von Balthasar captures this idea with his suggestion that the Holy Spirit is "the milieu in which the Resurrection takes place" in *Mysterium Paschale* (Edinburgh: T&T Clark, 1990), 211. Balthasar's own Trinitarian theology of Easter relies heavily on the influential exegetical work of David Michael Stanley, *Christ's Resurrection in Pauline Soteriology* (Rome: Pontificio Istituto Biblico, 1961), esp. 250-86. Although its exegetical method is dated, Stanley's work provides a thorough collection of the New Testament materials necessary for developing a Trinitarian theology of Easter.

18. According to Paul, the Father of Jesus will raise the dead by his Spirit (Rom. 8:11), resulting in Spirit-activated bodies (1 Cor. 15:42-44). For a pneumatological interpretation of the meaning of "spiritual bodies" in 1 Corinthians, see N. T. Wright, *The Resurrection of the Son of God* (Minneapolis: Fortress Press, 2003), 347-56 and idem, *Surprised by Hope: Rethinking Heaven, the Resurrection, and the Mission of the Church* (New York: HarperOne, 2008), 155-56.

(3) So far we have explored the claim that God's readiness for resurrection consists in his triune life from two perspectives: the oneness and threeness of the resurrected God. What else needs to be said? We cannot synthesize these two, but we can reassert the two at once in terms of the *livingness* of the resurrected God. To say that God is both one and three is to say that God is the living God.[19] And so my third and final exploratory thesis is that **God's readiness for resurrection consists in the** *livingness of God's triunity***.**

The God of Easter is the living God. The oneness of the resurrected God is not dead, but living. The God of Easter is not an immovable monad but mutual interpenetration of persons.[20] And the threeness of the resurrected God is not dead, but living. The Easter distinction between the Father and the Son is not a rigid separation, but a moving fellowship in the Spirit. In the Easter event, God's livingness is definitively revealed. In the resurrection of Jesus Christ, the triune God reveals to us his very own *life*. The living God is therefore antecedently fit for resurrection.

Because he is living, not dead, God can genuinely *activate* his being in time without diminution of his perfection. God's triune life is not diminished in repeating his internal relations, because God's being is always already in-act. Barth interprets the traditional doctrine of perichoresis in terms of this eternal being-in-becoming: each mode of being in God completely participates in the other two.[21] So God is always already a living, moving God—a God who is on his way from himself to himself. The livingness of God manifest in the Easter event is thus an outworking of God's eternal livingness. God is being true to himself when he activates himself in time, because God is in himself a living, moving, active being. The living God is ready for resurrection.

Furthermore, because he is living, not dead, God can anticipate and so *include* his temporal activation within his eternal being. In his eternal life, God anticipates his livingness in time. God's eternal livingness encloses within itself his temporal livingness. The resurrection of Jesus Christ from the dead took place *for us*, but it also took place *in God*, insofar as the triune God eternally willed to be united with Jesus of Nazareth. By way of anticipation, God is in

---

19. God's *livingness* and *triunity* are nearly synonymous in Barth's theology. The two are repeatedly found in apposition to one another throughout the *Church Dogmatics*. The most explicit discussion of their interconnection is found in *CD* II/1, §28.1.

20. Barth signals this consequence of divine perichoresis by the conflation *triunity*, which "indicates that we are concerned here, not just about unity, but about the unity of being one which is always also a becoming one" (*CD* I/1, 369).

21. See *CD* I/1, 370; and *CD* IV/3, 296.

himself for us. In other words, the living God is from and to all eternity also the God of the living.[22]

Finally, because the living God eternally anticipates his Easter self-activation, he is *"materially"* ready for resurrection. God's readiness is not a mere formal or structural fitness.[23] It is not just a happy coincidence that the threeness-in-oneness of God matches the threeness-in-oneness of Easter. Rather, God's readiness for resurrection has concrete content—the living Jesus Christ in his eternal fellowship with God the Father by the power of the Holy Spirit. God in his second mode of being identifies himself from and to all eternity with the man Jesus. The living God eternally determines himself to be present and active in the living Christ. And so the livingness of the triune God and the livingness of the risen Christ coincide materially. In this particular sense, God is "materially" ready for resurrection.

In this final chapter I have asserted that God's readiness for resurrection consists in his triune life. I have explored this thesis from three perspectives: the *threeness*, *oneness,* and *livingness* of the resurrected God. These exploratory theses are intended to highlight the prospective possibilities that flow from Barth's Trinitarian theology of Easter. In addition to opening up these constructive vistas, this chapter also serves to point us back to the assurance, joy, and hope of the Easter gospel. The resurrected God is the triune God; the triune God is the resurrected God.[24] In the resurrection of Jesus Christ we encounter the living God, and so we can confidently declare, "He is God not of the dead, but of the living."

---

22. This line of thought clarifies and deepens the sense in which Christ's resurrection is an "eternal event" on the one hand, and the eternal being of triune God is "historical" on the other. These sorts of phrases frustrate Barth's interpreters. But the former is not meant to deny the historicity of Easter and the latter is not meant to deny the eternality of God's triunity. Rather, they point to the enclosure of time within eternity. God's eternity is not a dead timelessness, but a living transcendence of the brokenness of time, i.e., the death that divides past and future.

23. This is the perpetual danger of the grammatical Trinitarianism of *CD* I/1. As I have tried to show throughout this book, the formal Trinitarian grammar of gospel proclamation is *the* starting point for theological reflection, but we must press on to the material ground of the gospel in the triune life of God.

24. This is a special application of what Barth calls "The Meaning of the Doctrine of the Trinity" (§9.4), i.e., that our God is *God*, and God is *our* God (*CD* I/1, 383).

Bibliography

Athanasius. *On the Incarnation: The Treatise De incarnatione Verbi Dei*. Crestwood, NY: St. Vladimir's Orthodox Theological Seminary.

Balthasar, Hans Urs von. *Mysterium Paschale*. Edinburgh: T&T Clark, 1990.

Barth, Karl. *Der Römerbrief*. Zürich: Evangelischer Verlag, 1922.

———. *Die Christliche Dogmatik in Entwurf*. Munich: Chr. Kaiser Verlag, 1927.

———. *The Epistle to the Romans*. Translated by Edwyn C. Hoskyns. London: Oxford University Press, 1933.

———. *Die kirchliche Dogmatik*. 4 vols. in 13 parts. Munich: Chr. Kaiser Verlag, 1932, and Zürich: Theologischer Verlag, 1938–65.

———. *The Church Dogmatics*. 4 vols. in 13 parts. Edinburgh: T&T Clark, 1956–69, 1975.

———. *The Humanity of God*. Richmond, VA: John Knox, 1964.

———. *Letters 1961–68*. Jürgen Fangmeier and Heinrich Stoevesandt, eds. Grand Rapids: Eerdmans, 1981.

———. *The Göttingen Dogmatics*. Vol. 1. Grand Rapids: Eerdmans, 1991.

Berkhof, Hendrik, and Hans-Joachim Kraus. *Karl Barths Lichterlehre*. Theologische Studien 123. Zürich: Theologischer Verlag, 1978.

Bornkamm, Karin. "Die reformatorische Lehre vom Amt Christ und ihre Umformung durch Karl Barth." In *Zur Theologie Karl Barths*, ed. E. Jüngel. *Zeitschrift für Theologie und Kirche,* Beiheft 6 (1986), 1–32.

Brodeur, Scott. *The Holy Spirit's Agency in the Resurrection of the Dead: An Exegetico-Theological Study of 1 Corinthians 15,44b-49 and Romans 8,9-13*. Rome: Pontificia Università Gregoriana, 1996.

Bultmann, Rudolf. *Faith and Understanding*. Philadelphia: Fortress Press, 1969.

Burgess, Andrew. *The Ascension in Karl Barth*. Hampshire: Ashgate, 2004.

Busch, Eberhard. *Karl Barth: His Life from Letters and Autobiographical Texts*. Philadelphia: Fortress Press, 1976.

———. *Karl Barth and the Pietists: The Young Karl Barth's Critique of Pietism and Its Response*. Downers Grove, IL: InterVarsity, 2004.

———. *The Great Passion: An Introduction to Karl Barth's Theology*. Grand Rapids: Eerdmans, 2004.

Calvin, John. *Institutes of the Christian Religion*. Edited by John T. McNeill. Translated by Ford Lewis Battles. London: SCM Press, 1961.

Carnley, Peter. *The Structure of Resurrection Belief.* Oxford: Clarendon, 1987.

Christian, William A. *Doctrines of Religious Communities: A Philosophical Study.* New Haven, CT: Yale University Press, 1987.

Coakley, Sarah. "Why Three? Some Further Reflections on the Origins of the Doctrine of the Trinity." In *The Making and Remaking of Christian Doctrine: Essays in Honour of Maurice Wiles*, ed. Sarah Coakley and David A. Pailin, 29–56. Oxford: Clarendon, 1993.

Dalferth, Ingolf U. "Karl Barth's Eschatological Realism." In *Karl Barth: Centenary Essays*, ed. S. W. Sykes, 14–45. Cambridge: Cambridge University Press, 1989.

———. *Der auferweckte Gekreuzigte: Zur Grammatik der Christologie.* Tübingen: J. C. B. Mohr (Paul Siebeck), 1994.

Dawson, Richard Dale. *The Resurrection in Karl Barth.* Hampshire: Ashgate, 2007.

Eitel, Adam. "The Resurrection of Jesus Christ: Karl Barth and the Historicization of God's Being." *International Journal of Systematic Theology* 10, no. 1 (January 2008): 36–53.

Farrow, Douglas. *Ascension and Ecclesia: On the Significance of the Doctrine of the Ascension for Ecclesiology and Christian Cosmology.* Grand Rapids: Eerdmans, 1999.

Flett, John G. *The Witness of God: The Trinity, Missio Dei, Karl Barth, and the Nature of Christian Community.* Grand Rapids: Eerdmans, 2010.

Frei, Hans W. *The Identity of Jesus Christ: The Hermeneutical Bases of Dogmatic Theology.* Eugene, OR: Wipf and Stock, 1997.

Greene-McCreight, Kathryn. *Ad Litteram: How Augustine, Calvin, and Barth Read the "Plain Sense" of Genesis 1–3.* New York: Peter Lang, 1999.

Guretzki, David. *Karl Barth on the Filioque.* Hampshire: Ashgate, 2009.

Hart, Trevor. *Regarding Karl Barth: Toward a Reading of His Theology.* Downers Grove, IL: InterVarsity, 1999.

Harvey, Van A. *The Historian and the Believer: The Morality of Historical Knowledge and Christian Belief.* Urbana, IL: University of Illinois Press, 1966.

Higton, Mike. *Christ, Providence & History: Hans W. Frei's Public Theology.* New York: T&T Clark, 2004.

Hunsinger, George. *How to Read Karl Barth: The Shape of His Theology.* New York: Oxford University Press, 1991.

———. *Disruptive Grace: Studies in the Theology of Karl Barth.* Grand Rapids: Eerdmans, 2000.

———. "The Daybreak of New Creation: Christ's Resurrection in Recent Theology." *Scottish Journal of Theology* 57, no. 2 (2004): 163–81.

———. *Let Us Keep the Feast: The Eucharist and Ecumenism*. Cambridge: Cambridge University Press, 2008.

Jenson, Robert W. "You Wonder Where the Spirit Went." *Pro Ecclesia* 2, no. 3 (1993): 296–304.

———. *Systematic Theology*. Vol. 1. Oxford: Oxford University Press, 1997.

Jüngel, Eberhard. "The Relationship between 'Economic' and 'Immanent' Trinity." *Theology Digest* 24 (1976): 179–84.

———. *Karl Barth, a Theological Legacy*. Translated by Garrett E. Paul. Philadelphia: Westminster, 1986.

———. *God's Being Is in Becoming: The Trinitarian Being of God in the Theology of Karl Barth*. Edinburgh: T&T Clark, 2001.

Keen, Craig. "Holy, Holy, Holy: The World Need Not Have Been." *Wesleyan Theological Journal* 44, no. 1 (Spring 2009): 200–218.

Kerr, Nathan. *Christ, Apocalyptic, and History: The Politics of Christian Mission*. Eugene, OR: Cascade, 2009.

Klappert, Berthold. *Diskussion um Kreuz und Auferstehung: Zur gegenwärtigen Auseinandersetzung in Theologie und Gemeinde*. Wuppertal: Aussaat, 1967.

———. *Die Auferweckung des Gekreuzigten: Der Ansatz der Christologie Karl Barths im Zusammenhang der Christologie der Gegenwart*. Neukirchen-Vluyn: Neukirchener Verlag, 1971.

———. "Die Auferweckung des Gekreuzigten." In *Auferweckung Jesu, Auferweckung der Toten, Auferweckung der Welt: Karl Barths Theologie aufnehmen und weiterdenken*, ed. Bertrold Klappert and Michael Weinrich, 7–22. Herrenalb: Evangelische Akademie Baden, 1989.

———. "Die Rechts-, Freiheits- und Befreiungsgechichte Gottes mit dem Menschen: Karl Barths Versöhnungslehre (*KD* IV/1-3)." *Evangelische Theologie* 49, no. 5 (1989): 460–78.

———. *Versöhnung und Befreiung: Versuche, Karl Barth knotextuell zu verstehen*. Neukirchen-Vluyn: Neukirchener Verlag, 1994.

Künneth, Walter. *Theologie der Auferstehung*. Munich: C. Kaiser, 1933.

Madigan, Kevin J., and Jon D. Levenson. *Resurrection: The Power of God for Christians and Jews*. New Haven, CT: Yale University Press, 2008.

Mangina, Joseph. *Karl Barth on the Christian Life: The Practical Knowledge of God*. New York: Peter Lang, 2001.

Marshall, Bruce. *Christology in Conflict: The Identity of a Saviour in Rahner and Barth*. Oxford: Blackwell, 1987.

---. "Absorbing the World: Christianity and the Universe of Truths." In *Theology and Dialogue: Essays in Conversation with George Lindbeck*, ed. Bruce Marshall, 69–102. South Bend, IN: University of Notre Dame Press, 1990.

---. "Israel." In *Knowing the Triune God: The Work of the Spirit in the Practices of the Church*, ed. James J. Buckley and David S. Yeago, 231–64. Grand Rapids: Eerdmans, 2001.

McCormack, Bruce L. *Karl Barth's Critically Realistic Dialectical Theology: Its Genesis and Development 1909–1936*. Oxford: Clarendon, 1995.

---. *"Justitia Aliena*: Karl Barth in Conversation with the Evangelical Doctrine of Imputed Righteousness." In *Justification in Perspective: Historical Developments and Contemporary Challenges*, ed. Bruce L. McCormack, 167–96. Grand Rapids: Baker Academic, 2006.

---. *Orthodox and Modern: Studies in the Theology of Karl Barth*. Grand Rapids: Baker Academic, 2008.

---. "Divine Impassibility or Simply Divine Constancy? Implications of Karl Barth's Later Christology for Debates over Impassibility." In *Divine Impassibility and the Mystery of Human Suffering*, ed. James F. Keating and Thomas Joseph White, 150–86. Grand Rapids: Eerdmans, 2009.

---. "Trinity and Election: A Progress Report." In *Ontmoetingen Tijdgenoten en getuigen: Studies aangeboden aan Gerrit Neven*, ed. Akke van der Kooi, Volker Küster, and Rinse Reeling Brouwer, 14–35. Kampen: Uitgeverij Kok, 2009.

---. "Karl Barth's Version of an 'Analogy of Being': A Dialectical No and Yes to Roman Catholicism." In *Analogia Entis: Invention of the Antichrist or the Wisdom of God?* ed. Thomas Joseph White, 88–146. Grand Rapids: Eerdmans, 2011.

Migliore, Daniel L. "Vinculum Pacis: Karl Barths Theologie des Heiligen Geistes." *Evangelische Theologie* 60, no. 2 (Jan 2000): 131–52.

Molnar, Paul D. *Incarnation and Resurrection: Toward a Contemporary Understanding*. Grand Rapids: Eerdmans, 2007.

---. Review of *The Resurrection in Karl Barth* by Richard Dale Dawson. *International Journal of Systematic Theology* 11, no. 2 (April 2009): 240–43.

Moltmann, Jürgen. *The Crucified God*. New York: Harper & Row, 1974.

---. *The Trinity and the Kingdom*. Minneapolis: Fortress Press, 1993.

Mueller, David. *Foundation of Karl Barth's Doctrine of Reconciliation: Jesus Christ Crucified and Risen*. Lewiston, NY: Edwin Mellen, 1990.

Neder, Adam. *Participation in Christ: An Entry in Karl Barth's Church Dogmatics*. Louisville: Westminster John Knox, 2009.

Newbigin, Lesslie. *The Household of God*. London: SCM, 1953.
———. *The Open Secret*. Grand Rapids: Eerdmans, 1978.
Newman, John Henry Cardinal. *An Essay on the Development of Doctrine*. South Bend, IN: University of Notre Dame Press, 1989.
Niebuhr, Richard R. *Resurrection and Historical Reason*. New York: Scribner's, 1957.
O'Collins, Gerald. "Karl Barth on Christ's Resurrection." *Scottish Journal of Theology* 26, no. 1 (1973): 85–99.
O'Donovan, Oliver. *Resurrection and Moral Order: An Outline for Evangelical Ethics*, 2nd ed. Grand Rapids: Eerdmans, 1994.
Pannenberg, Wolfhart. *Jesus—God and Man*. Philadelphia: Westminster, 1968.
———. *Systematic Theology*. Vol. 1. Grand Rapids: Eerdmans, 1991.
Rahner, Karl. *Theological Investigations*. Vol. 1. London: Darton, Longman & Todd, 1961.
———. *Theological Investigations*. Vol. 4. Baltimore: Helicon Press, 1966.
———. *The Trinity*. New York: Crossroad, 1997.
Ritschl, Albrecht. *The Christian Doctrine of Justification and Reconciliation*. Vol. 3. Edinburgh: T&T Clark, 1900.
———. *Three Essays*. Philadelphia: Fortress, 1972.
Roberts, Richard H. "Karl Barth's Doctrine of Time: Its Nature and Implications." In *Karl Barth: Studies of his Theological Method*, ed. S. W. Sykes, 88–146. Oxford: Clarendon, 1979.
Robertson, Gregory Alan. "'Vivit! Regnat! Triumphat!': The Prophetic Office of Jesus Christ, the Christian Life, and the Mission of the Church in Karl Barth's *Church Dogmatics* IV, 3. Unpublished Th.D. Thesis, Wycliffe College and the University of Toronto, 2003.
Robinette, Brian D. *Grammars of Resurrection: A Christian Theology of Presence and Absence*. New York: Crossroad, 2009.
———. "The Resurrection in Retrospect: A Response to Recent Criticisms of *Creatio Ex Nihilo*." Presentation at the Annual Meeting of the American Academy of Religion, Nov. 9, 2009.
Rogers, Eugene F. "Eclipse of the Spirit in Karl Barth." In *Conversing with Barth*, ed. John C. McDowell and Mike Higton, 173–190. Hampshire: Ashgate, 2004.
———. "The Eclipse of the Spirit in Thomas Aquinas." In *Grammar and Grace: Reformulations of Aquinas and Wittgenstein*, ed. Jeffrey Stout and Robert MacSwain, 136–53. London: SCM, 2004.

———. *After the Spirit: A Constructive Pneumatology from Resources outside the Modern West*. Grand Rapids: Eerdmans, 2005.

Schleiermacher, Friedrich. *The Christian Faith*. Translated and edited by H. R. Mackintosh and J. S. Stewart. Edinburgh: T&T Clark, 1999.

Schreiber, Tilman. *Die Soteriologische Bedeutung der Auferweckung Jesu Christi in gegenwärtiger systematischer Theologie*. Frankfurt am Main: Peter Lang, 1998.

Siller, Annelore. *Kirche für die Welt: Karl Barths Lehre vom prophetischen Amt Jesu Christi in ihrer Bedeutung für das Verhältnis von Kirche und Welt unter den Bedingungen der Moderne*. Zürich: Theologischer Verlag Zürich, 2009.

Smart, James D. *The Divided Mind of Modern Theology: Karl Barth and Rudolf Bultmann, 1908–1933*. Philadelphia: Westminster, 1967.

Sonderegger, Katherine. "Et Resurrexit Tertia Die: Jenson and Barth on Christ's Resurrection." In *Conversing with Barth*, ed. John C. McDowell and Mike Higton, 191–213. Hampshire: Ashgate, 2004.

Stanley, David Michael. *Christ's Resurrection in Pauline Soteriology*. Rome: Pontificio Istituto Biblico, 1961.

Thomas Aquinas. *Summa Theologica*. Westminster, MD: Christian Classics, 1981.

Thompson, John. "On the Trinity." In *Theology Beyond Christendom: Essays on the Centenary of the Birth of Karl Barth*, ed. John Thompson, 13–32. Allison Park, PA: Pickwick, 1986.

Trowitzsch, Michael. "Yes and No. The 'Strange Battle' of Jesus Christ according to Karl Barth." Public Lecture at Princeton Theological Seminary, April 7, 2009.

Vogel, Heinrich. *Gott im Christo: Ein Erkenntnisgang durch die Grundprobleme der Dogmatik*. Berlin: Lettner Verlag, 1951.

Volf, Miroslav. *After Our Likeness: The Church as an Image of the Trinity*. Grand Rapids: Eerdmans, 1997.

Webster, John. *Barth's Moral Theology: Human Action in Barth's Thought*. Grand Rapids: Eerdmans, 1998.

Webster, John, ed. *The Cambridge Companion to Karl Barth*. Cambridge: Cambridge University Press, 2000.

Weinrich, Michael. "Das prophetische Amt Jesu Christi und der Dienst der Gemeinde in der Welt: Skizzen zu Karl Barths Theologie der Geistesgegenwart." In *Auferweckung Jesu, Auferweckung der Toten, Auferweckung der Welt: Karl Barths Theologie aufnehmen und weiterdenken*, ed. Bertrold Klappert and Michael Weinrich, 61–88. Herrenalb: Evangelische Akademie Baden, 1989.

Wingren, Gustaf. *Theology in Conflict*. Edinburgh: Oliver and Boyd, 1958.
Wright, N. T. *The Resurrection of the Son of God*. Minneapolis: Fortress Press, 2008.
———. *Surprised by Hope: Rethinking Heaven, the Resurrection, and the Mission of the Church*. New York: HarperOne, 2008.

Index

Athanasius, 2, 40, 47, 57, 58

Balthasar, Hans Urs von, 21, 181
Busch, Eberhard, 18, 20, 122, 162

Calvin, John, 130
Coakley, Sarah, 7–8
creation, 20, 21, 30, 31–36, 108, 109, 140, 142, 156

Dalferth, Ingolf, 9, 127
Dawson, R. Dale, 6–7, 14, 17, 37, 40, 42, 46, 50, 75, 82, 152

ecclesiology, 14, 16, 18, 35, 37, 38, 43, 59, 63, 76, 79, 90, 92, 93, 95–99, 100–102, 119, 126, 132, 136, 145, 146, 147, 151, 166–67, 177
Eitel, Adam, 49, 53
election, 33, 58, 61, 73, 74, 76, 109, 112–13, 151, 152, 153, 157–60, 165
eschatology, 23, 31–36, 37, 127, 133, 140, 142–44, 147, 165, 166, 181

Farrow, Douglas, 76, 146
Feuerbach, Ludwig, 154, 166
filioque, 106–8, 116
Flett, John, 167
Frei, Hans, 4, 32

God the Father, 7, 9–11, 13, 15–18, 19–36, 37–40, 41–43, 44–54, 58–62, 67–69, 71, 74, 80, 82, 84, 85, 91, 95–98, 100, 104–9, 114–16, 128–30, 134, 137–44, 151, 156, 158, 169–72, 177, 179, 180–81, 182–83
grace, 2, 11, 13, 16–18, 26–27, 29, 32, 33, 37, 40–43, 44, 45–62, 63–70, 74, 103, 108, 110, 113, 114–15, 118–19, 128, 143, 147, 152, 157–60, 164

Harvey, Van, 3
Higton, Mike, 4
history, 2, 3–5, 9–10, 15, 17, 20, 28, 32–34, 43, 45–54, 55–58, 60, 64, 69, 72, 74–76, 94, 96–98, 99–109, 110, 112, 115, 117, 118, 121, 126, 127, 128, 131–33, 139, 146–47, 149, 150, 151, 153, 154, 156, 157, 160–64, 166, 168–71, 176, 178, 183
Holy Spirit, the, 1–3, 7–12, 13, 15–18, 19, 24–25, 30, 31–32, 35, 36, 37, 41–44, 54, 58–62, 63, 70, 71, 73–74, 76, 77–78, 79, 80–82, 85–98, 99–109, 110, 116–23, 125, 128–30, 132–33, 134, 136–37, 142, 144–150, 163, 165, 166–173, 177, 179, 180–83
Hunsinger, George, 17, 35, 64, 87, 110, 147–48, 153, 161, 164

Jenson, Robert, 2, 86, 129, 145, 147
Jesus Christ: cross, 2, 5–6, 9, 16–21, 23, 27–31, 39–40, 47, 50, 52, 55–57, 61, 65, 77, 79, 83, 86, 122; crucifixion, 5, 16–17, 20–21, 27–29, 35, 46–47, 54, 60, 61, 84, 115; exaltation: 11, 25–26, 59, 72–79, 80–85, 88, 93, 95, 108, 110–12, 114–16, 127–28; humiliation: 11, 17–18, 49, 55, 56, 59, 64, 67, 72–75, 80, 93, 110, 112, 114, 127–28; incarnation: 8, 14, 40, 46–47, 73, 74, 76, 77, 78, 163; *parousia*: 12, 35, 37, 63, 73, 76, 82, 125, 128–31, 132–33, 134–50, 151–52, 160, 164, 166–68, 169, 172;

prophetic office: 125, 127–33, 138, 146, 152–53, 172
Jüngel, Eberhard, 14, 36, 45, 79, 109, 179
justification, 11, 25, 27–31, 34–35, 54, 62–70

Keen, Craig, 34
Kerr, Nathan, 46, 52
Klappert, Berthold, 5–6, 11, 17, 37, 47, 61, 82, 135

Mangina, Joseph, 15, 88
Marshall, Bruce, 91, 122
McCormack, Bruce, 23–24, 64, 76, 89, 103–4, 112–13
mediation, 11, 99–109, 110
Migliore, Daniel, 59, 108
mission, 11, 53, 119–20, 125, 128, 132, 136–37, 144, 146, 149–50, 151, 167
Molnar, Paul, 7, 8, 46
Moltmann, Jürgen, 2, 19, 179
Mueller, David, 6, 37

Neder, Adam, 15, 136
Newbigin, Lesslie, 166
Newman, John Henry Cardinal, 122
Niebuhr, Richard R., 3

O'Collins, Gerald, 3, 27
O'Donovan, Oliver, 34

Pannenberg, Wolfhart, 3, 4, 178
perichoresis, 2, 12, 62, 129, 134, 137, 150–51, 160, 164–65, 182

Rahner, Karl, 2, 8, 25

reconciliation, 9, 13–16, 40, 43, 47, 54, 61, 72–75, 79, 86, 103, 109, 125, 126–30, 131–32, 135, 149, 150, 162, 163, 164, 173
Revelation, 4–5, 8, 20–27, 34, 36, 37, 42, 43, 52, 54, 55, 59, 75–78, 81, 83, 84–85, 91, 106, 127–28, 132, 139, 148, 153–54, 159, 162, 164, 169, 175–77
Ritschl, Albrecht, 130
Roberts, Richard, 164
Robertson, Gregory Alan, 127, 128, 153
Rogers, Eugene, 7, 8, 86, 129, 145, 147

Schleiermacher, Friedrich, 176
Schreiber, Tilman, 6
Siller, Annelore, 128, 166
Smart, James, 3
Sonderegger, Katherine, 76
soteriology, 5–6, 14–16

Thomas Aquinas, 2, 47, 147
Thompson, John, 104–5
transition, 6, 9–10, 13–18, 19, 27, 30, 36, 44, 61, 62–65, 71, 72–79, 80, 81–84, 85–90, 91–94, 95–98, 99–109, 113, 118–20, 123, 126–33, 135–37, 138–40, 144, 146, 147, 149, 152, 160
Trowitzsch, Michael, 167

vocation, 11, 87, 142, 166–73
Vogel, Heinrich, 37, 40, 55

Webster, John, 153
Wright, N. T., 181

www.ingramcontent.com/pod-product-compliance
Lightning Source LLC
Chambersburg PA
CBHW071200070526
44584CB00019B/2867